TURNING EDUCATION INSIDE-OUT

Confessions of a Montessori Principal

Judy Dempsey

J.ROSS
PUBLISHING

Copyright © 2017 by J. Ross Publishing

ISBN-13: 978-1-60427-131-7

Printed and bound in the U.S.A. Printed on acid-free paper.

10 9 8 7 6 5 4 3 2 1

Library of Congress Cataloging-in-Publication Data

Names: Dempsey, Judy, 1953–
    Title: Turning education inside-out : confessions of a Montessori principal /
    by Judy Dempsey.
    Description: Plantation, FL : J. Ross Publishing, 2016. | Includes
    bibliographical references and index.
    Identifiers: LCCN 2016028545 (print) | LCCN 2016030728 (ebook) | ISBN
    9781604271317 (pbk. : alk. paper) | ISBN 9781604277746 (epub)
    Subjects: LCSH: Montessori method of education.
    Classification: LCC LB1029.M75 D46 2016 (print) | LCC LB1029.M75 (ebook) |
    DDC 371.39/2--dc23
    LC record available at https://lccn.loc.gov/2016028545

Phone: (954) 727-9333
Fax: (561) 892-0700
Web: www.jrosspub.com

Dedication

This book is dedicated to my husband, Tom, and my mother and father, Joan and Bob Joyce, for their constant encouragement and support, without which, I would not be where I am today. They are my role models for showing unconditional love.

Contents

Preface vii
Acknowledgments. xiii
Author Biography xvii

Section I: Understanding the Montessori Approach **1**
    Chapter 1: Montessori 101 3
    Chapter 2: Why Montessori? 25
    Chapter 3: What Makes Montessori Work? 41
    Chapter 4: Montessori versus Traditional. 49
    Chapter 5: How to Recognize an Authentic Montessori
       School 53
    Chapter 6: The Importance of the Parent's Role in the
       Montessori Experience. 61
    Chapter 7: Montessori Educators 79

Section II: Montessori Curricula and Materials. 93
    Chapter 8: Infant and Toddler Years 95
    Chapter 9: Montessori Materials in the Early Childhood
       Curriculum (3-6 Years of Age). 103
    Chapter 10: Materials for the Montessori Elementary
       Curriculum (6-12 Years of Age). 129
    Chapter 11: Adolescent Years in Montessori 141

Section III: Spirituality and Montessori **157**
    Chapter 12: Spirituality in the Montessori Philosophy 159
    Chapter 13: Peace Education. 175

Section IV: Contemporary Issues in Education **187**
    Chapter 14: A Global Approach for the 21st Century. 189

Chapter 15: The Education of Boys. 195
Chapter 16: Testing, Grades, and Report Cards 201
Chapter 17: Special Needs in Montessori 209
Chapter 18: Technology and Montessori Education. 215
Chapter 19: Emotional Intelligence. 221
Photo Gallery 227

Section V: Reflections on the Montessori Experience. 233
Reflections on the Montessori Experience from Students,
Alumni, Alumnae, Parents, Montessori Educators,
and Specialists 235

References. 265

Index. 269

Preface

This book came to be because of a discussion that I had with a Montessori parent at a school social event. This parent, who just happened to be in the profession of publishing books, said to me, "Judy, I would really like you to write a book about the Montessori method. I have had my children in your school for years, I have watched them be transformed, and yet, I still have a hard time explaining to people why this transformation is happening. If you could reach prospective parents who are thinking about choosing Montessori, what would you most want them to know?" As is often true in life, opportunities will pop up when you least expect them; so I took advantage of this good fortune. Writing a book was definitely on my bucket list—so, thank you, Steve, for encouraging me to do so.

After some discussion with Steve, he suggested a title—*Confessions of a Montessori Principal*. At first my reaction was one of surprise...really, are we on the same page here? I do not intend to write about a soap opera version of Montessori. That outlook is in direct contrast to what Montessori is all about. Of course, Steve was coming from the standpoint of a professional in the business of selling books; that title will tend to catch people's attention. Okay, I thought, in true Montessori style, let me actually research the etymology of the word *confessions*, and I will go from there. Aha, research once again broadens our perspective—*a profession of belief, a confession of faith*; on to the thesaurus—*affirmation, acknowledgment, story, making public, avowal*. Okay, my first confession is that I jumped to a negative conclusion. In addition, if a catchy title to a book helps to bring more attention to the Montessori Philosophy, all the better. I am onboard, but I would prefer to lead into the reason as to why I am confessing. I am unashamedly pronouncing that I am proud to help the cause of educating people to understand that *true learning* must come from the inside out. I hope to also turn people's previous assumptions about education inside out as it is time to recognize that the traditional approach to education is backward.

This book is an overview of the Montessori method and philosophy as I have experienced it and lived it over the past 40 years. It is a summary of my journey in the world of Montessori. It is intended to help Montessori parents, and anyone else interested in education, to further understand this philosophy and how it is so relevant in today's world. Today, neuroscience is confirming much of what Dr. Montessori found over a century ago. It is vital to provide carefully prepared learning environments for children at every stage based upon the unique developmental needs of that stage. Only until education policymakers understand that it is imperative to appropriately nurture the development of the whole child and respect every type of learner, will traditional education reach the same level of success as the Montessori approach has in the past 110 years. In addition, this book is also intended to share the ups and downs, the mistakes and successes of my lifetime along the Montessori path—in the hopes that perhaps some of my experiences may be of support to other Montessori educators. If we truly want Montessori to help as many children as possible, then it is necessary to unite, support each other, and put aside any divisiveness that may have separated us in the past.

My journey as a Montessorian began in 1975 when I graduated from Wagner College in Staten Island, New York, with a degree in Elementary Education and, in a quirk of timing, teaching jobs were not available. I took the only job that I could find working with children and that was as an assistant in a lower elementary classroom at a small Montessori school. I was astounded by what I saw and experienced, and it determined the course that I would take for the rest of my life. I went on to take Montessori early childhood training at the Midwest Montessori Teacher Training Center in Chicago, Illinois, where I received American Montessori Society certification to teach children who were three to six years of age. I moved to South Florida to do my internship at Rosarian Academy in West Palm Beach, Florida, under the supervision of Sr. Jean Durrer, who later left religious life and became known as Barb Durrer. She was probably the best mentor I could have ever had to begin my Montessori career, as she had very high expectations and required me to devote my entire internship year to perfecting my craft. I am forever indebted to her for that. After a stellar internship, I was offered an intriguing opportunity by another Montessorian who would become another valued mentor to me, Elizabeth (Betty) Calabrese. Mrs. Calabrese was trained by Dr. Caspari, a direct student of Dr. Montessori's who came to South Florida and trained a group of people interested in opening Montessori schools. Mrs. Calabrese was a remarkable woman who took me under her wing and placed me in a position to learn directly from her how to open a Montessori school. She owned and operated a Montessori school in Homestead, Florida, but did not have a teaching position available for me. She wanted to open a Montessori school in the Florida Keys, so she bought a building, walked me through every step of opening the first Montessori school in Key Largo, and positioned me there to run it and teach. It set me on a course of teaching and working in administration from day one. It was an invaluable experience. I only stayed in Key Largo for one year, however, because I married and moved to Fort Lauderdale. Luckily, I found a job in an Association Montessori Internationale (AMI) school, where I worked for five years. I then went to work for an American Montessori Society (AMS) school at a position that led me directly to where I am today. I went to work for Jeanne Hudlett and worked as a teacher and administrator at four of her Montessori schools. In 1991, Jeanne decided to sell all but one school, and offered the Fort Lauderdale school to me. The name of each of her schools was Summit Private School. Jeanne continued to own and operate Summit Private School of Boca Raton, while I owned and operated Summit Private School of Fort Lauderdale. The Fort Lauderdale school was primarily early childhood education and my goal was to expand it to Montessori elementary, so I went to Barry University in Miami and took the 6 to 12 year old Montessori elementary training and received a Master's Degree as well as AMS Certification. Some of my instructors during that first year at Barry University were Dr. Ijya Tulloss, who directed the Montessori program, and veteran Montessorians, such as Harvey and Nancy Hallenberg, Beverly Mc-Ghee, and Dr. Pamela Zell Rigg. As my elementary school grew, so did the demand for a middle school. I went to Houston, Texas and trained with Dr. Betsy Coe for AMS Secondary I Certification for 12–15 year olds. I consider Dr. Coe a valuable mentor.

My school expanded to include middle school students and at that time, I decided to create a new corporation for it. I engaged the students in thinking about a name for the middle school; and in true Montessori fashion, they came up with a brilliant idea. Why not link our old name, combining the school's history with the new middle school? They looked at the meaning of *summit*, which is the *highest point* of something, and they researched the word *questa*, which means *forever seeking*. So, combining the two words resulted in a profound meaning—*our mission is to always seek the highest point of development in whatever we may pursue*. Thus, Summit-Questa was born.

Along with the growth of the school came a need to find a new location, because we literally outgrew our building. That led to finding the most beautiful ten acres I could ever have imagined. Our campus consists of gardens; multiple trees and flora from around the world; pigs, goats, rabbits, cats, fish, birds, and other multiple forms of life; and a live pond. We have added two swimming pools, a gymnasium, and a sports field. We have tried to provide multiple opportunities for our students to find their strengths and passions, and to have a well-rounded experience.

My Montessori life continued to expand because my school was growing faster than I could find trained Montessori teachers. Jeanne was experiencing the same thing at her school, so we decided to open a teacher training center. Summit Montessori Teacher Training Institute, an AMS-affiliated center that is accredited by the Montessori Accreditation Council for Teacher Education (MACTE) was created, and Jeanne and I are presently co-directors. It is housed at my school, Summit-Questa Montessori School, and it has been invaluable in providing enough trained Montessori teachers to support the school's growth. At this time, we offer infant/toddler, early childhood, and Elementary I AMS training.

Over the course of my 40 years as a Montessori teacher, administrator, principal, and teacher trainer, I have experienced just about anything that one could imagine would be a part of this journey. I have been blessed to have taught in early childhood, lower elementary, upper elementary, and middle school classrooms. I truly cannot say that any one was a favorite over the other—I loved them all. Each stage has its own unique and beautiful qualities. My excitement with life and learning grew right along with my students year after year. For the last 20 years, I have spent most of my time in middle school classrooms basically because it is so hard to find teachers who like to work with this age level. It brings me great joy when I find someone who is suited to that age group. Working with adolescents has probably taught me the most about myself because they do not let you get away with any inconsistencies…you must walk your talk every day when you live and work with adolescents. They love to zero in on your buttons, and of course, like all Montessori students, they are keen observers and know exactly which buttons to push! They delight in doing so because it satisfies that need in them to point out the hypocrisy in life.

I have attempted to share with the readers what I have seen, lived, researched, and loved about the world of Montessori. In Section I, I have given an overview of the Montessori philosophy, its origin, its history, comparisons of traditional and Montessori education, what makes it work, how Montessori teachers are trained, and the importance of the role of the parents.

In Section II, I delve a bit deeper into the Montessori Curricula for infant/toddler through adolescence in order to help Montessori parents become more familiar with the nomenclature as well as understand the scope of what the child is presented in the three-year cycles.

In Section III, I focus on spirituality in the Montessori philosophy. It is such an integral part of what we do and it needs to be included to assist parents in understanding how deep and far-reaching this approach is in terms of the full development of their child. It includes a chapter on peace education and, once again, why it is a necessary component in the healthy development, not only for the child, but for our teachers, communities, and ultimately, the world.

In Section IV, I have included contemporary issues in education. This includes how relevant Montessori education is for today's global society and the twenty-first century. I address the issues of testing, grades, report cards, and the recent findings in regard to the education of boys. In addition, I discuss special needs students, technology in Montessori classrooms, and the importance of the development of emotional intelligence for all students.

Last, but certainly not least, is my favorite section, Section V. In this section I share with you the reflections of Montessori students, graduates, parents, educators, and specialists. The words of the children and graduates who so sincerely express their feelings of gratitude and awareness of how this method has allowed them to become the best versions of themselves are what make this my favorite section. Their internal wisdom recognizes the gift that was given to them.

Acknowledgments

I am very grateful to many people who helped me along my path to this point. If I had not been hired by Building Blocks School in Staten Island, New York, as an assistant in 1975, who knows how long it would have taken me to discover Montessori. I am very grateful for that moment in time. I am indebted to all of the Montessori teacher trainers who imprinted their passion for this philosophy on my very soul. It began at the Midwest Montessori Teacher Training Center, and then on to Barry University, and finally, to the Houston Montessori Center. I am so grateful to everyone at those training centers who so joyfully shared their wisdom and knowledge.

I consider the following Montessorians and educators some of my most inspirational teachers and mentors: Barb Durrer, Harvey Hallenberg, Betty Calabrese, Beverly McGhee, Dr. Ijya Tulloss, Dr. Charaline Luna, Dr. Sarah Allison, and Dr. Betsy Coe. They have all touched my Montessori soul in extraordinary ways.

I am very grateful to Richard Ungerer, Executive Director of the American Montessori Society, for helping me make contact with very reliable and respected sources to ensure that the historical information about Dr. Montessori's life was as accurate as possible. There is conflicting information about her early years and events and Richard was kind enough to refer me to two outstanding resources. My gratitude goes to Francesco Mandolini and Lucio Lombardi from the Fondazione Chiaravalle Montessori in Italy. I learned things that I had never heard before about Dr. Montessori's early years. I hope to thank them in person one day at the birthplace of Dr. Montessori! Keith Whitescarver, Ed. D., the Executive Director of the National Center for Montessori in the Public Sector, was another invaluable resource for fact checking Dr. Montessori's history, especially in the United States, and I am very grateful for his input.

I am forever indebted to Jeanne Hudlett, my soul sister in the Montessori world. If it were not for Jeanne's friendship and support, I would not have accomplished as much in my life on so many levels, and in such remarkable ways.

It has been the joy of my life to own and operate Summit-Questa Montessori School. I am so grateful for an outstanding staff who supports me in more ways than I can share. If not for the business expertise, passion for Montessori, loyalty, and good friendship of Sherry McMullen, I would not have been able to take the time needed to write this book, nor would the school be as successful as it is today. Sherry is without a doubt, my right hand woman, and I consider her my Summit-Questa sister, closest confidante, and good friend.

I am blessed with an outstanding community of Montessorians who are second to none; they are my second family and consistently exhibit unconditional dedication to our children and school. I thank the staff for any contribution they made to the book and for holding down the fort while I was at home writing.

I am indebted to Shari Dickson, one of our artists in residence, for providing the beautiful pencil drawings of the early childhood Montessori materials. She is such a talented artist and we are very fortunate to have her as part of our Summit-Questa family.

I must also thank Patti Sands for providing the photographs from school. Patti is a Montessori teacher as well as a talented photographer, and we are so grateful that she captures so many wonderful moments of life at Summit-Questa.

Lisa Nalven, besides being a professional photographer extraordinaire, has also been a supportive Summit-Questa parent for 20 years. She has photographed 20 years plus of life at Summit-Questa capturing memories which bring us all so much joy. I thank her for that and for her efforts to make my personal photographs look as good as possible.

I am grateful to Charlene Strauss for helping me with all of the technology issues; particularly since I am somewhat of a dinosaur in this realm. Charlene created the outstanding charts used in this book and she is my go-to girl with all matters having to do with technology. Her help was invaluable to me.

The children and parents at Summit-Questa are also a vital part of our Montessori community and it is a privilege and honor to work with them every day—they are our Montessori family. I am so grateful for the heartfelt reflections from students, graduates, and parents that were shared with me for use in the book. Without our families continuously supporting our mission, we would not be able to do what we so passionately love to do. Our beautiful school exists because of the extraordinary support and generosity of the parents in multiple ways; whether it is financial, manpower, resources, or being ambassadors for the school, it was there from day one.

I want to thank my good friend Marcia Taebel for being my supporter and muse from day one of Montessori training in Chicago. She and her husband, Tim, have supported my vision for 25 years.

I want to thank Dr. Charaline Luna, president of the Association of Independent Schools of Florida (AISF), for stepping in and helping me with my AISF duties during the writing process. Without that support, it would have been much more difficult for me.

I am very grateful to Steve Buda, who offered this opportunity to me through J. Ross Publishing. I appreciate his confidence and trust in me to convey my Montessori mission and vision in such a public way. I am grateful to Steve and everyone at J. Ross Publishing who helped me through the entire process with every aspect. It was an exciting learning experience for me as well.

I owe a tremendous debt of gratitude to Dr. Douglas Faig, my oncologist. He played a vital part in helping me to beat cancer, and if it had not been for him, I may not have been here at all to enjoy the path my life has taken.

I must thank my husband, Tom, and my mother, Joan, for keeping our household together throughout the process of my writing this book. Without their unconditional love, support, encouragement, and patience, it would not have happened. My father, Bob Joyce, was my number one fan and losing him was one of the most difficult events that I have ever had to face. He would have been so proud of this accomplishment and I send him my love and gratitude every day. I was blessed with a very loving family and husband.

I thank Dr. Maria Montessori for her extraordinary vision. I can only hope that my personal interpretation and explanation of her method and philosophy would have met with her approval.

Finally, I must thank our Creator for this beautiful world, for gifting me with such an extraordinary cosmic task, and for all of the blessings showered upon me; I am truly grateful for my life.

Author Biography

Judy Dempsey is the owner and principal of Summit-Questa Montessori School in Davie, Florida—a Montessori school on 10 acres for students from the age of three through the 8th grade. She is also the co-director of the Summit Montessori Teacher Training Institute which offers training in infant/toddler, early childhood, and Elementary I levels. This institute is Montessori Accreditation Council for Teacher Education (MACTE) accredited and also an affiliate of the American Montessori Society (AMS) teacher education program. In addition, Judy was trained as an AMS consultant in 1990 and in 2003 as a MACTE Teacher Training Evaluation Committee member.

Judy held the officer's position of First Vice President and Director of Accreditation from 2010 to 2016 with the Association of Independent Schools of Florida (AISF), a state of Florida private school accreditation organization, where she has been a board member since 2006. She held the office of secretary for AISF from 2008 through 2010. Presently, she is a board member of the Montessori Florida Coalition, an organization that puts on an annual Montessori Conference in Miami, Florida. Judy also sat on the Board of Trustees for the Montessori Development Association from 1993–1995. She has been trained to serve on school evaluation teams for the Middle States Association of Colleges and Schools-Commissions on Elementary and Secondary Schools (MSA-CESS).

Judy graduated from Wagner College in New York City with a Bachelor of Science Degree in Elementary Education. She graduated Cum Laude with Departmental Honors in Education. In 1977 she received her AMS Early Childhood National Certification (for ages 3–6 years) through the Midwest Montessori Teacher Training Center, in Chicago, Illinois. In 1985,

Judy received Gesell Training for Early Childhood Educators through the Early Childhood Team, Broward County School System, Broward County, Florida. In 1994, she received an M.Ed. in Montessori Elementary Education from Barry University in Miami, Florida and received AMS National Certification for elementary (ages 6–12 years). Judy then went on to train in Houston, Texas where she received AMS National Certification for Secondary I (ages 12–15 years), through the Houston Montessori Center.

Ms. Dempsey is well-known in the South Florida Montessori Community where she has lectured at many local Montessori schools, held workshops for the Montessori community, and has presented the Montessori Philosophy to the general public. She conducts AISF training of educational evaluators for private school accreditation visits and has presented at numerous AISF and AMS conferences on adolescent development.

In 2009, Judy was awarded *The Alan O'Such Memorial Outstanding Service Award* by the AISF for outstanding service to the organization and the children of the state of Florida. In 2012, Judy was nominated for the Distinguished Educator of the Year Award through the AISF. She can be reached at Summit-Questa Montessori School, in Davie, Florida. Her e-mail is ms-judy@summitquesta.com.

™Web
Added
Value

Free value-added materials available from
the Download Resource Center at www.jrosspub.com

At J. Ross Publishing we are committed to providing today's professional with practical, hands-on tools that enhance the learning experience and give readers an opportunity to apply what they have learned. That is why we offer free ancillary materials available for download on this book and all participating Web Added Value™ publications. These online resources may include interactive versions of material that appears in the book or supplemental templates, worksheets, models, plans, case studies, proposals, spreadsheets and assessment tools, among other things. Whenever you see the WAV™ symbol in any of our publications, it means bonus materials accompany the book and are available from the Web Added Value Download Resource Center at www.jrosspub.com.

Downloads for *Turning Education Inside-Out: Confessions of a Montessori Principal* include a checklist to help parents looking for a Montessori school, articles on Montessori, and special material for Montessori educators.

Section I:
Understanding the
Montessori Approach

1

Montessori 101

A visitor to a Montessori school commented that this is where chil-dren do as they like, to which a child responded, "Excuse me, I do not know if we do as we like, but I know that we like what we do."
—Maria Montessori, *The Secret of Childhood*

When prospective parents visit my school, I am often asked, "Why should I choose a Montessori education for my child?" This is a question that is not easily answered in a short amount of time because there are so many layers to the Montessori experience that it is impossible to communicate all of them clearly in a snapshot. Even after many years and levels of Montessori training and teaching, it has taken me 40 years to assimilate this philosophy, and I am still having new experiences to this day! This is a rich and multilay-ered methodology, as well as a philosophy of education and life. With that said, let me give you a brief introduction to the Montessori Philosophy, or as I call it when I present it to parents at my school, *Montessori 101*.

Dr. Montessori was a remarkable and brilliant woman who was well ahead of her time. She was born in 1870 in Chiaravalle, Italy. Her parents were from the typical mode of thinking at that time, which was to encour-age girls to follow a traditional woman's role. They valued education and tried to steer their daughter toward the profession of teaching, which was basically the only acceptable career choice for women at that time. Maria, however, was having none of that; at age 13, she enrolled in the Technical School for Engineering and Math. She was a true pioneer in the field of women's liberation. She continued to fight for her rights when she enrolled at the University of Rome in 1890 and studied physics, math, and science; she was at the top of her class. In 1892, the battle continued until she was accepted as a medical student in Italy. Due to the fact that her father was not supportive of her choices, it was necessary for her to work throughout her schooling in order to pay her own expenses. In 1896, at the age of 26, Maria Montessori received her Doctorate in Medicine from the University of Rome, and became the eighth female physician in Italy. This in itself was a monumental feat at this time in history. This same year, she was chosen to represent the women of Italy at a feminist congress in Berlin, discussing such issues as women's rights and child labor laws. Aside from being an advocate for the rights of women and children, she was a scientist and a physician; not an educator by profession or choice.

In the course of her medical career in Italy, she was named the director of the State Orthophrenic School in Rome. It was here that she worked with a group of children in the hospital who were mentally impaired, and this contact changed the course of her life. As a scientist and physician, those children became the subjects of her observations, studies, theories, and finally, experimentation with unique learning tools, most designed by Dr. Montessori. She had studied the work of pioneers in this field, Jean Itard and Edouard Seguin, as a springboard for much of the material she later designed. She was ever the scientist, spending long days observing the children, and long evenings reviewing her observations and notes, and creating new materials. After two years of working with these mentally challenged children, those same children were able to pass a state exam that is given to normal children to enter public school. Dr. Montessori received international acclaim for this accomplishment. She chose at that point, however, to focus on brain development of the normally developing child as she was astounded that she was able to guide children who were mentally challenged to perform at the same level as was expected from children without any mental deficiencies. Her reflection was:

> *"I was searching for the reasons…healthy children of the common schools were on so low of a plane they could be equaled in tests of intelligence by my unfortunate pupils!…similar methods applied to normal children would develop or set free their personality in a marvelous and surprising way."*[1]

Hence, her quest began to study the growth of the brain in the normally developing child, in light of her previous experiences. She returned to the University of Rome in 1900 to study psychology and philosophy and in 1904, she became a Professor of Anthropology at that same institution. She did not remain at the University for long, however, as an opportunity presented itself in 1907 when Dr. Montessori was asked to direct a day care center for children from a poor housing project in the San Lorenzo Quarter of Rome. These children were seen as delinquents who were left alone during the day because they were too young for formal schooling, and their working parents could not afford day care; consequently, left to their own devices, they were vandalizing the area. The opportunity was too good to pass up and her calling to children was too strong. She opened the first *Casa dei Bambini* or *Children's House* in 1907 for approximately 60 of these children between the ages of three and seven who were the offspring of poor, illiterate parents. They were growing up in an area known at that time for crime, violence, and poverty. These children exhibited many negative qualities, such as destructiveness, greed, and violence, but some were also fearful, tearful, and shy. Yet another miraculous transformation took place in this setting; one that changed the course of life for these children, Dr. Montessori, and future children around the world. Dr. Montessori discovered through scientific observation that these children had within them what could be called an *inner life force* that brought them to a new and higher plane of existence—basically because they were given the freedom to explore their prepared environment and were held to a higher standard of behavior. These same children, who were unruly and exhibiting numerous negative behaviors, slowly transformed into children who cared about the environment, others, and about their own education. They concentrated; independently learned to read, write, and do advanced mathematics; but most importantly, they cared about their community. This was the secret that Dr. Montessori discovered—the spirit of the child when allowed to emerge in a safe, supportive, and loving environment will work miracles. She discovered that the actual life force (spirit) itself will work through the child, guiding the child toward his or her highest potential. We, as supporting and guiding adults in the child's life, should be there to be a *help to life*. Once again, Dr. Montessori received international recognition and the press wrote about these *converted children*.

"Finally, one day as I looked upon these children with great respect and affection, I placed my hand upon my heart and asked, "Who are you?" Dr. Montessori spent the rest of her life trying to find the answer to this question.

News of her work spread all around the world. In 1911, after a series of supportive articles were published in McClure's Magazine, interest in the United States was at a high level. Dr. Montessori received a warm and enthusiastic welcome to the United States during her first visit in 1913. A reception to introduce her to some of the most influential and powerful people in the country was held in the home of Alexander Graham Bell and his wife, Mabel, and she was the house guest of Thomas Edison. When she spoke at Carnegie Hall, it was filled to capacity. Dr. Montessori supported the formation of the American Montessori Education Association which had Margaret Wilson, daughter of the president of the United States, as secretary, and Mrs. Alexander Graham Bell, as president. The Bells were instrumental in bringing information about the method to the American public. Montessori schools began to open around the country and educational journals had multiple articles about the Montessori approach. This initial enthusiasm unfortunately waned, however, due to a number of factors such as the onset of World War I, a clash of strong personalities, and numerous influential critics, such as William Kilpatrick, a respected educator who wrote a book criticizing most of Dr. Montessori's theories. In addition, the educational climate at that time was moving toward a more *social* focus for education and the growth of kindergarten. As a result of all these factors, along with Kilpatrick's gross misinterpretation and short-sighted views of Dr. Montessori's work, most American educators discarded her theories. Time would tell, however, since the traditional educational focus, as we see today, clearly has become antiquated and ineffective.

Dr. Montessori moved on and continued her work. She focused on creating optimal learning environments based upon the needs of the developing brains of young children and the needs of the human spirit. She was able to scientifically understand and discern the unique periods of brain development in the child and developed a *prepared environment*, which was appropriate to the exclusive needs of that developing brain and spirit. Dr. Montessori called these developmentally appropriate learning times *sensitive periods*.[2] She taught that if a child is exposed to the appropriate types of experiences during the sensitive period, then learning is effortless and natural. You might also think of this as a learning *window of opportunity* that is wide open at certain times in the child's development. She discovered that young children can learn to read and write as naturally as they learn to walk and talk if they are in the appropriate prepared environment during their sensitive periods. The prepared environment was a term that she used to describe the ultimate learning environment for children at every stage of development, designed according to all of the specific needs of the child at that period. Of course, because the needs of children are different at each stage of development, the Montessori prepared environments will not look or feel exactly the same at each level. Montessori infant and toddler environments (birth through 3 years of age) are not designed the same as early childhood environments (3 to 6 years), and early childhood environments are not designed the same as elementary environments (6 to 12 years), and so on. Always constant, however, are the essential elements that should be a part of all Montessori environments regardless of age. These elements include:

- A multi-age mixture at each level:
  ◊ Infancy: birth through 18 months
  ◊ Toddler: 18 months through 3 years of age
  ◊ Early childhood: 3 to 6 years of age
  ◊ Lower elementary: 6 to 9 years of age
  ◊ Upper elementary: 9 to 12 years of age
  ◊ Middle school: 12 to 15 years of age
  ◊ High school: 15 to 18 years of age
- A classroom setting designed to allow children to work independently or in small groups, which allows for interaction of the children: the children choose to work on the floor on mats or at tables. The teachers are not standing in the front of the room lecturing to the students; they are immersed in the classroom, working with individuals or small groups of students on the floor or at a table. Quite often when I bring a prospective parent into a Montessori classroom for the first time, they will ask, "Where is the teacher?" At first they do not see or realize that the teachers are actually on the floor working with the students because they just blend in with the flow of the classroom.
- A full array of Montessori materials on open shelves available to all of the children: these materials will usually be organized by subject matter and have a definite sequence and order of presentation to the child. The Montessori materials should dominate any other resources that may be available to the children.
- Classrooms that are aesthetically beautiful, orderly, clean, and peaceful: anything on the walls is limited to a moderate amount of fine art reproductions or appropriate Montessori-related art work. The visual impact should be one of beauty, not clutter or overstimulation; where the Montessori materials are the prime visual focus calling to the children.
- Teachers who are fully trained and certified by an authentic Montessori teacher training center for the level that they are teaching: I will go into further detail about the training available in Chapter 7.
- A happy, positive atmosphere with children working together—teaching and helping each other—where students are fully engaged with the

Montessori materials: there should be a sense of calm and peacefulness exhibited by the students and the adults.

During the last three years of Dr. Montessori's life, she reflected upon her findings and in summary, three main theories surfaced:

1. Human development occurs in a series of formative planes, not in a linear, steady ascent
2. The development of human beings is made complete by their constant and repetitive urge to use very common actions in relation to their immediate environment
3. The most productive development of the individual occurs when the interaction with the environment is self-chosen and based on the individual's interest

Over the course of many years of working with children, she observed that there were four specific stages in human development. This led her to define human development in a radically different way compared to how traditional education and human development theorists typically looked at it. She described four planes of development, which included: two planes of childhood, from birth through age 12, resulting in a mature child; and two planes leading to adulthood, from age 12 through age 24, resulting in a mature young adult. Each of these planes is uniform in that they reach a summit, and then decline. So rather than looking at human development as a steady, or linear incline, Dr. Montessori saw it as the rise and ebb of the construction of the human being. She discovered that in each plane there was a dramatic appearance of a new development which steadily and strongly rose until it peaked, and then took a turn downward, where the slower, downward direction allowed the new development to be refined. Dr. Montessori stressed that in order for a child to move successfully to the next plane, the previous plane should have provided all that the developing person needed to continue to grow in a healthy and holistic way. Dr. Montessori was also one of the first theorists to stress how important childhood was in the development of the person. In past theory, childhood was not thought of as an important step in the process, but rather, a stage to get through in order to get to the more important, later stages of life. Dr. Montessori placed much more importance and emphasis on the value of childhood as its own unique building block of the person to be.

I have likened it to a *genesis*; the dawn of a new exploration of life as each plane emerges. For example: the first plane of life, birth to 6 years of age, is an explosion into exploring the actual, brand new, physical world. During the first half of that plane, from birth to 3 years, the child's unconscious psyche is working at internally answering these questions: Where am I? What is this world? How do things work? The next half of the plane, from 3 to 6 years of age, the child begins to consciously refine the knowledge that they have subconsciously absorbed in the first half. *"Before three, the functions are being created; after three, they develop."*[3] The changes in the child have affected all aspects of his or her development—physical, social, emotional, and intellectual—and the same pattern will continue with each subsequent plane.

The next plane, 6 to 12 years of age, follows the same sequence; only now there is an explosion into the intellectual world. The first half of the plane includes fiery energies focused on increasing their knowledge about the world. Why? How? When? Where? There are unlimited questions about every aspect of life, including social rules of society. Dr. Montessori likened it to the child's intelligence now becoming extroverted; whereas, in the earlier plane, the child's intelligence was growing internally—now it is launched out into the world with a fervent desire to accumulate as much knowledge as possible. This is the age of imagination where the child can imagine unlimited possibilities about the world. The second half of the plane, once again, involves refinement of the knowledge, reasoning, and thinking that emerged in the first half. This is where the child begins to make sense of the *cosmic order* of the world. They are fascinated with the universe, understand how interrelated all of life is, and how important interdependent relationships are within every aspect of our existence on the planet. The child has learned to adapt to the environment, has a broader and more protective and loving outlook on life, and is open-minded.

The third plane, 12 to 18 years of age, involves a new *genesis*—entrance into early adolescence—during the first half, 12 to 15 years of age, now involves a dramatic explosion into the social relationship part of life. Anyone who lives or works with adolescents is very aware of how dramatic and explosive emergence into this new phase can be. Children, in many cases, will become unrecognizable to their parents and teachers. This can become a very stormy and volatile phase for many adolescents. The first half, once again, is the most intense and dramatic part of the plane. The second half, 15 to 18 years, is a time for refinement, processing, and clarification of the individual's identity in society.

Finally, the last plane is emergence into young adulthood, 18 to 21 years of age—when they explode into adult life with all of its challenges, as they try to figure out their place in society. Then the second half, 21 to 24 years of age, hopefully melds together to help the mature young adult clarify his or her purpose and place in life and evolve into a person who is a morally, ethically, and socially responsible citizen. In addition, he or she should be a person who is a confident, competent learner, who is academically and emotionally prepared to succeed in whatever undertaking he or she may pursue, as well as being capable of sustaining healthy relationships. In other words, caring about the world and others in it.

Each plane has its own unique characteristics so the person is a very different being in each plane. The transition from one plane to another, as mentioned earlier, is likened to a *genesis* or *rebirth* of the new individual. Each experience in a specific plane will build the foundation for a successful transition into the next plane. In a future chapter, I will introduce Victor, who did not have any human interaction during his sensitive period for language in his first and second plane of development; he was never able to transition on to the next plane successfully in those specific areas. Dr. Montessori discovered that three consistent things happen during each of these four planes of development:

1. There is a distinct internal goal in development
2. There is a quickly recognized internal direction being followed to attain that goal
3. There are specific sensitive periods or opportunities given to people in each period of development to support the person in reaching the specific goal for that plane

Traditional education has a completely different view of child development. In most traditional schools, here in America and around the world, schooling before the age of six is not looked upon seriously as a critical opportunity for enhancing brain development. In many cases, schooling does not even officially begin until six years of age; and if it does begin earlier, the emphasis is primarily on social development and fantasy play. Dr. Montessori's first plane of development is virtually ignored. Fortunately for children around the world, change is happening. Research is supporting what Dr. Montessori found over 100 years ago, that children under the age of six should also be provided with a rich, developmentally appropriate learning environment in order to take advantage of this very fertile learning period.

In addition to this, traditional education looks at education and subsequent learning as a linear and lock-step ascent toward acquiring more knowledge and intelligence. Each year becomes more difficult because of subject matter that is externally imposed upon each grade level from experts in curricula. Students are tested on the material that they are fed, and those students who are proficient in memorizing and regurgitating information do well. This approach assumes that intelligence increases by the amount of information poured into the students. It is not an atmosphere conducive to thinking, problem solving, and collaboration. It is an environment rooted in conformity and memorization—not to mention, boredom.

I have included three charts to help explain some of the development theories that we are discussing. Figure 1.1 is indicative of Dr. Montessori's *Planes of Development*, which allows you to visually absorb her theory on how people develop from birth through adulthood. Figure 1.2 shows a linear ascent and indicates how traditional education looks at the developing child, continuously climbing a mountain of knowledge. The third chart, Figure 1.3, portrays the traditional approach as more of a lock-step process. Rather than assuming that all children are steadily inclining in intellect, I see it as a body of knowledge being presented at each plateau; all children

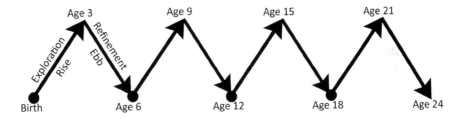

Figure 1.1   Dr. Montessori's Planes of Development

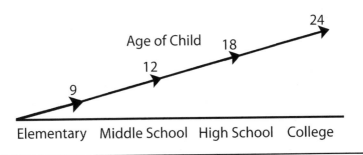

Figure 1.2   A traditional view of the developing child

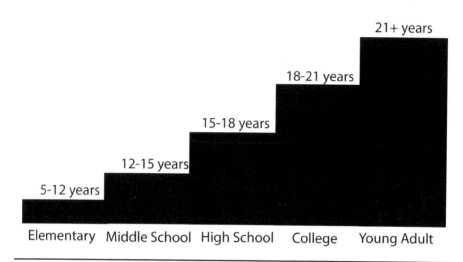

Figure 1.3   A body of knowledge as a plateau

must remain at that plateau until it is externally determined that everyone can move up to the next step. That plateau step is where everyone is put in a holding and waiting stage.

What is absolutely amazing is that Dr. Montessori discovered such in-depth and accurate truths about the brain development of children and that she did it without the benefit of technology. Today, advanced technology and brain research supports much of what Dr. Montessori intuitively and brilliantly deduced through her life's work and observations. One of her strongest proponents in the world of neurology today is Dr. Steve Hughes. Dr. Hughes, a board-certified pediatric neuropsychologist and past president of the American Academy of Pediatric Neuropsychology, is also a Montessori parent. He lectures around the world about the benefits of Montessori education and how it affects optimal brain development and subsequent learning. I would encourage you to visit his website, www.goodatdoing things.com in order to learn more about this exciting connection between Montessori and neuroscience.

Even though I will continue to use the word, I must admit that Dr. Montessori was not comfortable with labeling her work as a *method* because she believed that the term is too institutional; implying that there is a step-by-step, prescribed course of events that must be followed methodically in order to *teach* children facts. She did not want her method to be a fixed system. Conversely, being the scientist that she was, she knew that there needed to be constant experimentation based on the observation of the children. She wanted Montessori environments to be driven by the needs of the children and for her followers to be open-minded. Dr. Montessori stressed in her writings that she was more focused on her philosophy being one of freedom of exploration for the child and creating environments where the unleashed potential of the child is allowed to emerge without constrictions and interference. She believed we just needed to get out of the way of the child's emerging gifts and potential. Dr. Montessori had a much greater vision for her work; one which was a *help to life*, not just another method to teach children academically. She had a profound respect and love for the child and the innate potential within each one of them. She was one of the first researchers to recognize the *spiritual aspects* within the child and why it was important to create environments to allow for this aspect of development to emerge. This was one of her greatest contributions to children and the world. Montessori students truly emerge as well-rounded, self-knowledgeable, self-confident, and caring individuals due to their broad educational experience.

Dr. Montessori, always the scientist, tested her methods all over the world to validate the universality of her theories and method. She discovered that no matter what the country, culture, religion, or economic status was, her theories held true. This was confirmation for her that the needs of children were the same all over the world and that each and every child held the spark of life that was unique to them alone. These were not only Dr. Montessori's principles, but universal principles. Dr. Montessori was rare in that she definitely had the mind of a scientist, but also had a very spiritual nature as well. The combination of both natures of her personality led to the development of her very distinctive learning environments. She dedicated the rest of her life to the continued development of her method and philosophy for children at multiple levels of development.

Dr. Montessori had an illustrious and impressive history throughout the world, despite the rejection by American educators after their initial warm welcome. It is interesting to note that her method was recognized as an outstanding educational reform by some of the greatest thinkers of the time: Alexander Graham Bell and his wife, Mabel; Thomas Edison; Helen Keller; and President Woodrow Wilson's daughter Margaret. They all recognized the unmatched potential in her philosophy. She was invited to set up a demonstration class in a glass room at the Panama-Pacific International Exhibition in San Francisco in 1915, where she won two awards. In addition, she was a passionate advocate for women and children, and an eloquent speaker who spoke at international conferences on their behalf.

In 1922, Dr. Montessori was appointed as a government inspector of schools in Italy, but that changed when she opposed Mussolini's fascist regime. Her schools were closed and she was forced to flee Italy. She went to Laren, Netherlands, where she opened a teacher training center, then went on to open numerous other teacher training centers in India throughout the war. She was invited to speak at the League of Nations at Geneva in 1926, and was nominated for the Nobel Peace Prize three times—in 1949, 1950, and 1951. Dr. Montessori lectured and trained teachers worldwide and became internationally famous. She held many distinguished positions throughout her life and in 1950, at the age of 80, she was asked to be a member of the Italian delegation to the United Nations Educational, Scientific and Cultural Organization (UNESCO) conference in Florence. Over the course of her life, she wrote multiple books, which are listed in the bibliography of this book. Dr. Montessori died in 1952 of a cerebral hemorrhage, two months before her 82nd birthday. She had a fascinating life and holds the distinct honor of being a beacon of light for children and the world.

The tide began turning in the United States in 1958 when Nancy McCormick Rambusch opened the Whitby School in Greenwich, Connecticut. She introduced the Montessori method to America and the climate was right. Due to the rise of the middle class, and an interest in including more liberal and spiritual elements in education, there was a resurgence of interest in the method. Rambusch founded the American Montessori Society in 1960, in partnership with American Montessori Internationale. Later, the two organizations parted ways and became two entirely separate entities. Support of the Montessori method continues to grow in the United States.

Today there are thousands of both public and private Montessori schools all around the world in 110 countries. They exist on every continent with the exception of Antarctica. The method and philosophy have been successfully implemented into approximately 520 public schools and 5,000 private schools in the United States alone. In some countries around the world, the Montessori method is so integrated, it is not even called Montessori, it is merely their adopted educational structure. There is no doubt among the professionals who live and work in the world of Montessori that this approach works, and works well. President Obama acknowledged the success of Montessori education during a White House Summit on Early Education. Some other White House connections to Montessori have been Chelsea Clinton, who attended a Montessori school, as did former First Lady Jacqueline Bouvier Kennedy Onassis. There have also been many other distinguished people who have either attended Montessori schools or supported the philosophy, including: Fred Rogers, of *Mister Roger's Neighborhood* fame; Swiss psychologist, Jean Piaget, who headed the Swiss Montessori Society for many years; Larry Page and Sergey Brin, co-founders of Google; Jeffrey Bezos, founder of Amazon.com; Julia Child, chef and author; Katherine Graham, owner/editor of *The Washington Post*; Anne Frank, famous diarist from WWII; Prince William and his son Harry, English Royal Family members; George Clooney, actor; Helen Hunt, actress; Jerry Lewis, comedian; Jimmy Page of Led Zeppelin; Sean Combs, music mogul and fashion designer; Gabriel Garcia Marquez, Nobel Prize winner for literature; Sergei Bubka, Olympic Pole Vault Gold Medalist; Joshua Bell, American violinist; and Lea Salonga, multi-award-winning singer and Broadway actress. The list could go on, but it is obvious that the Montessori philosophy has impacted the world in many ways, and in some cases, as with Google and Amazon, world-changing ways!

Having the advantage of seeing our students go through the program from three years of age through middle school, I can attest to the fact that by employing the Montessori method for the past 25 years, we have seen confident, well-rounded students emerge from our middle school. The vast majority go on to be honor students in high school but even beyond that, and most importantly, they have an inner compass that points them in the right direction in many different ways. They become leaders, creative problem solvers, and mindful individuals who are adept communicators. They know how to work with different kinds of people and to use their strengths while being aware of, and continuing to improve on, their weaknesses. They have learned how to manage their time and be organized. They care about the environment, the world, and other people in it. To me and the rest of the Montessori world, the result of a Montessori education is so much more than the academic achievement (which is *very high*, comparatively speaking). Overall, the most important thing is that the whole person has been allowed to develop intellectually, socially, emotionally, and spiritually. The Montessori experience provides a safe and nurturing place for students to develop their unique gifts and their inner spirit. All human beings come into this world with their gifts. The world does not always understand or welcome them; and those gifts have often been squelched along the way. I have seen Montessori environments transform children who felt defeated at the age of six because of previous rigid, traditional learning environments that were not rooted in developmentally appropriate learning expectations. Dr. Montessori truly gave children a life-long gift.

Dr. Montessori's success is legendary and anyone interested in learning more about her can find multiple books dedicated to her fascinating life and work. Likewise, I will also share a timeline of Dr. Montessori's illustrious life.

"The unknown energy that can help human-
ity is that which lies hidden in the child."

—Maria Montessori

Timeline of Dr. Maria Montessori's Life

1870	Maria Montessori was born on August 31, in the town of Chiaravalle, in the province of Ancona, Italy. She was an only child. Her father had a military background, was a conservative government accountant, and was also a patriot of the Italian Unity. Her mother was more liberal in her views, but had to be respectful of her husband's conservative nature because women had no say in the family (or society) at the time. She did, however, encourage her daughter to be an independent thinker and focus on her studies at school. Maria was reported to be an average student in her early years in the traditional educational setting and preferred sewing and practical domestic duties, which she continued to enjoy all of her life.
1882	Even though her parents encouraged her to become a teacher, Maria had an aptitude for mathematics and science, and chose to focus on those subjects.
1883	Maria enrolled in a technical school generally reserved for men. She studied engineering and math.
1886	Maria graduated from *Michelangelo Buonarroti* Technical School with high marks. She then entered the *Regio Instituto Scuola Tecnico Leonardo da Vinci*, which had recently allowed the enrollment of women, and studied modern languages and natural sciences, but her favorite subjects continued to be mathematics and biology. She was one of ten girls that graduated from the institute.
1890	Maria enrolled in the University of Rome and studied physics, math, and natural sciences. She was at the top of her class.

1892	Maria was denied enrollment into medical school because that was a profession usually reserved for men. It was reported that she went to Pope Leo XIII to appeal her case, and won. She gained entrance into medical school. While in attendance, she faced much sexism from her classmates, and opposition from her father, who was concerned with the opinion of others, and kept hoping for her to choose a path in education. Due to the social climate at the time, women were not allowed to be in the presence of a dead, naked man while other men were in the room, so she performed her anatomy classes on cadavers alone in the darkness of the basement. On a lighter note, she was given the honor of presenting the award of a hand-painted banner and bouquet to her majesty, Queen Margherita.
1894	At the end of her fourth year at the university, she was in her second year in medicine and surgery. She won the coveted *Polli Prize* and the scholarship that accompanied it.
1895	Dr. Montessori started to work as an assistant to Professor Giuseppe Ferruccio Montesano at the University Psychiatric Clinic.
1896	There is a myth that Dr. Maria Montessori became the first female physician in Italy upon her graduation from medical school. There were actually seven other women certified before her. She graduated with degrees in surgery and medicine, began her medical career in a small clinic in Rome, and joined the staff of the University Psychiatric Clinic. It was here that she became focused on children with mental disabilities. This led to her researching the work of Itard and Sequin, French doctors who began to create hands-on materials for deaf and blind children. Their influence had a direct impact on her further creation of hands-on learning materials. In addition, shortly after her graduation, she addressed the International Women's Congress in Berlin, discussing issues such as women's rights and child labor laws.
1896	Dr. Montessori occupied the Chair of Hygiene at the Magistero Femminile in Rome, one of the two women's colleges in Italy at the time. She held that position for ten years.
1897	Dr. Montessori became a full-time faculty member at the University Psychiatric Clinic; in addition, she studied philosophy, education, social science, and pedagogy (which at that time was just a small portion of philosophy).

1898	Dr. Montessori became the co-director of the State Orthophrenic Institute, along with Dr. Montesano. She continued her work with mentally challenged children. On March 31, she gave birth to her son, Mario, born out of a relationship with Prof. Montesano. He was born out of wedlock. Mario went to live on a farm outside of Rome with a couple of peasants paid to take care of him, unaware that Dr. Montessori was his mother. According to Mario, only a few close friends and associates knew of his existence. Later on in life, Mario became her closest supporter and continued her work after her death. This was also the year that Dr. Montessori seriously turned her attention for the first time to the study of education. She audited courses in pedagogy and read all of the major works on educational theory of the past 200 years.
1899	Dr. Montessori was received at the Court of England where she addressed Parliament about child labor laws and exploitation. She gave a series of lectures in Rome to the teachers at the *Scuole Normali di Magistero* on special methods of education for mentally challenged children.
1900	Dr. Montessori returned to the University of Rome to study anthropology, psychology, and philosophy. She was appointed Director of a school developed to train teachers in the care and education of deficient children. The school had a practice demonstration room in which 22 young pupils were enrolled. She became a lecturer of Anthropology and Hygiene at the Royal Feminine Teacher Training College. She continued to practice medicine in clinics, hospitals, and private practice, and to lecture at universities in Rome.
1904	Dr. Montessori held degrees as a Doctor of Medicine, Surgery, Psychology, Anthropology, and Philosophy. She became very well-known at this time. Dr. Montessori believed that social progress depended upon the emancipation of women and that the attitude toward women and children were the reasons for society's failures.
1907	On January 6, 1907, the first *Casa dei Bambini*, or Children's House, opened with 60 children in a poor housing project in the neighborhood of San Lorenzo, Rome, in order to help the community and working parents. Dr. Montessori was commissioned by the City Council to "control" the children. In October, after receiving international notoriety for the amazing success of the Casa dei Bambini for normally developing children, Dr. Montessori allowed Anna Maccheroni to open a second Casa in Milan, in the blue collar neighborhood called Umanitaria.

1909	Dr. Montessori's first book, *The Montessori Method*, was published in Italy under another title (*Method of the Scientific Pedagogy*). The first American edition is dated 1912 and translated by Anne George. In addition, the first American article about Montessori was published in an educational journal.
1910	*Antropologia Pedagogica (Pedagogic Anthropology)* was published. This is the book that gave Dr. Montessori standing in the scientific world. An American elementary teacher from Chicago, Anne George, enrolls in Montessori's eight-month teacher training program in Italy.
1911	Anne George returns to America to open the first Montessori school in Tarrytown, New York and a second one in Boston. Over 400 public school districts requested information about the method. The Montessori method is adopted by schools around the world, including Italian and Swiss schools, and the method spread throughout Europe and as far as Australia and Argentina. McClure's magazine published articles on Montessori in America and London.
1912	Alexander Graham Bell's Washington, D.C. home became the new site of Anne George's Montessori school. *The Montessori Method* was published in English in America.
1913	Dr. Montessori made her first trip to America to give a series of lectures. Her method, however, became a subject of controversy in America. It became a target of attack, as well as a focus for reformer's hopes. In her personal life, she had her son, Mario, move in with her. Two years later, she publicly announced him as her adopted son.
1914	Dr. Montessori visited the U.S. and lectured at Carnegie Hall. She was a house guest of Thomas Edison during this trip. She had support from people such as Alexander Graham Bell, Thomas Edison, and President Woodrow Wilson's daughter, who requested that she start a school at the White House, but she declined. She published her second book, *Dr. Montessori's Own Handbook*.
1915	Dr. Montessori returned to the U.S. where she was asked to give a demonstration at the World's Fair in San Francisco. She set up a model Montessori classroom in a glass dome so the children could be observed, but not disturbed. Dr. Montessori won two awards. She also started the first U.S. training course in California.

1916–17	Dr. Montessori gave lectures and training courses in the U.S. and Spain. She was assigned by the Italian Ministry of Education to supervise the implementation of her method in several classes that had been established as an official experiment in the school of Rome.
1917	Dr. Montessori made her first trip to Holland. Montessori schools began to organize throughout Europe. In America, there was some discouragement among her supporters because of her tight control of the training and of the use of her name. Some American educators began to publicly criticize her methods for not providing enough opportunities for play and social interaction. This led to misunderstandings between Dr. Montessori and American Montessori associations. Dr. Montessori chose to focus her efforts in other countries. She published *The Advanced Montessori Method: Spontaneous Activity in Education* and *The Montessori Elementary Material* which led to the expansion of the Montessori method into the elementary years.
1919	Dr. Montessori held her first international training course in England.
1920	At this point, Dr. Montessori was internationally famous. She continued to travel, lecture, and train teachers around the world. She insisted on doing all of the training herself in order to stay true to her method. Traveling around the world gave her the opportunity to test her method and validate her research. She discovered that the method and the results were universal. For the next 10 years, Dr. Montessori gave teacher training courses throughout Europe. Her work influenced some of the leading specialists in the field of human development, such as Jean Piaget, Erik Erikson, and Anna Freud.
1922	Dr. Montessori was appointed government inspector of schools in Italy. She returned to Italy to continue to train teachers there.
1923	Dr. Montessori was honored with a Doctorate of Letters for her outstanding contributions to the fields of medicine, psychiatry, and anthropology.
1924	Italian leaders planned to reform the Italian educational system by using the Montessori method since Dr. Montessori had convinced the Italian government of its importance and success. There were many Montessori schools in Italy where the method was completely applied in accordance with Dr. Montessori's techniques. She creates the Opera Nazionale Montessori (ONM) in Rome and Naples. The ONM was an organization to oversee the activities of schools and Montessori societies around the world, and to oversee the training of teachers.

1926	A Montessori secondary school was opened in Amsterdam by parents and teachers and was supported by Dr. Montessori.
1929	Dr. Montessori founded the Association Montessori Internationale (AMI) with the same purposes of the ONM. She also wrote a new introduction to *The Montessori Method*.
1932	*Education* and *Peace* was first published in English in 1932, then in Italian in 1933.
1933	Hitler closed all Montessori schools in Germany. The fascist regime in Italy began to oppose her methods, burning her books in Italy, Germany, Austria, and Spain. Traveling became difficult. Dr. Montessori was convinced that if her method could create new children and new teachers, war could be a thing of the past. She and her son, Mario, walk out of the ONM.
1934	Dr. Montessori lectured at Congress; this was her last lecture before all of her schools were closed due to the regime. The Montessori method was banned by Mussolini in Italy, and in Germany and Austria. She leaves Italy and her headquarters were moved to Amsterdam.
1936	Dr. Montessori established her permanent residence in Holland. In the same year, Mussolini shuts down the ONM (which was reformed after the war in 1948).
1937	She lectured at the Second International Montessori Conference; its main theme: *Education for Peace*.
1938	Italy applies the "racial laws" and Dr. Montessori openly spoke against them on various occasions.
1939	Dr. Montessori went to India and gave the first training course there for over 300 teachers from all over the world. She remained there during World War II. She trained over 1000 Indian teachers during her seven year stay there. She started the first training course for elementary teachers and began to focus her interests on young infants.
1946	Dr. Montessori returned to Europe. While America had lost interest in her method, it was now flourishing in Europe. She ran a training course in London; and Scotland honored her with an honorary Fellowship from the Educational Institute of Scotland.
1947	Dr. Montessori returned to Italy to reorganize the schools after WWII. The first infant course (0–3 years) was started in Rome.
1948	At age 78, she taught one more course in India.

1949	Dr. Montessori held her first course in Pakistan; attended the International Congress in San Remo where she spoke on "the child as the constructor of peace"; and she was nominated for the Nobel Peace Prize in 1949, 1950, and 1951.
1950	Dr. Montessori continued to lecture in Europe for the next two years. Her last public speaking engagement was in London in 1951. She was asked to be a member of the Italian delegation to the UNESCO conference in Florence.
1952	Dr. Montessori died in Holland on May 6th, two months before her 82nd birthday, due to a cerebral hemorrhage. Her son, Mario was at her side. She was buried in the town of Noordwijk, where she resided at the "Villa Chiaravalle", an evident homage to her birth-place.
1957	Nancy McCormick Rambusch led a new movement in America, reintroducing the Montessori method.
1958	Rambusch opened the Whitby School in Greenwich, Connecticut.
1959	Mario Montessori appointed Rambusch as the AMI representative in America.
1960	The American Montessori Society (AMS) was founded by Rambusch in partnership with the Association Montessori Internationale (AMI). Schools and training centers were reestablished in the United States. Eventually, the two organizations parted ways and became two completely separate organizations.
1968	The first U.S. public Montessori schools were established.
1978	The first U.S. *Erdkinder* (12–18 years) was started.
1990	It is estimated that there are over 5,000 Montessori schools in America.

CONFESSION:

As a very young Montessori teacher, I intuitively knew that this philosophy had a much deeper meaning than any other educational philosophy that I had previously studied. My youth and inexperience with life in general, however, kept me from truly understanding the spiritual depth of the work I began to do. It was as if I was being drawn like a magnet to this powerful force, but had yet to recognize the source of that power. I was being pulled along a path to something very beautiful, although it took me many years to actually let go of the pull from other sources and go entirely with the flow that was leading me in the right direction.

REFERENCES

1. Montessori, Maria. *The Montessori Method*. New York: Schocken Books, 1964, pp. 38–39.
2. Montessori, Maria. *The Secret of Childhood*. New York; Ballantine Books, 1966, p. 37.
3. Montessori, Maria. *The Absorbent Mind*. Wheaton, Ill. Theosophical Press, 1964, p. 165.

2

Why Montessori?

"The things he sees are not just remem-
bered; they form a part of his soul."

—Maria Montessori

So, why Montessori?—besides the fact that it is one of the few educational methods used today that is scientifically based on the developmental needs of the child and the evolving brain. The *absorbent mind*, as Dr. Montessori described it, is in a prime mode for learning and the Montessori environment is specifically designed to appropriately meet its varied needs. That *sponge* of a brain is immersed in an ocean of learning—the Montessori environment. Interestingly enough, it also goes beyond simply the scientific knowledge of growth; it provides an experience in constructing the whole person, which is superior to just focusing on intellectual development. Children and adults who are immersed in this philosophy and methodology are given the unique opportunity to develop every aspect of who they were meant to be—not only intellectually but emotionally, socially, and spiritually. These different aspects of development cannot be separated in the Montessori experience.

Montessori paints a much bigger picture than just the method and the materials. It is a path to self-awareness, a path to finding what makes us unique inside; it gives us an opportunity to be everything that we could or were meant to be. This journey starts at birth and is driven by that spirit within all of us; that common, universal spirit that flows through all of us and is the potential for greatness that is within all of us—no matter who we are, no matter where we are, no matter what culture or country, no matter what religion. Unfortunately, if our immediate environments do not support it, then that greatness is often blocked, or in some cases, extinguished. This is the beauty of Montessori, the fact that Dr. Montessori recognized the innate nobility in all children. She perceived that this majesty needed to be given the right environment in which to grow and be nurtured. It needed to be given the ability to have life and flourish. The gifts bestowed upon each of us are as unique as the universe itself. When those gifts are allowed to flourish and are realized, then that person is able to give them to the world; and that is the ultimate goal—that our greatness contributes to the grandeur of the world (the big picture). Some of the world's most innovative thinkers have been greatly influenced by their Montessori education. In 2004, Barbara Walters interviewed Google founders, Larry Page and Sergei Brin, and asked them if they felt having college professors as parents was one of the main factors that led to their success. Interestingly enough, they both credited their Montessori experience as the foundation of their success: "*We both went to a Montessori school, and I think it was part of that training of not following rules and orders, and being self-motivated, questioning what's going on in the world, doing things a bit differently,*" answered Larry Page.

Will Wright, the inventor of famous video games such as *SimCity*, also attributed his success to his Montessori experiences: "*Montessori taught me the joy of discovery. It is all about learning on your own terms, rather than a teacher explaining stuff to you.* SimCity *comes right out of Montessori...*"

Jeff Bezos, founder of Amazon, is another Montessori alumnus. He describes his business strategy as one of experimentation and discovery. If exploration of the environment and discovery—*planting seeds* or *going down blind alleys*—sounds very Montessori-like, that is because it is. Jeff Bezos' early experiences in Montessori set him on a course which changed his life and the life of countless others in the world. He has said, "*But every once in a while, you go down an alley and it opens up into this huge, broad avenue.*"

Remarkably, two college professors, Jeffrey Dyer of Brigham Young University and Hal Gregersen of INSEAD, in a search to discover the similarities in how creative business executives think, discovered yet another link to Montessori. After surveying over 3,000 executives and interviewing 500 entrepreneurs and inventors over six years, they found something interesting. Gregersen sums it up this way:

> "*If you look at 4-year-olds, they are constantly asking questions and wondering how things work. But by the time they are 6 ½ years old they stop asking questions because they quickly learn that teachers value the right answers more than provocative questions. High school*

students rarely show inquisitiveness. And by the time they're grown up and are in corporate settings, they have already had the curiosity drummed out of them...

We also believe that the most innovative entrepreneurs were very lucky to have been raised in an atmosphere where inquisitiveness was encouraged... A number of the innovative entrepreneurs also went to Montessori schools, where they learned to follow their curiosity. To paraphrase the famous Apple ad campaign, innovators not only learned early on to think different, they act different (and even talk different)."[1]

When you think about that quote and understand how just these few innovators have changed the modern world, it is astounding to realize that the Montessori method played an important role in *planting those innovative seeds*.

This leads to reflecting about how the Montessori experience allows children to develop a completely different perception and experience with what is called *work*. Montessori children actually think of their work as play. They enjoy the process, get excited about exploring new things, and want to continue to learn more about the world. Dr. Montessori observed that children have an innate understanding of the nobility of work. When one is truly engaged in something that is of value to the individual, there is a deep sense of satisfaction and accomplishment that feeds the soul. Erik Erikson, a theorist in child development, actually believed that the child's choice of work was the beginning of their search for identity and realistic self-esteem.

Our traditional culture disregards and disrespects the young child's innate capabilities and desire to learn. As mentioned previously, one of the reasons traditional educators rejected the Montessori philosophy in the past, and some still do today, is that they see young children very differently. They believe that childhood should not be taken that seriously, that it should only be a time for play and social interactions. Then there is the opposite extreme, where once again, adults impose externally what they think the young child may be capable of, and try to control the experience. This would include trying to force infants, toddlers, and preschool children to do things that are developmentally inappropriate before their time of readiness. For example, an adult may want their infant to be the youngest child to walk, therefore intervening in an effort to try and skip the crawling stage and jump right into walking. The adult robs the child of the natural cycle that needs to take place in order to develop in a healthy way, all for the adult's satisfaction of telling people that their child is ahead of other children. Unfortunately, I have seen this type of behavior in parents in other areas as well, such as in learning to read, write, and perform mathematics at the time the parent wants the child to do it. This is exploitation of children, along with being a dangerous practice in exerting inappropriate external force. This type of external intervention on the part of the adult is unhealthy for the child, and can cause actual damage on many levels. This is a gross misinterpretation of not only what Dr. Montessori was telling us, but also of what the young child's developing brain and body needs. Dr. Montessori greatly respected children and encouraged adults to safely prepare appropriate environments that allowed for the natural internal exploration process completely forged by the child. Once again, current brain research supports Dr. Montessori's findings.

In many ways, our world is going through a cultural revolution. It is very clear that the traditional educational approach is not succeeding in preparing students for this new world. The value of work and the concept of success have been narrowed down to very shallow notions. It has been culturally ingrained in us that success depends upon the size of your bank account, the type of car you drive, and the grandeur of the house in which you live. Work is what allows you to attain all of these material status symbols. I am not suggesting that people should not enjoy owning nice things, but when it becomes our reason for being, then we are out of balance. These things are neither permanent nor long-lasting, and if we place the foundation of our self-worth and happiness upon this sandbar of a foundation, we are setting ourselves up for a potentially unhealthy and unhappy life. This is precisely what we are seeing in our culture today; people working only because it will bring success as defined by our culture. In many cases, people hate what they do; they have no love or passion for it. It may bring material success, but it rarely brings true happiness. Allow me to share a personal story that demonstrates the ramifications of this view.

I was diagnosed with cancer in 1986, and during one of my oncology appointments, I was talking with another cancer patient who was there for a check-up. He was actually a physician, and during the course of our conversation, he shared with me that his true passion in life was music. He had wanted to be a musician his entire life, but that was not an acceptable choice in his family. His grandfather was a doctor, his father was a doctor, and the list went on. He had believed that there was no choice other than following in his family's footsteps. After many years of doing something that certainly brought him material success, but brought him little joy, he was diagnosed with cancer. It was a pretty serious battle, so he gave up practicing medicine while he attempted to fight the disease. In its place, he began to fill his time with what he loved—music. He surrounded himself with music, learning to perfect his craft with musical instruments, and it brought him great joy. His joyful state of mind definitely helped strengthen his immune system and improve his health (eventually he went into remission). He also decided to give up medicine and pursue music full time. I do not believe this is an isolated incident for I have read many similar stories during my fight with cancer. Finding your passion in life and loving what you do is vital to a happy existence.

When children go through the Montessori experience, they discover that work, their personal gifts, and passions, can bring joy not only to themselves, but to others as well. They learn to value other rewards besides just the accumulation of money and things. The irony in this is the fact that when people find and follow their passions, based on their self-knowledge and the determination to follow their dreams, they can achieve financial success beyond their wildest dreams—just look at Larry Page, Sergei Brin, and Jeff Bezos! It is not the fact that we should not value the success of our accomplishments in whatever form it may come, it is that when we place our value system *only* on the accumulation of wealth, we are not allowing ourselves to develop in a healthy and balanced way. Many Montessori students go out into the world and are highly successful in many other areas as well; they are spiritual leaders, educators, philosophers, and advocates. The satisfaction of helping others and the world is the kind of success that makes them feel happy and fulfilled.

Unfortunately, our traditional educational system has not been structured in a way to allow children this freedom to explore their environments. Therefore, we haven't always seen people getting in touch with, or living up to, their potential. There is a reason for this. If we look at the history of our traditional educational system, we discover that it was established for a specific purpose that was relevant for that time. During the Industrial Revolution in our country, there was a need to provide training to millions of immigrants coming into our country in order to teach them English, acclimate them to our country, and prepare them to work in the factories. Thousands of factories were in operation and the need for workers was great. People needed to have a competent grasp of our language, understand directions, accept conformity and change tasks at the sound of the bell. This system was not designed to create leaders or innovative thinkers, merely people who would accommodate the needs of the current society. This is the same system that has remained in place to this day. Obviously, the needs of society have changed so the traditional structure is no longer relevant or useful. Educational reform was a topic that Dr. Montessori and other educational theorists have been proposing for over one hundred years.

It is also relevant to address the impression that many people have that Montessori is a new-age, *granola crunch* kind of philosophy, where children have complete freedom to do whatever they like without any boundaries. Perhaps as you read the earlier paragraph, when my thoughts began to take a more esoteric tone, it was very easy to interpret the information in different ways based upon your personal beliefs. If we go back to the early 1960s when the Montessori philosophy was reintroduced to the United States, the time was one of rebellion against traditional thought in our country. It was the right time for a different philosophy of education to be embraced and many *out-of-the-box* thinkers became the champions of growing the Montessori method again in the United States. That impression of free-spirited, free-thinking hippies aligned itself in some cases to this philosophy, which was certainly a very different approach to that of the conservative, highly structured traditional approach to education. False impressions of the Montessori philosophy ranged from the belief that children were allowed to do whatever they liked, to the opposite extreme; that they were little soldiers, deprived of the opportunity to be creative or spontaneous. Neither of these impressions was correct and was based on a misunderstanding of the philosophy. In addition, because of the nature of the *whole child* being developed—which is what attracted the free-thinkers—some traditionalists believed this was too much of a touchy-feely kind of method; that children had to be exposed to the *real world*, which is a world of competition and hard knocks where only the strong survive. Many traditional educators still hold these beliefs, verbalize them, and are very steadfast in their opinion. This, of course, continues the false impression of Montessori education among some people and educators. The interesting thing is that if traditional educators actually researched and observed authentic Montessori schools in action, it would be very hard to believe that they would not be impressed with the method or at least be willing to agree that it works and is a viable choice for many children. Old structures and belief systems are often very hard to surrender and there is always fear of the unknown.

The good news is that many educators today embrace the true Montessori philosophy in both private and public schools. The method has certainly moved beyond the impression of bare-footed, long-skirted flower children of the '60s, into a time where world-renowned brain specialists, scientists, educators, entrepreneurs, and philosophers are singing the praises of the impact of a Montessori education on children and the world.

The simplicity and brilliance of Dr. Montessori's work is what makes it so intriguing. The idea of providing hands-on learning materials certainly seems like a simple concept, but the brilliance behind it is in the complexity of actually doing it, doing it effectively, and seeing the big picture. Dr. Montessori discovered through her astute observations exactly how children's brains work. That is one of the most captivating elements of the Montessori experience and one that took me many, many years to understand—and I confess, I have still not mastered complete understanding. It is an on-going evolution of not only internalization of this philosophy, but personal development in relation to it.

To continue with more factual reasons as to "Why Montessori?," I will go into some of the details explaining how it provides a well-rounded experience for the child on many other levels. Socially, children are grouped into three-year age groupings, which provide a family-like experience for them. Children experience being the youngest in the class and are nurtured by their older, more experienced peers. The older students act as role models and teachers, and their self-esteem and confidence are strengthened when they are looked up to as teachers and mentors. In their roles as teachers, they take the younger students under their wings, presenting lessons to them that they themselves have mastered. This is a valuable way to reinforce their learning as well as develop the brain even further. Teaching something to someone else exercises a completely different part of the brain compared to being on the receiving end of the experience.

Parents will often ask if there is a danger of the older children regressing in behavior because of the presence of younger children in the classroom and that does not typically happen. One reason is that most children cherish the role of being the *elder* and definitely do not want to be thought of as babies. They take pride in their leadership roles. This pride in their roles, without a doubt, increases their self-esteem and puts them on the path to being future leaders. In this family-like grouping where the students grow up together, it is easy to see the advantage this holds for an *only child* in a family, but it adds another valuable occurrence for children with siblings. This is because they will always be the oldest, youngest, or middle child in their own family, and that place will not change. In the Montessori classroom however, they encounter being the youngest, middle, and oldest in the community in each cycle of the three-year experience. This is a very valuable social experience since it allows them to see life from many different perspectives; something that builds critical thinking skills as well as appreciation of people's differences and abilities. Montessori children have been shown to have very high critical thinking skills in comparison to many of their traditionally educated counterparts. This is a direct result of being exposed to so many different levels of abilities, the use of questioning as a constant means to create thinkers and not just give children answers, and the continual interaction of the children and adults in the environment.

It also gives children a very strong sense of community. A community is a living, breathing thing that allows all of us to have opportunities to grow and mature in many ways. Students grow in their emotional development as well. They learn how to handle their emotions and to understand that emotions are part of being human. At times, we all get angry, hurt, jealous, fearful, anxious, frustrated, impatient, *and* we all experience joy, courage, empathy, compassion, patience, thoughtfulness, and love. A Montessori community allows children to learn how to be patient, considerate, and respectful of others' needs, along with how to handle their frustrations and communicate those feelings when they need to. They learn how to overcome conflict because, in an interactive community, conflict is inevitable and actually normal. How do we react when we want a lesson that someone else is using and we need to wait our turn? How do we learn to communicate in a positive, respectful, and proactive way when someone hurts our feelings, either intentionally or unintentionally? It is a constant exercise in self-awareness and learning to use our personal power for our own good and for the good of others.

The children are given the opportunity to make mistakes and to learn from them in an atmosphere of forgiveness, love, and respect. When they do make a mistake, and all of them will, by either hurting someone else with their words or with their hands, we want them to become proficient in understanding their role and responsibility in every altercation. The discipline approach is a positive one and its goal is for the children to develop an inner self-discipline and moral compass. We focus on helping the child to express him or herself as to what led to the choice that they made. The discussion would continue as to how a different choice could have led to a different outcome. They are given the opportunity to come up with appropriate solutions to the issue at hand, while also hearing about how the other involved child felt about the situation. That gives both of the children an understanding of other people's perceptions of a situation. We help guide them to understand the natural consequences of their choices. This is real life; there are always consequences to the choices that we make, so we want to do our best to make positive choices. This dialogue about interactions between others, both good and bad, is what builds the child's skills in self-awareness, awareness of others, and the need to be a good community member for the benefit of all. Just giving a child a punishment for poor behavior, as occurs in most traditional settings, does not have the same overall positive, long-range results as the discipline approach used in Montessori classrooms. Good communication, collaboration, and cooperation are necessary in order to build students' internal self-discipline and to have a functioning classroom. These real-life skills are built upon, year after year, as the children continue their journey though Montessori levels; and when the students emerge as young adults, these skills are a part of who they are. They are life-changing skills and will certainly pave the way to success in future endeavors. Montessori students learn how to work with all different types of students and adults, to communicate what they need, to problem solve, to manage their time, and to accomplish goals. They learn to be responsible and respectful individuals and community members. They are also self-aware; they have learned what kind of learner they are, what their strengths are, what their weaknesses are, and how to navigate life and learning through this personal awareness.

One of my favorite stories about Montessori students using their self-awareness is that of Skylar, who went through the entire Montessori experience from preschool through eighth grade. He was in our very first graduating class of 1998, a group of seven graduates! He was accepted into a prestigious local private high school, one which was much larger than anything he had ever experienced in Montessori. On the first day of classes, after sitting in the back of a class with 40 students in it, Skylar went up to the teacher and told him that although he understood that the teacher did not assign seats, Skylar requested that he be allowed to sit in the front of the class. When the teacher inquired as to why he wanted to sit up front (not typically something most high school freshman would request!), Skylar told the teacher that he was a visual, kinesthetic learner, not an auditory learner, and if he remained in the back, he would be too distracted to really focus on the lecture. He needed to be up front in order to see the board and stay engaged in the class. The teacher was so impressed with Skylar's self-confidence and self-awareness that he called Skylar's mother to find out how he acquired these skills. Skylar's mom told the teacher that it was his Montessori experience that helped with this realization.

Skylar was not unlike many boys in Montessori classrooms; he was active, athletic, and needed to move. There are many studies today indicating that the traditional educational system is leaving boys behind because of the current expectations of students in terms of testing and higher language expectations. This will be addressed in further detail in Chapter 15, but in general, Montessori classrooms have given boys, who are particularly in need of movement, the ability to learn by moving. They are not confined to a desk all day, which is a very unnatural constraint for young boys in terms of their overall development. All students are able to move about and make choices in the course of their day. This freedom alone can be life-changing for all students in their educational journey, but it is most impactful on boys.

Skylar went through all the typical challenges of adolescence and his experience in this particularly difficult stage of life led him to a career where today, he helps young people navigate their journey through it. In addition, his love of the environment has had profound effects on the world. Today, Skylar holds a Master's Degree in Philosophy, Cosmology, and Consciousness. He co-founded a nonprofit organization dedicated to environmental education for sustainable development. He has guided and educated youth in middle school, high school, and college in topics ranging from ecology to self-awareness. Skylar has guided wilderness trips all over the world, ranging from back-packing and canoeing expeditions to managing ecological restoration teams in damaged areas. He is a cultural ecologist and meditation teacher who works to help people become self-aware and to celebrate life and their place in the world. Skylar is helping young people and the environment, and, at the same time, is enjoying life to the fullest. One more example of how the Montessori experience has positively impacted young people's lives and the world.

As indicated in Skylar's passion for nature, the Montessori experience leads to a heightened respect of, and concern for, nature, its creatures, and the environment in general. Dr. Montessori was one of the first environmentalists, in that she created a curriculum based on the interconnectedness of all things in the universe. Her *cosmic curriculum*, which brings to the children inspirational stories about the universe, our planet, and all the creatures on it, has instilled in Montessori children a mission to be good stewards of the earth. The children learn that every creature has a job and should be respected for its contribution to the environment. The students are excited and often in awe after researching each creature's special and unique gift to the world! It is not unusual to see our students go to great care to rescue an insect that is in the classroom and return it to its natural habitat. They are aghast and greatly disturbed when they see anyone carelessly or cruelly kill, abuse, or injure any creature. Montessori children actually experience a close relationship with nature and have intense respect for it. Montessori students know much more about botany, zoology, and earth science than most adults. Conversely, when children in traditional educational settings are not given the opportunity to interact with nature, or delve deeply into learning about the interconnectedness of life, it is not surprising that there is little connection to it. That lack of connection leads them to unconsciously pollute, harm, and destroy nature as children and to continue that behavior even when they grow into adulthood. We critically need our Montessori young people to lead us into a future where the planet is not stripped and depleted of its resources, habitats, and creatures. More than any other time in the history of our world, our planet is on the brink of unprecedented changes that will eventually alter the lives of all. Our students will need to rise to the challenge of helping everyone to overcome these obstacles; Montessori students have the skills and the passion for nature to do that.

A favorite story of mine that shows the depth of sincere caring and empathy of which our Montessori students are capable, is that of the bus driver on one of our middle school field trips. The middle school students and teachers were on a five-day trip when some of the students discovered that it happened to be the bus driver's birthday. On their own, they came up with a plan to make his day special. There was a planned stop at one of the historical gift shops later in the day, and the students pooled their money and bought the driver small gifts, a card, and treats to substitute for a cake. They boarded the bus, sang happy birthday to him, thanked him for spending his birthday with them, and presented him with their birthday gifts. The entire plan originated from the students; the teachers and I were as surprised as he. The driver was almost brought to tears by the kindness, thoughtfulness, and generosity of the students, as was I.

Another very critical reason that the Montessori approach is such a positive experience for children is the high level of positive self-esteem and confidence that we see in our students; and those traits are a direct result of being in a Montessori environment. There are many reasons for this. First of all, the goal of the Montessori method is to allow children to become completely independent. Dr. Montessori told us that we should never do anything for a child that they can do for themselves. Allowing children to be completely independent builds their self-esteem; with every success, they begin to see that they are very competent and do not need adults to do things for them or to solve all of their problems. This is why you see open shelves in Montessori classrooms where children have access to all that they need in the course of their day. The adults are there to guide and support them, not dictate what they are to do. Children have choices within their day, which is very empowering to them. Learning to use this empowerment responsibly in a community of learners is a process that builds their communication skills and their sense of competency as individuals. They are allowed to make mistakes, because mistakes help them to learn. This is the message that is constant: we are all learning and growing, we all have strengths and weaknesses, we are all here to help and support each other as we learn and grow.

When children understand that everyone makes mistakes, they are not so hard on themselves when they make one; and they can then pick themselves up, brush themselves off, and move on with a better understanding of how they can create a different outcome next time. There is no referral to *good* or *bad* children. There will, however, be a discussion that may include *good* and *bad* choices. This is a very important distinction! Adults must make it clear to the child that it is *the action* that is the problem, not the child. I will often say to students who may come into my office because of misbehavior, "I love you, but I do not like hitting. Your choice of behavior is what we are concerned about." Children will not automatically understand this distinction. Sadly, more often than I would like to see (and hear) young children have come to my office and when I asked them what happened, their response was, "I was a bad boy (or girl)." I tell them, "You are not a bad boy, you just made a bad choice. You are a good boy, and good boys need to make good choices." Children need to know that we love them, and that because we love them, it is our job to help them remember to make good choices for the benefit of everyone. When children are told over and over again that they are bad, they believe it and act accordingly. They sometimes actually use it as an excuse as to why they behaved the way that they did, as if it is a given *because* they are a bad boy. When you separate the behavior from the child, responsibility is placed directly on the choices that they make, not on who they are. This also builds the child's self-esteem as they see that they have direct power over the choices that they make.

Another element in building the child's self-esteem is the absence of grades for children in our early childhood and elementary Montessori programs. Our children learn for the love of learning, not for an external reward, such as grades or stickers. This internal sense of accomplishment allows children to feel successful and have a natural desire to learn more and take on challenges. When traditional programs give young children grades, those young children do not have the emotional maturity to understand that if they don't get all "A"s that they are not stupid or slow. Of course, all of the "A" students do not have a problem with self-esteem, but what about all of the other students? They now begin to think that they are not as smart as others and their concepts about themselves and learning start to deteriorate. Some of these students may begin to show physical signs, actually becoming ill with constant headaches or stomachaches. They may become extremely fearful or anxious, not wanting to attempt anything new or something they perceive as challenging. Some will become defiant and act as if they do not care or become the class clown to deflect attention away from their deficiencies. Others will just give up and not try. This is an educational disservice to all young children. Children in a Montessori classroom are treated and respected as individuals with unique learning styles.

Montessori classrooms were designed to meet the needs of all kinds of learners. Typically, learning styles are categorized into three main areas: auditory, visual, and kinesthetic. Auditory learners will easily process any information that they hear. Students who do well in traditional classrooms are usually strong auditory learners for obvious reasons. In most cases, the teacher is lecturing in front of the classroom and if a student is good at listening and processing what they hear, then a traditional classroom easily works for them. Visual learners need visual stimulation in order to process information, so pictures, a board, charts, videos, mind-maps, posters, drawings, etc., will all help the visual learner to process and retain information. This approach may also be used in a traditional classroom, but only when the teacher decides to use it. Kinesthetic learners have the most difficult time in a traditional classroom because they need to move! Their brains process information when some part of the body is moving. Think back to those poor students sitting in a desk and their legs were kicking or their hands were in constant motion, perhaps tapping a pencil, and they were constantly getting in trouble for not sitting still. I once had an elementary student come into my class who had failed terribly in traditional school; he was a kind boy but had given up on himself and learning. He was a kinesthetic learner and felt like a complete failure as a student. He literally had to move to remember anything. So we proceeded to come up with a plan for him to succeed through movement. Other than our community meetings, when everyone needed to sit and listen, he could walk around the classroom to study as long as he did not distract others. He would take his vocabulary words and walk as he studied them. He would also put his work into music and memorize facts to song, dance, and poetry. He began to feel successful as he was able to remember much more. As his academic success grew, so did his self-esteem. The shy, defeated young boy who entered our classroom was being transformed into a witty, confident student. His fear and avoidance of challenges began to disappear. He stayed with us through middle school and emerged as a confident young man who became much more self-aware and self-accepting. He is one example of why children with traditional backgrounds should not be excluded from joining Montessori classrooms. I have seen too many children be transformed for the better to not allow them this opportunity.

Montessori classrooms are stimulating environments that allow all children to learn through their own individual combinations of learning styles. There are ample opportunities and activities in all three styles: freedom of movement and hands-on learning materials for the kinesthetic learners, a rich array of visual materials for visual stimulation, and unlimited opportunities for auditory learners to discuss information and ideas with both teachers and classmates.

In a final answer to "Why Montessori?," perhaps the real question to answer is: "What kind of young person do we want to emerge from this educational experience?" If we want a young person who is happy, self-confident, and self-aware; good at communication, time management, and goal setting; who cares about the world, the creatures in it, and other people; is a kind, respectful and caring community member who is able to form healthy relationships; and is a self-motivated, life-long learner, and functioning adult; then Montessori is the answer.

I would like to end this chapter with another story about a quintessential Montessori student. She is yet another positive example that helps answer the question of "Why Montessori?"

Anna started Montessori at age three and eventually graduated from middle school. As far back as I can remember, Anna had aspirations of being a neurosurgeon. She was a gifted student who worked hard and always set high goals for herself. She thrived in the Montessori setting where she was allowed to pursue her interests and have lively debates on topics that interested her—and there were many! She was passionate about many things, one of which was to always be true to herself. Anna graduated and went on to a very prestigious private high school where she was a well-rounded honor student, who was involved in many activities and continued on the path toward her medical aspirations. She was accepted into many colleges upon graduating high school, but was offered a substantial academic scholarship into a prestigious Florida university's pre-med program. Anna accepted the scholarship and remained on her path to the goal of being a neurosurgeon. After her first year in college, she wrote a letter to me explaining why she was choosing to leave the university. She told me that she felt the need to research the country for a university that was more Montessori-like. She missed the interaction of like-minded students on a quest for knowledge and making a contribution to the world. She felt the more traditional approach to education was not where she thrived as a student and a person. She felt passionately about being true to herself and what she believed would contribute to her greater good, and then ultimately to the greater good of the world. Her parents were proud of her decision and fully supported her. She wanted me to know because she felt the Montessori environment played such a critical role in developing who she became as a person. So Anna did her research and found just what she was looking for, St John's College in Annapolis, Maryland. It was the closest thing to a Montessori experience that Anna could find in the college world. Anna was accepted and found her academic home. St. John's entire curriculum is based upon the greatest books ever written, from Plato to Socrates to Shakespeare and beyond. The students discussed the writings in seminars. Anna invited me to visit her on a Parent's Weekend so that I could see what type of experience she was having. To say that I was impressed would be a gross understatement. What I witnessed was some of the brightest minds in the country reading these brilliant works and discussing them from many points of view and levels of understanding. The critical thinking power in those rooms could have fueled a rocket into space! It gave me such hope and excitement for these young people and for the future of our country.

Here is my point concerning the final story about Anna. This is an example of how the Montessori experience so affected this brilliant young woman to accept nothing but the best for herself and her goals in life. She was self-aware enough to know that she needed something different and had the self-confidence and courage to pursue it. In the end, Anna changed her goal to become a neurosurgeon and is a Harvard Law graduate, currently practicing Energy Law in Washington D.C. She is working for change in the world and I have no doubt she will succeed.

> *"My vision of the future is no longer people taking exams and proceeding on that certification...but of individuals passing from one stage of independence to a higher (one), by means of their own activity through their own effort of will, which constitutes the inner evolution of the individual."*
>
> —Maria Montessori, *From Childhood to Adolescence*

CONFESSION:

In my early years of being a Montessori teacher, when asked by parents, Why Montessori?, my immediate response would be primarily concerning academic reasons. Your child will learn to read, write, and do advanced mathematical operations at an early age! This was my automatic go-to response. Of course, although this is very true, over the many years of Montessori and life experience, I have come to realize that the academics, while a wonderful byproduct of the Montessori experience, are not the most important aspects of this method. I now put many other skills acquired by the student ahead of the academics, such as self-awareness, high self-esteem, communication, creativity, critical thinking, empathy for others, and a love of nature, self, and others.

REFERENCE

1. Fryer, Bronwyn. "How Do Innovators Think?" *Harvard Business Review,* September 28, 2009. https://hbr.org/2009/09/how-do-innovators-think. org.

3

What Makes Montessori Work?

As my experience as a Montessori educator grew, it became very apparent that what Dr. Montessori discovered about the nature of the child was, in fact, very true. That is, children have an innate desire to learn and to grow, and they follow their own timetable as to what calls to them. This is one of the most important and amazing facts as to why Montessori works. My doubts melted away as, time after time, I witnessed children immersed in work of their own choosing, fully concentrating and doing it joyfully, and with a sense of accomplishment.

How could this be possible with children as young as three years of age? Through Dr. Montessori's many years of observations and the subsequent work of her followers, it became very evident that there is a force within children that pushes them forward. Anyone who has had a child knows that the infant, from the very first day of life, begins observing and exploring the world around them and imitating adults. Parents do not need to *teach* their children to talk and walk; it is a natural process that emerges because of this life force, or inner intelligence, that pushes them forward. As long as the parents are providing a safe, loving, and nurturing environment where the child is allowed to observe, interact, and explore, the child's development moves forward in a healthy and positive way. This force, or inner intelligence, will continue to push the child to seek more and more knowledge until he or she is satisfied and then moves on to something else at the appropriate time. Unfortunately, if that *prepared environment* (as previously described) is not available to the developing child, then that life force gets blocked and the emergence of a specific skill at a particular time might be jeopardized. Let me give you the example of the infant's acquisition of oral language. The child's *sensitive period* for the acquisition of oral language is between birth and three years of age. If a child, for some reason, is deprived of the opportunity to hear the spoken language of their native tongue, or has limited exposure to it, that child will be affected greatly. In some rare cases where a child was totally deprived of the human voice at this sensitive period, the child was never able to develop the skill of speaking a language. Of course, this is a very extreme example that unfortunately has been true for a few children but has taught scientists the importance of nurture in the development of the child (I will share a specific example of this in a following chapter). If we examine children who have been deprived of the opportunity to be read to or hear nursery rhymes and songs, their language development will be stunted; hence, the importance of the *prepared environment*.

Another critical element in what makes Montessori work is the teacher. The Montessori teacher must be someone who has absolute respect for children and the inner force directing them. They must be the complete opposite of what many traditional educators are: people who think they are wiser than the children, and want to control them and what they learn. Montessori teachers must be humble, wise enough to trust and be in awe of the inner workings of the child, and flexible enough to observe and adapt to the individual needs of the children. Montessori education is an indirect style of teaching; the teachers are there to be role models, and to guide, inspire, and support. The teacher must be diligent in preparing the environment for learning based on the knowledge of the Montessori materials and the developmental needs of the child. Dr. Montessori stressed that teachers must be keen observers in order to know their children and what it is they need. She also felt that Montessori teachers should be generalists; meaning that it is not necessary to be a specialist in any one field of education. She considered it more important to be a role model to the children, being in awe of life, and modeling a passion to learn about every aspect of it. The Montessori teacher also understands that Montessori materials were not designed to be used as a rigid, step-by-step curriculum as in traditional education, but as a series of exciting discoveries made by the child and guided by the observations of the teacher.

In a Montessori classroom, children are surrounded by a rich array of appropriate, concrete learning materials—the next element necessary in making Montessori work. These materials are so attractive to the children that there is no need for the teacher to force children to use them. The materials actually pull the children to them like a magnet. This same inner intelligence that pushes infants to watch their parents' mouths and faces and imitate the sounds that their parents make in the process of developing oral language skills, also drives the child to work with materials that actually call to the child. They are answering that inner call. This inner call is very intelligent and knows exactly what the child needs. Classrooms need to be fully equipped in every area. If a parent visits a school and sees very few Montessori materials on the shelves, this is an indication that it is not an authentic Montessori classroom. The materials are the link between the child's hands and mind. They are a necessary ingredient in the process of exploration by the child and in providing a prepared environment for all of the children.

Many years ago, when I was first working with three to six year old children, I had a student who was five years old and in his third and final year of the early childhood classroom. This was long before today's common use of occupational therapy (OT) for students who have poor motor skills. This child could barely write legibly and had poor fine motor skills. He was naturally drawn to the lesson area called Practical Life, which is the area of the early childhood classroom that is designed to strengthen fine motor skills among many other important skills. He consistently chose to scrub tables, chairs, and floors; polish silver; clean the windows; fold the classroom towels and mats; care for the plants; and was fully immersed in every aspect of Practical Life without me having to ask him or force him. In fact, it seemed to be his passion, and without a doubt in my mind, it was calling him. Since this was in the beginning of my career, I would sometimes be nervous about allowing him to so passionately and single-mindedly spend so much time in the Practical Life area at his age. Well, my worst fears were realized when sometime in November, the boy's father came to see me and angrily stated, "I am not paying all of this tuition to train my son to be a janitor! I want him to be practicing his handwriting, not playing with these silly lessons." Well, I confess my inexperience and fear of upsetting the parent got the better of me, so I told him that I would make sure that his son did more academic tasks before moving to the Practical Life area. So, I interfered with the boy's natural choice and imposed *the rule* that he could not choose any Practical Life lessons until he did some *harder* work and practiced his handwriting. The boy was respectful and complied, but I watched his frustration grow and the joyful light in his eyes start to diminish as he painfully struggled to trace his letters over and over again on his handwriting sheets. I could see that his joy was being tampered with. I called the father back in and told him what I should have said initially, that I needed him to trust the method—and me. I explained that his son had a delay in his fine motor skills and that he needed to do Practical Life lessons in order to strengthen them, as they were designed to do. I told him I would not keep him from choosing the Practical Life lessons before any other lessons, and I assured him that I would continue to guide him to choose other lessons as well, but that Practical Life was very important for him right now. Fortunately for his son, the father was willing to listen and do as I asked. It was a lesson for me as well. I learned that I can't allow my fear of parents' reactions prevent me from doing what I believe is right for the child based on our Montessori philosophy. I learned to stand up for the philosophy and the children in my care. The happy ending to this story is that although the boy's fine motor skills still needed work, his extensive work in Practical Life certainly did improve them. The boy, on his own, moved away from Practical Life and began to work diligently in all areas. It was a great example of seeing a child instinctively know what it was that he needed, follow that inner intelligence, and then move on to another calling. He graduated from kindergarten with a great deal of self-confidence and prepared for the elementary level.

> *"Respect all the reasonable forms of activity in which the child engages and try to understand them."*
>
> —Maria Montessori

A common misconception about the Montessori method is that it is just for exceptional learners; either gifted or learning disabled. In reality, it is designed to be successful for most children. All children are treated as individuals in Montessori classrooms. No two children are exactly alike, so therefore, should not be treated exactly the same. Children are allowed to develop at their own pace and ability. This allows for the gifted children to move ahead without being bored and conversely, when a child needs more time to master a concept, they are given it, and not made to feel badly about themselves because the whole class is *getting it* and they are not. This individualized approach allows all students to feel successful and therefore builds their self-esteem at a time in their development that it is very important for them to feel confident and excited about learning. The prepared environment allows all children to build their knowledge and develop at their own unique rate.

Another misconception about the Montessori method is that there is no structure. This belief comes from the untrained eye comparing the Montessori classroom with a traditional classroom. There are no desks lined up with assigned seating as in a traditional classroom, nor is there a teacher standing in front of the classroom lecturing and controlling every aspect of the classroom and the day. Although the Montessori classroom doesn't follow the traditional model, there is, in fact, a structure to it, which is what makes it work. We know it is a much more natural structure for learning, and it is based on the developmental needs of the child at that stage. Children are able to freely choose constructive, purposeful activity and destructive or disturbing behavior is redirected. Children cannot just do *whatever they want*; they have freedom with limits. So, how can it be structured when it appears to be just the opposite? Well, on the very first day of school, the students come together as a community and discuss what it is that everyone in the community needs in order for the classroom to be a safe, productive, nurturing, and positive place for learning and living together. All children and adults in the classroom community have a voice and express their needs. From that discussion, a community agreement may be drawn up and everyone signs it and agrees to abide by these *agreements* or *ground rules*. The foundation of the structure is in place now. Generally, these agreements will cover the basic needs of everyone and may look something like the following:

COMMUNITY AGREEMENT

Our classroom community agrees to be respectful of everyone's needs and will do so by:

- Behaving in a way that everyone feels safe
- Using inside, quiet voices so that everyone may concentrate
- Moving our bodies in a slow, careful way so as not to harm or interfere with others
- Using only kind words when we communicate
- Helping everyone to feel included
- Using our hands to help, not hurt
- Being respectful of personal space
- Helping others
- Being kind

There may be different variations on this theme, but in general, it is about establishing an atmosphere of respect, comradeship, and collaboration. All of the students sign the agreement. The boundaries are now in place and the Montessori structure allows for the children to learn through their mistakes, and develop a deeper understanding of what it means to be a member of a community. Students are not automatically given freedom, but rather earn it through their responsible behavior as a community member. This evolution of learning by being in a community is one of the most important ways that the child learns to become self-disciplined. It is an inner awareness of what needs to be done in order to be able to meet all of the agreements. This is an intrinsic control as compared to the extrinsic control in traditional education. If a teacher walked out of the room for a moment in a traditional classroom, we all know what would typically happen; the children would lose control, papers may fly, etc. Children will usually take advantage of the extrinsic control agent (the teacher) being absent and some will react in inappropriate ways. In a Montessori classroom, when a teacher walks out momentarily, nothing changes. The classroom goes on as usual because the children are not controlled outwardly by the teacher, but inwardly by their own compass. In fact, many of the children could successfully run the classroom without the teacher even being present. The community as a whole respects their agreements and the Montessori structure. The children actually take pride in how their classroom works and are protective of it.

> *"To let the child do as he likes when he has not yet developed any powers of control is to betray the idea of freedom."*
> —Maria Montessori

All of this goes on without the need for rewards. Children in Montessori classrooms do not get grades, stickers, happy faces, or prizes for good behavior. Their reward is intrinsic as well. They feel good about being a responsible community member and student because that is what we value in the Montessori method. So because we place no emphasis on rewards, neither do the children. Their reward is in feeling safe, contributing to the community, and feeling competent and successful. We believe that this internal drive is what leads to being life-long learners, responsible community members, and leaders—now and in the future.

No matter what age they are, children are keen observers. They rarely miss anything that is said or done. The Montessori method takes advantage of this element of the developing child. This is one of the reasons that Dr. Montessori mixed the ages of children in a classroom. This exposure to multiple levels of abilities, thinking, and points of view contribute greatly to the overall development of academic advancement, intelligence, and critical thinking by children in Montessori classrooms. Due to the fact that children are keen observers, the level of learning and interaction that goes on in any Montessori classroom far exceeds any traditional one. Younger children are observing the advanced lessons of the older students and are absorbing the information. Dr. Montessori taught us that the child's brain from birth through six years of age is like a sponge and will effortlessly absorb and be affected by that to which it is exposed. One of Dr. Montessori's books, *The Absorbent Mind*, goes into great detail and should be required reading for any Montessori parent. Basically, during this very critical stage of brain development, much of the wiring in the brain is being developed and will deepen with every experience to which the child has been exposed. Therefore, Dr. Montessori created this rich, substantial classroom that exposes the children to a vast array of appropriate learning tools and experiences to enhance the development of the brain. Dr. Montessori remarkably took many advanced concepts, such as geometry, algebra, square roots, chemistry, botany, zoology, and physics and created concrete, developmentally appropriate learning tools that allow children to be successful in understanding these concepts on a sensory level, not an abstract level, in the early years. Later on, when students are working abstractly on those more complex concepts, the earlier solid, sensory experiences allow for a deeper understanding of the concept.

Parents will often ask me about class size when inquiring about Montessori. I explain that in the Montessori world, we want to have larger class sizes because it allows for the children to have more exposure to different abilities and experiences. A typical Montessori classroom, depending on the appropriate square footage, would have approximately 25 to 30 students with two Montessori trained teachers—or at the very least, one Montessori trained teacher and a trained assistant. Dr. Montessori herself, in her initial work at the Casa dei Bambini, had approximately 60 students. As long as there is enough square footage and work space, along with enough Montessori teachers, and materials, I have seen class sizes of 50 to 60 students that operated seamlessly, where most visitors would never guess at the number of students present. This is Montessori in action. It works because the students are engaged, committed, and independent workers who are proud of their community.

I like to think of the Montessori experience as a beautiful quilt being sewn together; many different textures, colors, patterns, and designs coming together with the final result a rich, vibrant, unique, and beautiful collection melded into one extraordinary work of art. This analogy hopefully helps show that what makes Montessori work is the compilation of many different experiences as the child and adult move through his or her Montessori journey.

CONFESSION:

Originally, I received my degree in elementary education and after being trained as a traditional educator, when I first began my Montessori journey, I had doubts as to whether children, when really given the freedom to choose work, would actually do that. Don't all children want to just play and have fun? And, left to their own devices, wouldn't they just waste their time and not really accomplish what we, as educators, believe they should accomplish at a given time? The fear existed; what if they don't learn what they need to know? This fear takes form in a belief in the theory that adults must somehow "fill up" children with knowledge at certain times in their educational journey and that children are unable to accomplish this unless we force them to do it. My work with children in Montessori classrooms allowed me to see that this theory is incorrect—and made me a true believer in the Montessori method.

This book has free material available for download from the
Web Added Value™ resource center at *www.jrosspub.com*

4

Montessori
versus Traditional

I am sure that many readers will have had a traditional education and do not need a review of how it works. However, for purposes of comparison, I will list descriptions for Montessori and traditional schooling procedures. This should also benefit Montessori parents, by giving them specific details about the differing structures so as to be better versed in their understanding and explanation to others.

THE CLASSROOM

- **Montessori:** Montessori classrooms are referred to as *prepared environments*. They are designed for the developmental needs of the children at a particular stage. Children work at their own individual pace and the lessons are child-centered. Open shelves, with the full array of Montessori materials placed on them in an orderly way, are available to all of the children. Children are active learners, able to move around the classroom, choose their own lessons and workplace—usually at a table or on the floor with a floor mat. Lessons are hands-on and children explore and discover information on their own. Children are able to talk to each other and have discussions without disturbing others. Due to the interaction and exposure to many different perspectives, ways of thinking, and learning, Montessori children typically have high critical thinking skills.
- **Traditional:** Children are all sitting in assigned desks or at tables with very little or no movement allowed. Lessons are teacher-directed.

Children are passive learners in that they have no choice over what they will learn at any given moment. The teacher chooses the course of study for everyone. Most of the time, teachers are lecturing to students who need to listen, take notes, memorize, and take tests. All students need to work at the same pace. The classroom is typically silent. This approach tends not to build critical thinking skills.

TIME ELEMENT

- **Montessori:** There are usually long blocks of time scheduled to allow children to work on lessons for as long as they need and to have a minimum number of interruptions in their work cycle.
- **Traditional:** There are predetermined and set class times which are usually divided by subject.

TEACHER'S ROLE

- **Montessori:** Dr. Montessori did not like the term *teacher* as she did not feel that anyone can actually *teach* anything to anyone else without the complete engagement of the learner. Therefore, she chose to call the teachers, *directresses*, or to use the more contemporary term, *guides*, because their role is to actually direct or guide the children in their care and learning on a one-on-one basis. Each child will have a different pace and path, therefore they will all be directed and assisted individually along that path. The learning is child-led.
- **Traditional:** The teacher typically gives the same lesson to all of the children at the same time and in the same order. The learning is teacher-led.

AGE GROUPINGS

- **Montessori:** Children are typically grouped in three-year age groupings, based on developmental stages and the child's development within those groupings. For example: birth–3, 3–6, 6–9, 9–12, 12–15, and 15–18 years of age.
- **Traditional:** Children are placed strictly by chronological age in a specific grade level. The grades are typically *stand-alone*, not mixed.

CURRICULUM

- **Montessori:** The Montessori curriculum is individualized in that it is comprehensive, open-ended, and expansive and is designed to meet the particular needs of each individual. There are hundreds of hands-on, Montessori materials and activities dominating the curriculum because the best kind of learning takes place when physical, concrete exploration is linked to cognition. The child individually works their way through the curriculum based on their interests, but needs to meet minimum requirements for each subject area.
- **Traditional:** The curriculum is predetermined for the grade level based on lock-step, traditional national standards without consideration of students' individual needs or interests. Abstract materials such as whiteboards, worksheets, and textbooks are the main tools used for teaching.

DEVELOPMENT OF SELF-ESTEEM AND SELF-MOTIVATION

- **Montessori:** The Montessori approach allows for the child to build their own self-esteem and self-motivation from within. They acquire a strong, positive self-esteem and self-motivation by becoming more independent in their work, choices, and accomplishments and the satisfaction and sense of pride that is a result of successfully going through that process. The child's own feeling of success is the reward that builds this self-motivation.
- **Traditional:** A traditional approach places most of the emphasis on external pressures to conform and get good grades. A child's self-esteem and self-motivation is determined by how those external controls interpret the child's performance. Motivation is usually achieved by a system of rewards and punishments.

CHILDREN'S ATTITUDES ABOUT LEARNING

- **Montessori:** The philosophy is based on the belief that children have an innate desire to learn, and there is an intelligent internal force that guides them on that path. Children love learning because their choices are respected and encouraged. This leads to a love of learning that continues throughout their life.
- **Traditional:** This approach focuses primarily on standardized test results and memorization for grades—not true learning. Children have

no choice in their learning, so it is not as enjoyable for most. Only the students who are good test-takers typically enjoy the competitive aspect of it—because they usually excel.

DEVELOPMENT OF THE WHOLE CHILD

- **Montessori:** The approach takes into account the importance of the development of the child in all areas: intellectual, social, emotional, physical, and spiritual. Children are given ample opportunities to develop practical and real-life skills. Communication and conflict-resolution through peaceful means build strong character.
- **Traditional:** The main emphasis is on intellectual development and academic performance.

DISCIPLINE

- **Montessori:** The sense of community, the peace curriculum, along with the Montessori environment and method in general, lead to children developing an *internal* sense of self-discipline. Even though unkind behaviors emerge periodically due to the nature of being human, children learn to resolve conflict, forgive, and move on cooperatively.
- **Traditional:** The teacher primarily acts as the external enforcer of rules and discipline. Children are either rewarded or punished, depending upon their compliance. This can lead to resentment, anger, and revenge. There is usually much more bullying because very little emphasis is placed upon building community or peaceful conflict resolution.

CONFESSION:

I still become very impatient with some traditional educators and policy makers when they make inaccurate assumptions about the Montessori method. It amazes me that Dr. Montessori's work has been virtually ignored or dismissed by professionals for the wrong reasons. Even today, when we see brain research validating most of what Dr. Montessori discovered, it is very sad that educators still bury their heads in the sand in light of current research. I do not understand that type of denial when it so greatly impacts the lives of children. In addition, I have a great deal of compassion for traditional teachers who are dedicated to children but have their hands tied by an antiquated and developmentally inappropriate system.

5

How to Recognize an Authentic Montessori School

This request by parents may seem simple in theory, but it can be one of the most difficult to answer in some ways. The reason for this is that Dr. Montessori never trademarked her method, so virtually anyone can put up a sign advertising a Montessori approach. It is really up to the parent to know the difference between an authentic Montessori program and one that uses the name, but does not fully embrace the philosophy or methodology. This surprises many parents, and of course, makes their job much more difficult because they are not Montessori trained and can't always differentiate between a real Montessori school and one that may be a blend of different approaches. I will share the story of my history in discovering the method, along with the challenge of finding an authentic school in which to work.

I first became involved with the Montessori method in 1975. I had just graduated from a great college in New York City with a degree in elementary education. I had some misgivings, however, when I graduated as to whether I had chosen the right career path. I had just finished my student teaching year in a traditional New York City public school working with second and fifth grade students. Although it was a lovely school, with dedicated and wonderful supervising teachers, and had a very successful track record, I was disenchanted. It is in my nature to have a more creative or *out-of-the-box* view of the world. In fact, in my last semester of college, one of my education professors assigned a final essay asking us to write about our educational philosophy. I struggled with this assignment because I could not sincerely write that I agreed with the traditional approach to which I had been exposed. The college trained me well as a traditional teacher but the approach did not resonate with me. I had initially wanted to go to college and major in art since that was my first love. My parents, understandably, wanted me to have a more solid foundation to fall back on, so they encouraged me to pursue another major. I also loved children, so it seemed that education would be the natural choice for me. I could always teach the creative arts, and the combination seemed perfect for me so I minored in art. I absolutely loved my art classes and immersed myself completely in them. I would spend hours on the potter's wheel, drawing, painting, or developing my photographs. I diligently completed my education assignments, however it became apparent that while art was my passion, education was what I needed to do to get a regular paycheck.

My assignment was due and I decided to paint a picture rather than submit a written essay. I handed in a painting that showed a sunrise among dark clouds. I named it, *The Rebirth of Education.* Of course, my professor did not know what to do with this, so she called me in and asked me to explain my submission. I told her that I chose to use a medium that I was passionate about in order to express my feelings about what I believed had to happen in the field of education. I explained to her that although I felt the college did an excellent job of training me to be a traditional teacher, I believed that there had to be a better way to excite children about learning and to help all students to feel successful—not just a percentage who do well with others left behind. My submission was my small way of protesting precisely that; that all students are expected to produce in exactly the same way. During my student teaching experiences, I could see that although some students were very successful in the traditional setting, some students were just lost—and the saddest thing to me was that they seemed to accept the situation. They assumed they just were not smart and had to live with that view of themselves. As a young, idealistic, and slightly rebellious college student, I felt we needed to find a better way. I can clearly remember my professor looking at me with bewilderment; she did not know what to do with me or my painting. She kindly told me that she would need to give it some thought. I told her I understood that I did not do the assignment as requested so I may not receive a passing grade. Remarkably, my professor came back to me and told me that she felt the need to encourage my passion about changing education and gave me an A.

I have discovered in my life that the universe somehow intercedes and amazingly offers us opportunities when we most need them. The year I graduated from college, there was an unusual lack of teaching jobs available in New York City. I could not find a job. I came across an ad for a teaching assistant in a Montessori elementary classroom. I was intrigued! I did not know anything about Montessori, but I was drawn to the ad. I interviewed and got the job. Of course, they were delighted to hire someone with a degree in elementary education, but I was only eligible to work as an assistant because I was not Montessori trained. This position changed the course of my life. I had found what I was searching for! Here I saw students fully engaged in their own learning, working at their own rate and pace. They loved school and the materials that they worked with were beautiful and awe-inspiring—even to me. Children were free to explore their environment and create their own path of learning. My thirst for freedom and creativity in education was quenched. I did not understand what I was seeing and experiencing, but I knew that it was working. Children were learning without desks lined up or teachers lecturing all day! The children excitedly made beautiful drawings and artistic renderings of maps of the world rather than dryly answering questions in a geography workbook! I was hooked. My Montessori experience began.

The school in which I began my Montessori journey was affiliated with the American Montessori Society (AMS). The AMS was established in 1960 by Nancy McCormick Rambusch. Dr. Rambusch was instrumental in opening a Montessori school—the Whitby School, in Greenwich, Connecticut, in 1958. In 1959, Mario Montessori, Dr. Montessori's son and successor of the Montessori movement, appointed Dr. Rambusch as the United States representative of the Association Montessori Internationale (AMI). The AMI was, and is, the original Montessori organization that was created by Dr. Montessori and continued by her family and followers. Dr. Rambusch broke away from the AMI in 1960 to create the AMS. She believed that there needed to be adaptations made to bring Montessori into mid-twentieth century American culture. Some of those changes were that the AMS required teachers to have a college degree, to be open to new research about child development and learning, and to broaden the curriculum based on those findings while still remaining true to the Montessori method and philosophy. At that time, Mario Montessori disagreed with these changes, and as a result, in 1963, the AMS and the AMI discontinued their collaboration. It is exciting to note that currently the two organizations have worked through their differences and are once again collaborating in a relationship of mutual respect. This will undoubtedly lead to the strengthening of the Montessori method in this country and the world on many levels. Both organizations are dedicated to educating the public about the value of a Montessori education and focus on supporting Montessori schools and teacher education. Today, the AMS is the largest Montessori organization in the world with 100 AMS-affiliated teacher education programs worldwide, over 1300 member schools, with 400 of them being public, and 13,000 members.[1] There are many other Montessori organizations in the world, which you can find on the AMS website: amshq.org.

My experience with the Montessori world has been primarily with the AMS, however I have worked with many excellent and dedicated AMI teachers. Although my first work experience in Montessori was in New York City, the women who ran the school were both trained in Chicago so they recommended that I go there to train. At that time, there were approximately six training sites in the United States so I took their advice and headed to the Midwest for my training. When I completed my training, once again, my restless nature led me to accept an internship in sunny South Florida so that I could escape the cold winters of New York. The training center approved of an AMS school in West Palm Beach, and my immersion into the curriculum and philosophy was life-altering for me. I had found my home. After my internship, an opportunity was offered to me to open the first Montessori school in Key Largo, Florida. That offer was too intriguing to pass up, and it certainly was a learning adventure.

In 1978, I moved to Fort Lauderdale. Up to this point, I had only experienced interactions with AMS Montessori schools in New York City, Chicago, and West Palm Beach. So, when I opened the Yellow Pages (for the younger generations, that's what we used to look up businesses, before the internet) looking for Montessori schools, imagine my delight when I saw pages and pages of Montessori schools listed in the Greater Fort Lauderdale area. There should not be a problem finding a job in this oasis of Montessori schools! Of course, once I started to visit those schools in my quest to find employment, I was astounded that the vast majority of them were not Montessori at all. Almost without exception, when I would visit one of these schools, as soon as I said that I was an AMS-trained and certified Montessori teacher, the school representative would tell me that they didn't follow *only* the Montessori philosophy, but a combination of philosophies, and that Montessori was just one of those. The catch phrase used by most of these types of schools was: "Well, we only use parts of the Montessori philosophy." The classrooms may have had a few pieces of Montessori materials here and there, but in general, they were not fully equipped, nor were the teachers Montessori trained and certified. Probably my most horrifying experience was at a school that interpreted the Montessori principle of *freedom* paramount to anything else; thereby allowing children to do whatever they wanted, whenever they wanted—including drawing on walls, floors, shelves, and tables. To say that it was chaotic and unattractive is an understatement. I politely excused myself and left. What disturbs me greatly, and contributes to the general public's misconceptions about Montessori, is that the parents in this school actually thought that this was a valid Montessori experience. With these types of programs calling themselves Montessori, it was no wonder that some parents might have had a negative experience with the Montessori method. In addition, these misconceptions contributed to the negative reputation that South Florida had at that time in the rest of the country in terms of not providing authentic Montessori school options. Much to my relief, after many visits, I finally found a school that was AMI and an authentic Montessori school! I worked there for quite a few years before branching out on my own.

Today, many parents find themselves in the same situation I was in—looking at schools and trying to find an authentic Montessori program. I am happy to say that in South Florida those *anything-goes* types of Montessori schools are few and far between thanks to the growth of authentic Montessori schools and training centers in the area. Once parents see the real thing, it is much easier to tell the difference between the authentic and the quasi-Montessori approach. With that said, let me give you guidelines to assist you in searching for an authentic Montessori school:

- The very first thing you should do, and continue to do, is make yourself familiar with the Montessori philosophy by reading Dr. Montessori's books and researching as much as you can about the Montessori method.
- When you visit a school, ask them if they are affiliated with any of the nationally or internationally recognized Montessori organizations such as AMS or AMI. You can visit the AMS website and get a list of the organizations as well as a list of AMS member schools in your area.
- Ask them if their teachers are Montessori trained and certified, or are in the process of training, and with which training center. Most authentic Montessori teacher training centers should be accredited by the Montessori Accreditation Council for Teacher Education (MACTE).
- Ask the school if they are accredited by any organizations. Accreditation by an organization is an affirmation that the school has met all

of the standards of that organization. Not all schools can afford the process of accreditation, and some schools are strongly independent; so if a school is not accredited, it does not necessarily mean that the standards are not being met. If a school is accredited, you have more of an assurance that it is authentic.

- Ask to see a Montessori classroom. You should see a room fully equipped with a full array of Montessori materials—in very good condition and on open shelves. There should be clearly defined sections for each area: practical life, sensorial, language arts, mathematics, geography, history, science, art, music, and a peace table or area. There should be open floor space in order to accommodate floor work and child-size tables for individual work.

- The classroom should be aesthetically pleasing. It should be orderly, neat, clean, and attractive. Typically, you should not see clutter, disorganization, or an over-stimulating environment. You should not see traditional toys or play areas.

- Ask to observe a classroom. Most authentic Montessori schools have observation guidelines for observing parents so that it is not disruptive to the class.

- When observing, you should see happy, busy, and peaceful children. There will be a busy hum to the room—as it is interactive—but not enough to distract children from focusing and working. Children should be working on their own individual task, or in some cases, in very small groups. You should see children helping each other and being very respectful of each other.

- Children should be moving and working carefully and respectfully throughout the environment; you should not witness running or yelling. The students are taught to respect each others' personal space.

- Ages should be mixed according to the three-year cycles described previously. If a school separates each grade level or age, they are not adhering to a basic tenet of the Montessori philosophy and the children will not have the same experience or results. There must be a mixture of older and younger children in order to allow the older students to act as role models and experience leadership and mentoring.

- The teachers will be working with individual students or very small groups on the floor or at a table. They will blend in with the children and act as a guide for each child. You should not see a Montessori teacher standing in front of the class and lecturing to the group. The teachers will be treating students with respect and communicating with them in a respectful way.

- The atmosphere of the classroom and school should be warm, nurturing, peaceful, and positive. You would not typically see anxious, fearful, or bored students in an authentic Montessori environment. In fact, they should be most gracious and proud, typically welcoming you to their classroom in a polite and confident manner. They are given lessons in grace and courtesy, and they delight in sharing their good manners with visitors.

- My final suggestion is to pay attention to how you *feel* when you visit the school. Do you feel welcomed? Do the children seem relaxed and happy? I am a great believer in the power and importance of energy. Do you feel a positive or negative energy? Does your energy resonate with the school's energy? It should be a match. If you do your homework and it feels right, then you are on the correct path to finding the perfect school for your child and your family.

CONFESSION

*Respect and nonjudgment are two cornerstones of our Montessori philosophy, and I was guilty of ignoring them on occasion when I spoke of quasi-Montessori schools. In the somewhat arrogant, self-righteous attitude of my youthful sense of idealism, I felt completely justified in bashing these types of schools to parents or colleagues. I hadn't quite attained a sense of humility or wisdom in recognizing that I was acting in a superior way, and not living our Montessori principles. That is not to say that I shouldn't educate parents, it was just that my attitude needed an adjustment on the peaceful and loving side of the philosophy which I so revered. I have humbly come to realize that we are all on our own unique journey—individuals, as well as the schools that I so vehemently criticized. Today, I merely explain to parents what **does** constitute an authentic Montessori school without going into any negative discourses as to what is wrong with those other types of schools. Focusing on the positive and what is right with our world, rather than disparaging others is such an integral part of Montessori. It took me a while to realize that I needed to change that focus in order to actually become a true Montessorian.*

REFERENCE

1. American Montessori Society website: www.amshq.org.

6

The Importance of the Parent's Role in the Montessori Experience

"The child's parents are not his makers but his guardians."

—Maria Montessori

It goes without saying that the role of the parent in any experience that a child is exposed to is critical in the development of the child. As we all know, parents are the child's first teachers. They are responsible for introducing the world to their child, and this is such an awesome and intimidating responsibility for most parents. It is probably the most important job in the world, and sadly, it is one of the only jobs that requires no training or education. Of course, it is everyone's biological right to give birth to their offspring, but without some sort of knowledge of child development and what is necessary in order to raise a healthy human being, we end up with a world filled with woes that could be directly linked to the fact that children were not being given what they needed at critical times in their development. In most cases, parents just continue the same type of parenting that they were raised with and the cycle continues. I can't tell you how many times I have heard this statement, "Well, I am using the same methods my parents used with me and I turned out okay." This is usually in the context of trying to come up with solutions to a problem their child has—either socially, emotionally, or cognitively. Some parents still do not see that simply using the same methods (that are not working) over and over again only continue the difficult cycle of not overcoming issues that have arisen over the course of the child's growth. In fear of labeling their child, some parents will resist the recommendations to educate themselves more on what the child's challenge is or to seek professional guidance from a specialist who is trained to help. It seems as if parents will often take their child's challenges as a personal failure that is very hard to admit. I do not mean to indicate that all of the challenges that children encounter are related only to how they are raised—that would be an unfair statement. Many challenges that children face are genetic, and even though the child has been raised in a loving, proactive, knowledgeable, and positive environment, some challenging behaviors can still emerge because of this genetic factor passed on to them somewhere along the line.

Sadly, there are some parents who think of their children as clones of themselves. They are just *chips off the old block*, or even worse, a vehicle to relive their own lost dreams and aspirations. I once had a father come to meet with me who was very upset that his son's teacher was not pushing him enough in the academic areas. His son was four years old. He actually said to me, "My son will be going to Harvard to become a lawyer, and he has to start on a very strong academic path now." After being stunned into silence for a few seconds, I responded by asking him, "Well, what if your son does not want to be a lawyer or go to Harvard?" "It is not his choice," he told me. There was no arguing or convincing this man; his mind was made up. I told him that we would not push his son based on his father's aspirations for him. Needless to say, Montessori was not the right match for this father. I have thought about that little boy quite a few times, hoping that his father gained some wisdom along the way. Parents should not live vicariously through their children. Children are unique personalities with their own passions and purpose. Even if this father was not living vicariously through his son, he was certainly determining ahead of time what his son's life path and purpose should be. This type of interference rarely leads to a good situation. How many left-handed people were forced to be right-handed with very negative consequences because it was believed to be a better hand preference? The same thing occurs when parents discourage their children's natural talents or tendencies because they do not believe it is in the child's best interest, such as not supporting a child's artistic, dramatic, or musical talent to avoid what the parents believe would be a hard life for the child. It is important to stress that your children are completely unique individuals, with their own passions and purpose in life. It is a mistake for the parents to assume that their children are their property to mold into what they want or *miniature versions* of themselves. Too many times, to the detriment of the healthy development of the child, a parent imposes their dreams or aspirations on their children, completely ignoring or disregarding the talents, interests, personality, or passion of their child. There is a great deal of heartache inherent in this situation for the child and parent alike. It is much wiser for the parents to love and accept their children as the unique individuals that they are, and support them on their journey. When parents are not aware of the damage that can be done by disregarding the developmental or emotional needs of the child, the more apparent it is that parents need more education about this topic. Most parents begin their very important role without a guide or user's manual, which can make the journey very daunting for all concerned.

In a very simplistic summary, starting from the very beginning of conception, if the mother is not aware that good nutrition and abstinence from potentially damaging elements such as cigarettes, alcohol, and over-the-counter medications are vital to the health of the fetus, the developing child can be forever impacted in a negative way—cognitively, physically, and emotionally. Infancy is the stage where we know that it is critical for a child to be held and nurtured in order to develop trust in the world and the people in it. If infants are left for long periods of time with little or no human interaction, their emotional psyche is damaged, not to mention their language development—in many cases for life. Moving on to the toddler years, a period where children need to explore their environments in order to develop normally, parents who are unaware may keep their toddlers virtually trapped in playpens or high chairs for long periods of time, inhibiting their natural exploration of their surroundings. Dr. Montessori reminded us that in many other countries and cultures around the world, babies are constantly with their mother or care-giver; they go everywhere with them, which was a reason, she believed, why they would rarely cry. In her words:

> "...the crying of children is a problem in Western countries....the child is bored. He is being mentally starved, kept prisoner in a confined space offering nothing but frustration to the exercise of his powers. The only remedy is to release him from solitude, and let him join in social life."[1]

Dr. Montessori also stressed to parents how important it was to allow their children independence at home. She was very concerned that parents do *too much* for their children and thereby rob them of the opportunity to become independent, a very necessary skill to develop in order to live a full and healthy life.

> *"… to teach a child to feed himself, to wash and dress himself, is more tedious and difficult work, calling for infinitely greater patience, than feeding, washing, and dressing the child one's self…the former is the work of an educator, the latter is the…work of a servant…Needless help is a hindrance to the development of natural forces."*[2]

If the environment in which the child is developing is one of love, nurturing, and peaceful energy, then the child will develop an attitude of trust in the world, self-confidence, and will continue to have that natural inquisitiveness to explore the world around him or her. This is what we all hope for. Unfortunately, if children experience tension, impatience, criticism, fear, anxiety, and aggression in their environments on a consistent basis, including violent video games, cartoons, or television (often used as babysitters), then the child's overall development will be impacted negatively. The child may also become fearful, tense, and show signs of aggression in different ways. They will not feel the confidence to naturally explore their world and they will be in more of a survival mode than an exploration mode. This impacts healthy cognitive development as well.

Parents must consistently guide their children to be responsible for their actions. As the child grows, if she is not required to be accountable for her actions by her parents and the parents always blame others for their child's shortcomings, then the child develops into a person who does not accept responsibility for her own actions and continues to blame others. Those children actually develop into self-absorbed individuals who begin to feel entitled and then expect the world to cater to their needs. As Dr. Montessori stated, the child's mind is like a sponge and will absorb all to which it is exposed. Therefore, we need to be sure that we are properly preparing our children's environments at every stage of their development. This takes knowledge that is not required for most parents to engage in or to master. Wouldn't it be wonderful if parents could get a significant discount in their health insurance premiums or be offered more services if they completed courses on child development and parenting? If we want to put a practical price tag on it, imagine the potential future savings, not only for health and emotional care, but avoiding future criminal activity in our society as well.

> *"The things he sees are not just remembered; they form a part of his soul."*
> —Maria Montessori

With that said, if a parent is reading this book, it is obvious that they are aware that the Montessori experience for children is something worth exploring. As they continue to educate themselves, it will become evident that this experience is a life-changing one for their child, and for the family as a whole, if they fully embrace the philosophy. I always encourage every parent in my school to read and make themselves aware of this philosophy for many reasons. First and foremost, the more aware parents become of the Montessori philosophy and adopt it as a general philosophy of child-rearing, the more their child benefits. Secondly, parents are often asked to defend their choice of education by grandparents, other family members, professional colleagues, and friends. Parents are often at a loss as to how to do that effectively. Once the parent begins to see the changes in their child and have a deeper understanding of what is happening to them, they usually develop a genuine awe and appreciation of the experience their child is having. The parent gains not only confidence in their choice, but usually has a fervor that is contagious to other parents and family members. I will never forget when one of those parents said to me, "Ms. Judy, I drank the Montessori Kool-Aid and love it! I am trying to get all of my friends to drink it too!"

HIGH RISK—HIGH REWARD!

The choice of a Montessori education for a child can seem very *high risk* to many parents. It is often a leap of faith to trust that the Montessori method is actually working because parents do not receive constant traditional feedback in the form of grades, worksheets, tests, etc. It is not a *product*-based system. In addition, nothing looks the same as most parents' experience with traditional education. There are no desks lined up in a row with silent students restrained by them, no teacher standing in front of the class teaching everyone at the same time. It is a very unfamiliar experience for most adults. They need to trust that the method and philosophy is working through sheer observation of their child. This however, is probably the most important and effective way to assess the success of this method. Here is where the *high reward* applies. Parents see that their children love learning and enjoy going to school. In fact, when children first begin school in our Montessori early childhood programs, I have had numerous parents tell me that they actually had to bring their child to school on Saturday to show them that no one was in school, because the child was insistent that they wanted to go and not miss anything! This love of school is the first clue to parents that this is, indeed, a very natural and comfortable learning environment and that the children are reacting to that inner guide that is effortlessly leading them to their potential. Children are encouraged to follow their own interests, to move about the classroom, to work at their own pace, and share ideas with others. They are using the hands-on materials that Dr. Montessori created, which leads to a whole different level of brain development and thinking. Montessori students' critical thinking skills are much higher than most traditional students because of this interactive environment. They are exposed to different points of view, different problem-solving skills, different thinking and learning styles. The process of exploration and inquiry that go on in the Montessori classroom allow students to fully engage in their own learning. Due to the fact that this experience is *process*-based, rather than *product*-based, the child's self-esteem is protected, leading to very self-confident, enthusiastic, and courageous learners. I use *courageous* because Montessori students are not afraid of challenges or trying new things—learning is an adventure to them, not something that is anxiety-ridden because of the fear of poor grades or low self-esteem. This *prepared environment* is meeting the needs of the child and the child is joyful. Montessori schools are happy places because the nature of the Montessori philosophy is to provide joyful experiences for the child. I was once giving a tour to a prospective parent and I was discussing this factor of happiness in the Montessori experience. The parent turned to me and said, "I do not care if my child is happy, I am only concerned that he is learning what he needs to learn." I respectfully responded that I thought the parent should do more research on the Montessori philosophy because in order for this method to be effective for the child and the family, it needs to be a match to the philosophy of the parent. If it is not, then it can become a very negative experience. If a parent cannot move beyond the reliance of strictly measuring their child's learning by grades and test results, those parents may not be fully satisfied with the Montessori approach. It was not surprising that the parent never returned. As I answer the question often asked of me by many people, "Is Montessori for every child?" My answer is, "I believe Montessori can be successful for most children, but it is definitely not right for all parents." Mark Twain had an amusing comment about traditional education, "*I have never let my schooling interfere with my education.*" I do believe Mark Twain would have been an enthusiastic supporter of a Montessori education.

It is hard for any parents to witness their child making a mistake. It is, however, vital to allow children to make them; for in making mistakes, valuable lessons are learned. In my experience as a Montessori educator, this has been one of the most challenging aspects for most parents to accept. Even our most dedicated Montessori parents can become unraveled when they realize that their child is not perfect and can make foolish, even dangerous, mistakes. They want to swoop in to the rescue and help the child avoid the pitfalls of life. This may emerge in the form of *advising* the child's teachers as to how their child reacts to certain situations and to please make exceptions for them. This kind of overprotective, constant parent intervention is what some refer to as *helicopter parenting*, and it is not beneficial to the development of the child. An even more frightening term, the *zamboni parent* has also emerged in the world of parenting. These are the parents who will aggressively steam-roll their way into actually removing any evidence of mistakes that their child has made; it is always someone else's fault, their child never lies, and all imperfections need to be removed from their child's record. One can only imagine the kind of harm that is done to a child with this kind of consistent and inappropriate interference on the part of the parent. I am very glad to say that the occurrences of this type of parent have been few and far between in our Montessori community.

Of course, under other circumstances, certain important communication on the parent's part may benefit the child when there are special needs. However, for most students, making the mistakes and moving past them teaches the child valuable life lessons. The message to the child should be consistent from parents and teachers: mistakes are a normal part of the learning process, they are valuable for helping us to evolve beyond behaviors that do not work for us, and everyone makes them. Challenging ourselves and moving out of our comfort zones often leads to mistakes. How people grow because of their mistakes is what develops their knowledge, independence, strength of character, work ethic, and self-esteem. If children get the message that making mistakes is a normal process of learning, they will not feel like a failure when they make one. They should respond by asking themselves, "What can I do differently to solve this issue?" and, "What was my part in this conflict?"

I came across another term that certainly is more appropriate and indicative of how most Montessori parents see their role in the healthy growth and development of their child. *Hummingbird parent* refers to the type of parent that does not hover over their child constantly to intervene and fix the child's problems, but observes from a healthy distance and allows their child to work on finding a solution to the problem on their own. They only zoom in after they see that their child may need assistance in finding a way to solve a problem. The parent then tries to guide the child in looking at different perspectives of a situation, coming up with possible options to overcome the problem, and then having the child follow through on their own. When a child goes through this process and is able to overcome a challenge without the direct intervention of a parent, the child's confidence and self-esteem will be strengthened and they will then be stronger and better equipped to handle the next challenge that will come across their path. Children who need to consistently depend upon their parents to solve their problems do not develop the confidence or feel the success of being strong enough to problem solve on their own; their self-esteem will not develop in the same way. What many parents are often confused about is the role of feeling capable on the part of the child in developing their self-esteem. There is a great deal of research out there that tells parents their child needs to be happy in order to develop strong self-esteem, and as I said earlier, happiness is an important factor in the equation. The conflict arises, however, in how to guide the child to true *inner* happiness, which is what we strive for in the Montessori philosophy. Too often, parents misinterpret this need and go to all costs to minimize any disappointments for the child and will rarely say no to the child's demands, feeling this will cause the child to be unhappy. When this occurs, children will often grow up feeling entitled, unhappy when things do not always go their way, and will actually have much lower self-esteem because it is directly dependent on external factors, i.e., other people making sure that they are happy. In the Montessori philosophy, children are faced with the everyday challenges and disappointments that are a natural part of life, but the difference is that the child is given the opportunity to overcome these challenges—with guidance, but primarily on their own. It is this experience of discovering that they are capable of being successful on their own that develops strong self-esteem. Montessori parents know the value of allowing their child to be independent in every aspect of their growth and development. Dr. Montessori advised parents and teachers to never do anything for a child that they are able to do for themselves. If we step in and do not allow them the independence of discovering their own capabilities, we are actually robbing them of valuable and sometimes irreplaceable learning opportunities.

One piece of advice I give to parents that I feel is probably the most important element in raising healthy, happy children is consistency. Consistency should be a staple in everything that goes on with your child. As much as is possible, children need consistent rules, routines, caregivers, and schedules, along with positive emotional behaviors on the part of the parents and adults in their lives. They absolutely need boundaries and guidelines and it is the job of the adults in their lives to provide them. As children, they cannot do it on their own. As a family, the parents need to be the role models and facilitators of creating the healthy climate that they want to exist in their home. The parents need to guide a family discussion as to what values are the foundations of their family. Based on those values, then just as we do in a Montessori classroom, a family agreement should be created stating what those family values are, how everyone is expected to support those values through their behavior, and the consequences for not doing so. For example, a family agreement might state something like this:

> *In our family, we will always use love as a way to overcome challenges that we will face in life. Therefore we will think, speak, and act in loving ways. We understand that we are not always our behavior; we love each member of our family, however, we may not like the behavior of a family member. If we are very emotional over a conflict, we will always wait until we are calm before speaking or acting. We will be respectful of everyone in the family and work together to fairly distribute the work involved in running a household. As much as possible, we will consider the individual needs of each member of this family as long as it does not disrupt or harm anyone else in the family or elsewhere. Our goal is to all live in a cooperative and collaborative home, fueled by love and respect for each other.*
>
> *If any one of us fails to follow our family agreement, there will be a consequence. It is important to understand that every choice in life will result in a consequence. The consequence will be determined by each individual situation, and it may not be the same for everyone. Sometimes it will be a very natural consequence and other times it may be more complicated than that. The important part of the agreement is that the consequence will always occur because that will lead to everyone in the family growing in self-awareness, self-discipline, and character building. These are traits that are necessary for a successful and happy life.*

As I said previously, this is just an example of a possible family agreement. Each family agreement should be different—because all families are different. They should be based on positive values and appropriate consequences. I personally do not condone corporal punishment as I believe it does nothing to prepare children for facing the world with confidence, enthusiasm, and joy. It is a fear-based method of intimidation and is not a healthy consequence on any level. The key to success is consistency of enforcement of consequences. If you, as a parent, consistently threaten to enforce a consequence, and do not follow through, then you will make your job much harder in the long run, which will negatively affect your child's development toward being a responsible, empathetic, and respectful person. If you say something is going to happen, *it must happen*; which is why it is a good idea to always wait until everyone is calm before having a discussion and coming up with consequences. Too often, parents will make a grand statement while they are angry, and it is almost impossible to follow through with some emotionally charged and unrealistic consequence. Create calm, and then create peace.

PRAISE VERSUS ENCOURAGEMENT

These two ideas may seem interchangeable to most parents and adults, but they are not the same concept. Praise is very much like giving rewards for good performance. It does not build a long-term set of skills for making the right decisions for the right reasons. In the case of constant praise given to children in the hopes of building self-esteem, it can have some dramatic and negative side effects. When children are constantly given praise for being smart, or beautiful, qualities that require little effort on their part, they will eventually come to expect that same kind of praise from everyone without ever having to work for it. There have been multiple studies showing that these children will eventually develop character traits that avoid hard work, expect special treatment, and will want others to take care of their problems. They will go to different extremes to make sure that their label stays put, by not taking any chances to disturb it. This could be by stepping back and refusing to take on new challenges, or just refusing to work any longer. It could also take the form of lying or blaming others for causing their inadequacies.

Conversely, when encouragement is used with children, it sends an entirely different message. Here the child is being acknowledged for the behavior being exhibited, which is hard work and determination. When we recognize the efforts that are being made, the child begins to realize that he or she has control over that and can choose to work hard and make an effort. Most children will realize that when they do make an effort, then usually there are good consequences. This builds a good work ethic, which builds good self-esteem. It also builds students who are not afraid of making mistakes and learning from them. They are more willing to take on new challenges because they realize that unless one tries, very little is gained. Encouragement helps them through the mistakes that they will make, without taking it personally.

One of our Montessori parents, Dani Bastos, is a professional Life Coach. She spoke at one of our parent education meetings and had this to say about *praise versus encouragement*:

"There is a distinguished difference between praise and encouragement. With encouragement, you are acknowledging your child's achievements, emphasizing the work applied to the results. It is concentrated on the act, so it values the effort, the action, and the work. Praise has a negative effect on children. It is the applause of the innate capacities of the child, like intelligence, giftedness, or beauty, something that they did not develop, so they do not feel in control of it. They cannot improve something if they don't know how they received it in the first place; but effort and hard work are things that they have done and understand. This attitude empowers children, instead of giving them empty applause. The term *praise junkie* is used for the child who is naturally a people pleaser and wants to do everything they can to get the attention and rewards that come with praise. They do not do things for the fun of it, or to improve their skills; they tend to be recognized for being intelligent. As a result, they tend to do the things that they are naturally good at and have no intention of choosing harder or more challenging things. This is because they do not want to have to struggle, or risk their *reputation as a smart person*. They are terrified of failing, so they do not take as many risks."

"When we praise a student and say they are smart, they get addicted to the praise. Intelligence and giftedness is a God-given ability, and they did not conquer that ability themselves, therefore they don't have any control over it. The praise boosts their egos and makes them feel entitled to it. Specialists use the term *praise junkies* precisely because that is the feeling that they are after."

There have been many research studies that focus on praise and the effect that it has on student's developing self-esteem and work ethic. One of the most interesting studies was done by psychologist Carol Dweck and her team at Columbia University. They performed a series of experiments with 400 randomly chosen fifth-grade students at a dozen schools in New York. They specifically divided the students into groups where, after a puzzle was completed successfully, some were praised for their natural intelligence while others were praised for their effort. "You must be smart at this" versus "You must have worked really hard." One of the conclusions of the study was that students, who were praised *only* for their intelligence, when given the option between two later tests of different difficulty levels, would tend to choose the easier one to protect their self-image of being smart and not risk being embarrassed. "When we praise children for their intelligence," Dweck summarized, "we tell them that this is the name of the game: Look smart, don't risk making mistakes." Those students who were praised instead for their effort exhibited a "stick-to-it" attitude until they could figure the problem out. "They got very involved, willing to try every solution to the puzzles," Dweck said. "Emphasizing effort gives a child a variable that they can control. They come to see themselves as in control of their success. Emphasizing natural intelligence takes it out of the child's control, and it provides no good recipe for responding to a failure."[3] The unfortunate result in many cases for students who are continuously praised for their natural intelligence is that they often fall into the habit of not choosing difficult tasks where they could fail and/or not putting forth much effort in overcoming challenges.

Here are some examples of language that parents can use with their children in order to encourage, rather than praise. I would also recommend the book, *Talk So Kids Will Listen & Listen So Kids Will Talk* by Faber and Mazlish, the source from which some of these suggestions have been adapted. Focus on your child's effort and improvement with statements such as these:

- Great effort!
- I can tell you spent a great deal of time thinking/working on that.
- Your effort is really paying off.
- Great solution! I don't think I would have thought of that.
- That work is much neater than the last one you showed me. I see improvement.

Also, describe what you see.

- Oh my goodness, this room is so clean; your books are put away and your bed is made!
- I like your choice of colors, they are so bright!
- I can see that you enjoy creating things.
- I see that you are serious about your work.
- I see that you really stick with things.

- I can see that you really care.

Similarly, describe how you feel.

- I love spending time with you!
- Your artwork makes me feel so happy!
- I am so proud of how you always do your best.
- I enjoy working on things with you as a team.

Show appreciation and gratitude for the child's contributions.

- I appreciate your help, it would have taken me much longer without it.
- Thank you for cooperating, it was very helpful.
- I am so grateful when you choose to be cooperative.
- Wow, you are very observant!
- I am not surprised that you are so considerate of your friend's feelings.
- It is so much fun spending time with you because you are so good at getting along with others.

Show your child that you have confidence in their choices.

- I trust that you will choose to make the right decision.
- I know that this is a big challenge, but you will do the right thing.
- Wow, how did you do that?
- Good choice!

Remember to put the focus on your child's control of the situation.

- Tell me how you feel about this.
- What are you thinking?
- Tell me about the solutions that you came up with.
- You must feel good that you were able to handle this on your own.
- You made the right decision to ask for help.

Finally, label the quality that you want your child to acquire.

- Wow! Now that's a great example of leadership, honesty, integrity, creativity, teamwork, sticking to it, being a good friend, etc., (just fill in the blank).

MONTESSORI PHILOSOPHY AT HOME

I will share with you some ways that you can bring the Montessori philosophy into your home. I do not mean that you should buy the pink tower or any other Montessori materials to set up a classroom because that should be their work at school. It is much more important to establish a Montessori *atmosphere* at home; one of independence on the part of the child, appropriate experiences for exploration, establishing a family *community* with responsibilities, expectations, rules, and guidelines—and you, as parents, acting as positive role models for your children.

ESTABLISHING INDEPENDENCE

> *"...provide objects he can handle by himself and that he can learn to master. This principle can be applied, and must be applied, in the child's own home. From the earliest possible age, the child must be provided with things that may help him to do things by himself."*[4]

The first thing to keep in mind when preparing your home with the goal of building your child's independence is to make sure that things are child-sized. Wherever possible, such as in the child's bedroom, the furniture and shelving should be in proportion to the child's size and ability. A child's bed should be low enough for the child to independently get in and out of it. Closets and drawers should be low enough so that the child can have easy access to clothing; for taking out and putting away. Low hooks will also help the child to organize their belongings. You could also use a language tool that we use in the classroom—labeling things—perhaps label the drawers where certain clothing or items go, etc. Children should have a place to put their dirty laundry, they should help sort it before and after washing, and finally, they should put the clean clothing away in the correct place. The child's clothing should be such that it is easy for the child to dress and undress independently.

Children should learn how to make their own bed. It is much easier for young children to do this with a comforter rather than a blanket and sheet. You will need to give them a *lesson* on how to do it, but they are very capable of learning it and doing it on their own as their skills improve.

It is a good idea to provide open shelves in your child's bedroom, similar to those in a Montessori classroom, so that their things (books, favorite things, toys) can be displayed or stored in an aesthetically pleasing and organized fashion. They should also be easily accessible by the child. Small storage boxes are good for this, which again should be labeled with their contents, such as blocks, toys, paints, crayons, puzzles, etc. It is not a good idea to have a large *toy box* because then everything is thrown into the box in a disorganized fashion. In addition, it would be helpful to have a small desk or table where the child can work, draw, read, and write. The chair also needs to be child-sized. A place to display some of his or her work, such as a bulletin board or just an empty wall space for that purpose, is a good idea. It is also wise to give the child colored pencils or wax crayons rather than markers with indelible ink to avoid permanently damaging furniture or carpet. Finally, this family rule should be similar to the classroom rule: finish your task and put it away before you choose something else.

If your child does make a mess, he or she should clean it up. Don't get upset; just teach them how to wipe down tables and chairs, to sweep with a child-size broom and dust pan, and to clean the floor with a small mop or cloth. Children often love to polish furniture and other household items such as silverware and glassware.

There are many activities you can share with your child in the kitchen. Some excellent practical life activities would include: preparing food, washing dishes, loading the dishwasher, drying dishes, and loading the washing machine and dryer. Make sure that there is a step-stool so that your child can work at the sink washing dishes or vegetables and is able to reach the counter. Put the stool in a place where your child can independently retrieve it. Have a waterproof apron for your child to wear in the kitchen while helping, and a low hook to store it so it is reachable by your child. Children can set the table with dishes and silverware. They can help you with cooking and will learn how to use measuring cups and spoons.

In the bathroom, children should be encouraged to be independent in caring for themselves—brushing teeth, washing his hands, and keeping the bathroom clean and tidy. Teach him how to use faucets in the sink, tub, and shower and how to manage the cold and hot water. They will also need a step-stool in the bathroom to reach the sink and see the mirror. Teach him how to use the door handle and to understand how to lock and unlock it. Children can also be of help with the cleaning jobs in the bathroom: washing the bathtub and sink, polishing the faucets, using the toilet brush, folding the towels, and wiping surfaces. Children should have a place to hang their own towel.

Some other areas in which you could encourage growth in independence might be trips to the supermarket where your child helps you to find the items that you need. Yes, it will take longer, and you wouldn't be able to do it every time, but it can be a very valuable experience for your child in many ways—and fun for you, if you are not in a rush. Children can also help with the yard work, raking, piling leaves, maintaining a bird house, or gardening. Being in nature is a very valuable experience and you can demonstrate your respect and enjoyment of it. Observing the seasons and changes in nature, measuring rainfall and temperature, and recording weather conditions are all valuable learning experiences. Also, caring for the family pet (or pets) is another way to teach responsibility and care of others.

Let this be your mantra: Dr. Montessori reminded us that we should never do anything for a child that they can do for themselves.

GRACE AND COURTESY

Children need to be taught proper social behavior in their own home so they can carry those skills elsewhere. Teach children proper table manners and where and how it is appropriate to eat. They should also be made aware of *restaurant manners*, where they need to be considerate of other diners. Teach your children to greet people and respond appropriately when they are greeted. In addition, expect them to say please and thank you at the appropriate times.

There should be guidelines as to safe and respectful behavior in your home and at other people's homes. You should teach your child not to jump on sofas and chairs. You should also allow young children to carefully handle *breakable* valuables with two hands—and only while you are there monitoring them. The standard rule for other valuable items—in your home or someone else's—is to look at them, but only touch them when an adult is there to help. Children will learn to be respectful of other's things when you model that respectful behavior.

SAFETY ISSUES

As discussed, it is always the job of the adult to prepare the environment in a safe way. There are things that you as the parent need to do in order to make the home environment safe. If your child is young, all electrical outlets should be covered. Make certain that all wires or cords are not left out where anyone can trip on them. If you allow your child to use any electrical devices, be certain to teach them how to use them properly and safely.

In the kitchen, be sure to keep your child safe from hot ovens and always turn saucepan handles inward. Make sure that the first rule in the house is to not touch the stove or oven because it can be hot and cause a burn. Never leave your child alone in the kitchen when the oven is on or something is cooking. Be sure to keep all dangerous items, such as cleansers, bleaches, etc., in a locked cabinet or completely out of reach.

Make sure that there are safety stops on windows so that your child cannot crawl out. It would also be wise to put safety stops in your child's drawers so that they do not pull out completely and fall on him or her.

Be certain that all medications in the bathroom are in a locked medicine cabinet. Remove all dangerous chemicals from the bathroom. Teach your child proper handwashing techniques, using soap and water.

I have just summarized some things that you can do as a parent to build and encourage independence in your child. It is actually unlimited in scope and experience depending upon what your families' interests and talents are.

If a parent chooses Montessori as the path to educate their child, it is absolutely necessary for them to research and understand what the method is about and how it works in order to fully appreciate and support the work that goes on in the Montessori classroom. Their child will fully reap the benefits of this unique experience by having an informed Montessori parent. Read Dr. Montessori's books and attend the parent education lectures that your Montessori school provides.

CONFESSION:

I have not always been patient with parents over the years when I have tried to explain the Montessori philosophy, or if parents did not always see our Montessori perspective because they were blinded by their emotional connection to their child (which is absolutely understandable). It took me many years to gain the patience and the empathy to really put myself in their shoes to determine that yes, it is very hard when they are in the role of the parents, to be completely objective because it is their child and there are strong emotional ties (as there should be!). So, therefore I confess that in my early years, I could be self-righteous and judgmental, blinded by what I thought was obvious and right. It wasn't always fair or right on my part for my attitude to have touched parents in a way that possibly made them feel like less of an effective parent. It has taken me many years to temper my idealistic and almost cult-like passion for trying to impart upon parents what I thought was best for their children.

REFERENCES

1. Montessori, Maria. *The Absorbent Mind.* Wheaton, IL: Theosophical Press, 1964, p. 109.
2. Montessori, Maria. *The Montessori Method.* New York: Schocken Books, 1964, pp. 96–99.
3. Bronson, Po. "How Not to Talk to Your Kids," *New York Magazine,* August 3, 2007. http://nymag.com/news/features/27840.
4. Montessori, Maria. *What You Should Know About Your Child.* Wheaton, IL: Theosophical Press, 1963, p. 12.

7

Montessori Educators

"To aid life, leaving it free, however, to unfold itself, that is the basic task of the educator."
—Maria Montessori

MORE THAN JUST A METHOD OF TEACHING

Montessori educators have a wonderful world in which they live and work. This philosophy is all about the love of humanity and love is truly the operative word. Dr. Montessori had such a transcendent, all encompassing love for the child, and not only for the child itself, but also for the person whom the child could become. She loved the potential individual within the child, the one who could grow to contribute their unique gifts to the world, hopefully for the world's good. One of Dr. Montessori's most cherished goals was to bring peace to the world through these new children. She knew that the only way to possibly create change in the world was to start with the children, who would then emerge as new adults. And that is what Dr. Montessori was trying to unleash—that magnificent human spirit that could lead to creating a new world. Her followers have the honor and privilege to continue with Dr. Montessori's work in a world where it is as relevant, if not much more, than at any other time in the history of humankind. Most Montessorians are passionate about their calling. This is not just a method of teaching for most of us, it is a lifestyle choice. In an age where at the push of a button, the world could cease to exist, or just as disastrous, be totally stripped of its resources, Dr. Montessori's contribution to the world has the potential to actually save it. Is there a more passionate calling than that?

Dr. Montessori chose not to call her trained teachers by the label, *teacher*, but by the name, *directress*. Today, another term widely used in the Montessori world is *guide*. She believed that no one could truly *teach* anything to anyone else; the best we could do was to *direct* or *guide* them along their own path of acquiring knowledge. Once again, that journey was an inner one; the directress's job was to prepare the learning environment so that the child could educate himself from the inside-out. I have used the commonly understood term *teacher* throughout this book—mainly to avoid confusion for parents and people who are unfamiliar with Montessori. Be aware however, that many Montessorians still refer to their teachers as directresses, directors, or guides.

CONFLICT AS AN OPPORTUNITY FOR GROWTH: CHANGING THE CHANNEL IN YOUR MIND

The reality of implementing this beautiful philosophy, however, can be an arduous journey. We cherish an idealistic theory and the path is perilous at times because what we want and what we see and deal with everyday are sometimes at extreme polar opposites. All we need to do is watch the news for a few minutes and it seems as if the world's problems are overwhelming and terrifying. Our media tends to keep us focused on what is wrong with the world, not what is right. This negative attitude is insidious in that it permeates so much of our culture. Most adults are affected by it, so therefore our parents, our families, and our staff will be affected by it as well. Fear of something being missing or wrong, cynicism, and a fascination with the negative and frightening aspects of life can be very difficult to ignore, and can actually be contagious. Negative energy generates more negative energy. So therefore, as Montessorians, it is vital to place our focus on the right energy—the energy of love, not fear. We need to constantly remind ourselves to go back to the roots of our philosophy: it is rooted in love, it is rooted in peace, and it is rooted in respect. That is the journey we are on, the path that we choose to take. Not always an easy path, but certainly a highly rewarding and hopeful one.

> *"The study of love and its utilization will lead us to the source from which it springs, The Child."*
>
> —Maria Montessori

I do my best to lead at my school in that place of love, peace, and respect. Personally, I have to work on it every day; it is a constant battle between the energy of fear and love. As the head of a school, all of the serious conflict within our community usually ends up at my door. In any community, when people interact, there will be conflict. It is a natural and normal part of human interaction. People think differently, communicate differently, problem solve differently, and ultimately perceive all of it differently. When teachers come to me upset and wish that there would be no conflict, I do my best to help them see that what they are wishing for is unrealistic. Wishing that conflict would not exist is buying into the fearful energy that tells us that conflict will always be painful and too difficult to overcome. Many adults live in this energy and therefore ignore any conflict, hoping that it will go away. The energy that is generated with conflict will never go away; it will morph into something else if the parties involved choose to ignore it, but it eventually raises its persistent head at another future opportunity. And because many people choose to avoid conflict, they also avoid communication. This is what I have learned about the importance of communication and conflict after my forty years of living in the world of Montessori: communication is the only way to use conflict as an opportunity for growth, and without a doubt, conflict is an opportunity for growth for all involved. If we use the energy of love when communicating during a conflict, the growth can be tremendous and transformative.

So let me talk about some down-to-earth, real-life conflict that goes on everyday in all Montessori communities. One of the most common discussions to arise in a staff meeting or at a meeting with other heads of school is, "Our job would be so much easier if we didn't have to deal with the parents!" And parents, while you read this, I certainly do not intend for this to be disrespectful or critical, I just think it is important to have the dialogue. I think that many educators live in the fear of how parents are going to react—will the parents be upset with them or blame them for the children's shortcomings? That fear does not encourage a strong bond or build strong relationships. That is why there are many school administrations, Montessori and traditional, who say to the parents, "Please just drop your child at the door; do not come in and disrupt our day or our classrooms. We are here to teach your children and you are here to drop them off. Please let us do our job." I have heard different versions of this message many times from parents who were at the receiving end of this type of message, or from other school heads who feel some parents can cause too much of a disruption or distraction to their school day—and in some cases, there is truth to what they say. In fairness to this standoffish attitude, I can tell you quite a few stories where parents have caused a huge disruption to the successful administration of school policies or just disturbing a peaceful, calm school day. I can understand that attitude by some school communities; however, my personal belief is that I chose *to live* our Montessori philosophy, not merely to use it as a method of teaching children. I believe that includes treating everyone in our Montessori community with respect, and the parents are a vital part of our community. Parents are always welcomed at our school and we have many parents who are on our campus everyday providing some form of community service or giving the school volunteer hours. With that said, we do have guidelines; parents *are not* allowed to just walk into classrooms and disrupt them. The truth of the matter is that when you welcome parents and give them an opportunity to be a part of the community, they will be very respectful of those guidelines and boundaries. When parents feel that they are a respected and valued member of the community, a stronger relationship is forged among everyone. We call everyone a member of our Summit-Questa family. A very positive result of this relationship is that there is an atmosphere of trust, support, and confidence in each other. The vast majority of our parents feel comfortable enough to come and voice their concerns or questions because our philosophy is one of listening to each other, putting ourselves in each others' shoes, and being respectful of differences in opinion. It does not mean that they will always get the answer that they want, but I do believe they appreciate that fact that they are given the opportunity to have a voice. This willingness to listen and always putting the needs of children first builds a level of comfort and confidence that you do not always find in other schools that do not place emphasis on close communications and relationships with parents.

The opinions of all members of the Montessori community—parents and staff alike—are always valued, even though we do not always agree with them. On the other hand, the varied perceptions of life at Montessori schools also helped me to build a stronger community through improvement of the school systems and policies. Much of the feedback provided by parents helped to build better school policies, which resulted in an improved school. In addition, our families literally helped to physically build our school from day one. We constantly had groups of families that would help us paint, lay sod, make repairs, and clean up after hurricanes on weekends, after school, and evenings. This was especially helpful in the beginning years when we could not afford to pay professionals to do much of that work. Our families showed up, rolled up their sleeves, and pitched in. The school was their second home, and they were there to help. It went even further than that when families went above and beyond the call of duty to raise funds for the growth of our school. Our parents have dedicated thousands and thousands of hours toward raising funds in many different ways. One unbelievable undertaking was by a group of families who committed to running a concession stand at Dolphin Stadium for the entire football season over fifteen years ago. We had enough parents to literally give up every Sunday to spend the day in preparation, selling, and cleaning up in the concession stand. They raised approximately $25,000, and it was a huge amount of money for the school—so helpful in allowing us to improve and meet goals. They did such a great job that the stadium wanted them to continue! One year was enough however, as that kind of commitment was more than anyone anticipated; but no one backed out, they honored their commitment. There were other types of support that went on in our community as we continued to grow. Many parents contributed expertise, guidance, money, or in some cases, moving mountains of bureaucratic obstacles when the school would hit county or city snags in the process of growth and construction. One parent made a networking phone call and said in effect, "This is family, so you need to find a way to help the school get what they need." That kind of dedication to the school by parents still goes on today; our PTO continues to put on events to not only raise money for the school, but to also enhance building of the Montessori community. When parents feel connected to their school community, there is tremendous support that shows up in many ways. That is the power of community.

I know that the strength of our school community is directly linked to the strength of each link in our community—students, parents, teachers, administration, and leadership. I would never want a community where everyone thinks, behaves, or perceives things in exactly the same way. We value open-mindedness, collaboration, creativity, and communication, while still holding strong to our respect and belief in our Montessori philosophy—that is our guiding light.

I think my journey to this point has been a unique one in some respects, but overall, no different from most people walking the planet. My perspective has certainly been affected by the emphasis on the energy of love in our Montessori philosophy. Everyone has personal challenges to face but the difference is in how we choose to handle those challenges, based on our belief system. If we choose to stay in a place of fear, then that fear overwhelms us, guides us, and leads us to continue to choose from a fearful place. It's that journey from fear to love and making choices based on the positive place of a loving attitude that is the most difficult part of the journey. It is difficult, but certainly possible, to create our own world of peaceful conflict resolution.

People flourish in such an atmosphere. Just as we see children flourishing in our Montessori classrooms through the use of peaceful conflict resolution and the positive energy of love and acceptance, so too, can the adults. There have been times when I have stepped back and wondered, "How can some Montessori teachers be so good at lovingly helping their children learn to resolve conflict peacefully, but then are often unable to do it themselves with their coworkers?" In addition, during some of my interactions with other Montessorians, I have seen divisiveness when there are differences of opinion on the implementation of the Montessori method or philosophy. I have come to understand that many of the adults of which I speak did not have a Montessori upbringing so therefore still default to old behaviors and habits of communication. Human beings have a dual nature and being imperfect beings, we can flip-flop back and forth. As much as we may want to choose a peaceful response and stay calm and loving, all it takes is that button being pushed and we revert back to that survival place, that ancient response of fight or flight— yes, even peace-loving Montessorians! Dr. Montessori wanted the educators who followed in her footsteps to become those agents of peace; absorbing and being role models for loving and peaceful strategies to overcome conflict and develop better human beings.

So, how does one go from the initial reaction of, "Oh no, not another conflict!" to "What can I learn from this conflict?" The answer lies in our reactions and attitude. As Lou Holtz, retired American football coach, author, and motivational speaker, once said, "Life is ten percent what happens to you, and ninety percent how you react to it." No truer words were ever spoken. If we let go of the initial negative reaction of "Why again?" and switch the channel in our mind to a more positive attitude, "Ok, let's see how we can all learn and grow from this," then we are on the path to creating a more positive habit which benefits all involved. This creation of a new habit takes time and practice like any other skill.

Let me give you an example from school. Parents who are not familiar with the Montessori approach will often question certain aspects of the program. A new parent came to me concerned because her child's teacher was not pushing her child in a certain subject area. The parent felt that her child's personality was such that she would always take the path of least resistance and was therefore concerned that the teacher would not keep her child on the right track. The parent said she had a conference with the teacher already to discuss it, but after a few weeks, it did not seem to be getting any better, so she came to me. The first thing I always do when meeting with a parent is to thank them for sharing their feelings. I let them know that it is important to me to know how and why they feel the way that they do, so that we can get to know each other better as we focus on what is in the best interest of their child. I have found that when I actively listen, without reacting defensively, and show genuine interest and concern in their opinion, the energy of the parent immediately becomes more comfortable and positive. In this case, the parent actually expressed how grateful she was that I was so open to listening to her and that conversely, was not as comfortable with the teacher's reaction, which was defensive. Without judging any behavior, I told the parent that I would look into the situation and would meet again with her once I had enough background information to suggest the best plan for her child.

When I approached the teacher, her first reaction was defensiveness and she said something to the effect, "Oh my goodness, this parent is a helicopter parent! She is constantly interfering with the child's choices and telling me what her daughter should or shouldn't be working on; I am exhausted from the constant pressure!" I told the teacher I understood why she felt that way and until we came up with a solution, she would continue to feel pressured and the parent would continue to push. I always ask my staff for their perception of the situation and if they have any solutions in mind that we could discuss. In this case, the teacher shared that even though the parent felt her daughter was gifted, the child had some learning challenges in certain areas, and did indeed, shy away from them out of avoidance. I asked the teacher if she had shared this with the parent—and she had—only she felt that the parent really did not hear it or want to accept it. The parent felt the child was just being lazy and needed to be pushed more. The teacher asked for my help in handling this parent. I asked the teacher to join me in another conference with the parent and this time to be very careful not to react defensively in any way. Often a teacher's body language or facial expressions will speak volumes beyond their words. This is almost always in response to what a parent says. I further asked the teacher to stay calm and positive, no matter what the parent may say, and lovingly describe the positive qualities of the child, while also sharing her observations of the child at work in the classroom. I reminded the teacher that parents are usually acting out of a sense of fear for their child when they react in this manner. It could be a fear of their child not getting what she needs or a deeper fear that perhaps all is not right, and that is a very difficult fear for most parents to accept. If we look at the parent's reactions in that way, it is easier to be compassionate and supportive, rather than feeling threatened and defensive. Of course, because the teacher is a Montessori teacher, she agreed that being compassionate, forgiving, and supportive was the right thing to do for the parent and the child. So she went into the meeting with a different attitude. I am sure that you can guess that because the teacher went into the meeting with a different attitude, there was a different outcome. This time, the parent felt that the teacher really was a nurturing and competent teacher (which she was) and was much more willing to listen to the teacher's observations and recommendations. This occurred because the teacher first spoke of all of the beautiful qualities and strengths of her daughter, expressed how much she admired and cared about her daughter, and then shared the weaknesses she observed. I supported the conversation by stating that every child, no matter if they are gifted or challenged, has their strengths and weaknesses. Our job as Montessori teachers is to direct them to use their strengths and work on their weaknesses. I encouraged the parent to trust the process because it is definitely a process that the child will go through in terms of self-awareness and independence. I also reassured the parent that the teacher knows each child very well because they are specially trained to do so. The mother left the meeting with an entirely different attitude. She became very supportive of the teacher and as the child grew in not only her strengths, but also in overcoming her challenges, that parent became one of the teacher's greatest supporters. This is an example of how important attitude and energy is in the quality of communication. As soon as the teacher changed the channel in her mind from being defensive and impatient, to being compassionate and supportive, that shift in energy affected the parent. The parent went from being critical and fearful to supportive and happy. It seems like such a simple thing, however, it takes practice and control in learning to change the channel in your mind. So in this case, the teacher learned the power of words and attitude in communication. The parent learned to be more open-minded in regard to the strengths and weaknesses of her child, and that it is perfectly normal for all children to be wavering in both of those as they grow and develop. This shift in energy absolutely helped the child, most importantly, because her parent was more relaxed and so was her teacher! The big picture here is that when we try to put ourselves in another person's shoes, listen with respect, show compassion, and problem solve with a sincere desire to support the growth and well-being of the child—miracles do occur.

A CALLING AS WELL AS A PROFESSION

Montessori educators are a very special group of individuals. I believe that most teachers, whether they are Montessori or traditional, do not go into the teaching profession because they want summers and holidays off, but because they love children and want to help them become successful people. Montessori teachers have a system that works and for this fortunate reason they tend to have long, happy careers in teaching; whereas their traditional counterparts, unfortunately, often burn out in the first five to ten years because the system is not effective. The reason for this discrepancy is that Montessori learning environments are a very natural way for children to learn and therefore, children are happy, cooperative, and successful. Unfortunately, traditional classrooms are typically not natural learning settings that are based upon the developmental needs of children. When students are immobile, and classrooms silent, the atmosphere is counterproductive to deeper thinking and true learning, which is *not* rote memorization or learning to pass a test.

In my experience, it seems that Montessori teachers are following a *calling*. This is not just a job to them; they experience a greater purpose to what they are doing. I would hope that by the time you finish reading this book, the reasons for being *called* to this philosophy will be evident to you. Montessorians have often been referred to as being *cult-like*; a term that could imply a negative, mindless following, however, we are the furthest thing from negative or mindless. The cult-like behavior, which is a misinterpretation, is actually a passion for what we believe and what we do. I have never met such a diverse, creative, free-thinking group of people who are dedicated to a common cause as I have in the world of Montessori. It has been a privilege and honor to share the mission with them. At my own school, the melting pot of personalities is our own special Montessori family. Many of the teachers have been at our school since its inception 25 years ago. It is not an institution, it is a home-away-from-home for the staff, children, and families, where they feel supported, welcomed, and appreciated. Many of the students and families find life-long friends in our Montessori community. They share common values and goals, and learn and grow together. I have actually had numerous parents tell me that they have passed up jobs that would take them away from their *second home*, their school. We share the ups, downs, laughter, and tears that go hand-in-hand with a dynamic and growing community.

PARENT EDUCATION

One of the ways that we help parents to feel connected to our community is to offer parent education classes. There are some parents who come to us who are very familiar with Montessori and know exactly what they are looking for. The vast majority however, know a little bit about Montessori, they know it is a good educational choice, and for the most part, found their way to us through word of mouth. Either family, friends, coworkers, or neighbors have told them how happy they have been with the Montessori approach for their children so they are seeking a similar experience. Whether parents are familiar with Montessori, or not, they all need on-going and quality education about this philosophy. I have had many parents, informed and not, come to me with questions and concerns that show that they really do not understand our philosophy beyond knowing it is an individualized approach based on children working with hands-on materials. This is understandable because it is such a multi-layered philosophy and it takes a great deal of study and experience to get to the point where anyone would be very knowledgeable about the tenets of the method and philosophy. In my experience, the more we educate parents about the Montessori philosophy, the more supportive they become. When they grasp the extent to which their children can be transformed, they are usually in for the long run.

I have tried many different approaches for providing parent education. We have offered multiple lectures, newsletters, workshops, and reading assignments with discussions. What I have discovered is that when we involve the children, the participation is always much better. We have had evening sessions where the teachers and I would present different aspects of the curriculum and would have students be presenters. We have also had parents come into the classrooms after school or in the evenings, and their children take them through a *mini-morning*, explaining their daily routines and giving their parents lessons. This has been very successful, but the evening events do seem to add a bit of a challenge for families. I have also brought in related specialists, such as psychologists, nutritionists, or doctors for evening presentations. We always provide babysitting—as this is a must if you want as many parents as possible to attend. What has probably been the most successful approach, however, is what I call, *Montessori Mornings with Ms. Judy*.

Montessori Mornings with Ms. Judy came about as I observed that the PTO meetings were much better attended when they were held the first thing in the morning at drop-off time, rather than in the evening. It seemed that many parents, even if working, could schedule themselves into work an hour later. So, I tried the same approach and I included the students as presenters. Each morning meeting was a different topic: Montessori math, Montessori language, Montessori cosmic education, to name a few. I asked students from each level—early childhood, lower elementary, upper elementary, and middle school—to present materials in each specific topic area. The first morning, Montessori math, had approximately ten to twelve student presenters and approximately forty to fifty parents in attendance. I considered this a very successful turn out! The success of this approach was not only in the increased amount of parents in attendance, but also the fact that those parents were not just listening to me or the teachers espouse the benefits of the Montessori method, they were actually seeing it in action! I literally watched some of the parents' mouths drop open in astonishment because of what they were witnessing. Why hadn't I thought of this sooner? The excitement of the parents was palpable. Talk about word of mouth, at the next session a month or so later, the attendance was even higher. I could see that this was a very successful venue for reaching the parents. It only lasted an hour, from 8:15 to 9:15 a.m., which was enough for everyone. Little bits of quality Montessori time for the parents was working wonders for their understanding and support of the philosophy. The children presenting were also very proud of their role in the event, and I had to make sure that I rotated students in order to give as many children as possible the opportunity. I highly recommend it.

Another very successful parent education class was when a panel of Montessori graduates from our school returned to share with the parents how Montessori benefited them as they moved on to high school and college. This really resonated with the parents because it was very affirming to hear how well the graduates were doing, and how self-assured and confident they were. The graduates answered a barrage of questions from the parents, and they did it with grace, composure, and intelligence. It was a highly successful event.

The more parents are offered information about their developing children, the more we are directly helping children. Parenting is a very difficult job today. They need all of the support that we can give them.

MONTESSORI TEACHER TRAINING: BEYOND THE NORM

When I received my bachelor's degree in education, I was given a broad repertoire of how to give lessons across the curriculum and assess students' learning in a traditional classroom. Basically, I was given the same toolbox to use with all children, no matter what age or grade. I earned a New York State Certificate to teach grades K–8 in traditional settings. When I discovered Montessori, I was not qualified to teach in a Montessori school, even with my degree in education, until I trained specifically in the level that I wanted to teach in the Montessori environment. In other words, if I wanted to teach at the elementary level, I would need to take Elementary I (ages 6–9 years) and Elementary II (ages 9–12 years) Montessori training. At the time that I was interested in taking elementary training, it was also required that I take the full foundational early childhood training (ages 3–6 years) before being allowed to take the elementary level training. This was a requirement even if I was not planning to teach at the early childhood age because that is how important the foundation is to this method. Many parents do not realize the level of training that goes into preparing a Montessori teacher. I had to take three levels of Montessori training before I was nationally certified to teach Elementary I and II. I then went on to take Secondary I training (ages 12–15) as Summit-Questa grew into middle school. So, to summarize, after my bachelor of science in education, I had to take four levels of training, which entailed an additional one-to-two years for each level. The American Montessori Society (AMS) requires all adults who are going into Montessori training to have a minimum of a bachelor's degree in order to receive a full, nationally recognized Montessori certification.

Montessori training is very intense, academically rigorous, and includes the education of the whole child, as well as the professional and inner growth and development of the teacher. Each level of training is comprised of an academic section, where the adult learners spend a year being presented the Montessori materials, course by course, by highly experienced Montessori educators. Once all of the core subject areas are successfully completed by the adult learners, they are then required to go into an approved Montessori classroom at the level of training they are taking, and do a year-long internship while they are mentored by an experienced Montessori teacher in their school. At the completion of both segments of the training, they must pass both practical and written exams and hand in their manuals for each subject area, which in some cases can number over twenty or more manuals. It is a tremendous commitment in terms of time, resources, and dedication to the cause and children. Successfully finishing those four levels of training was one of the most difficult *and* most rewarding accomplishments of my life. I had epiphanies about life, learning, and just about every academic content area. I could not believe what I did not know. I thought I was well-educated, but the Montessori approach is more than education, it is life-changing. Montessori teachers are truly specialists in their fields. After completing the Montessori training, I felt much better prepared to enter a Montessori classroom than I did after my traditional training.

Dr. Montessori stressed that the adults who work with children in Montessori environments must possess certain qualities. They need to have a deep understanding of what is needed for the healthy development of the child at every level. They must have a profound respect for the child and the developing spirit within. They must be keen observers of the children, getting to know them better on a daily basis by observing their interactions with the environment and others in it. They must be passionate defenders of the rights of the children in their care. Dr. Montessori wanted teachers to behave as more of a generalist in education, not showing favoritism or being a specialist in only one subject. Rather, she wanted her teachers to model a passion for all learning and to have a sincere awe about life and everything it includes. She wanted the educators to demonstrate that even if they did not know very much about a specific subject or something of interest, we would actively and enthusiastically model the process of research while guiding the student to follow their interests. In addition, Montessori educators must always be on a path of self-reflection, self-knowledge, and self-growth. There is a focus on the inner and spiritual development of the adult in the Montessori classroom as well, for how can we guide children if we are not familiar with the process of our own inner development?

So, parents, rest assured that you are working with an expert in the field of education and a passionate child advocate when your child's teacher is Montessori trained and certified. My training was always through an AMS training center; one in Chicago, one in Miami, and the third in Houston. I chose the AMS because that was the organization that was recommended to me by the first Montessori school I worked in as an assistant. I have been a proud member of the AMS throughout the course of my career and as I continued on to open an AMS Montessori teacher training center, accredited by the Montessori Accreditation Council for Teacher Education (MACTE). There came a time, as my school grew, that I was not able to find enough Montessori teachers to support this growth. So my friend and colleague, Jeanne Hudlett, who also owned a Montessori school and was facing the same problem, partnered with me in opening Summit Montessori Teacher Training Institute, which is also housed at my school. Despite the tremendous amount of work involved, it was necessary in order to remain true to keeping our Montessori philosophy in place. I can understand why many Montessori schools transition into traditional methods when the children grow older because of the shortage of trained Montessori elementary and secondary teachers. I was tempted many times to give up my beloved method in the upper grades because of the difficulty in finding Montessori teachers as compared to traditional teachers. Today, I am so glad that I stuck with my passion. It would not have been possible however without the training center. Now, if I lose a teacher, I can put someone through training to work with an experienced, certified teacher. This advantage has allowed us to grow into a stronger Montessori school.

I mentioned previously that there is another major Montessori organization that trains teachers, and that is the Association Montessori Internationale (AMI). This is the original organization that Dr. Montessori started and her family continues to run today. There have been many disagreements over the years between the AMS and the AMI, but I am happy to say that they are in collaboration presently. This will only strengthen and unify the Montessori movement—as division only weakens and hurts the cause. We all look forward to working together for the greater cause—the child.

CONFESSION:

Becoming an experienced Montessori educator was a long and arduous journey for me. I made many, many mistakes along the way and still do. Some of those mistakes, i.e., when I unintentionally hurt people due to my fear or misperception of a situation, I regret greatly to this day. I have had to self-reflect, self-correct, and self-forgive, so many times; it seemed that I would never attain the level of inner and outer peace that was my goal as a person and Montessorian. I felt as if I was emotionally and spiritually challenged many times while traveling my path. If it wasn't for the awe that I have for children, nature, and life in general, along with my passion for the Montessori philosophy, I could have easily lost my way.

Section II:
Montessori Curricula and Materials

8

Infant and Toddler Years

THE ABSORBENT MIND

From the time of birth until three years of age, Dr. Montessori referred to this period as the *unconscious* phase of the absorbent mind. The child does not consciously choose to learn about their environment, it just happens. Things just seem to *sink in*; the brain absorbs every impression to which it has been exposed. If you think about how a child acquires their own native language, a large vocabulary, and their social and cultural behaviors before the age of three, it is an awesome and effortless accomplishment that seems to just happen. I go back to our discussion of the absorbent mind, and that inner force that is guiding the child's development. The child's brain is wired to focus on certain things at certain times. It is evident when you watch an infant's focus on the adult caregiver's mouth, specifically their tongue and lips, as they speak. That inner intelligence is helping the child to do exactly what the brain needs at that time. Notice that the child does not imitate the other myriad of sounds to which they are exposed, such as the dog barking or the phone ringing because that innate wisdom directs the focus to the right source. This is why it is so important to be aware of the child's developmental needs. If the child is not exposed to the proper experiences when they need them the most, then that sensitive period is lost forever.

We all understand what it is that we are referring to when we hear the word embryo. We immediately think of the physical embryo, which is the developing human being within the mother. That embryo is developing with all of the predetermined physical characteristics from both sides of the parents' families. In essence, the child in the womb is the miniature adult that will emerge and grow into adulthood according to the DNA plan set in motion for the child at conception. Dr. Montessori added another element of development that she called the *spiritual embryo* of the child. She believed that, similar to the physical development within the child, is a predetermined *psychic* plan that is unique to each individual. This spiritual embryo is not visible at birth but is in fact, present, with its own unique blueprint for the child's spiritual development. The development of the spiritual embryo is also dependent upon the quality of the child's physical environment and the interactions that he or she has within that environment, along with the people within it. Just as with the physical, intellectual, and social development of the child, if these conditions are not met, or are of poor quality, the spiritual development of the child will be stunted and not manifest to its full potential.

From the moment of birth, the child needs to be held and nurtured in order to develop a sense of trust with the world and in those caring for him or her. The child needs to be spoken to frequently, read to, even sung to, in order to acquire their native language and develop that area of the brain. They need to hear nursery rhymes and lullabies. All of these activities nurture the further development of language patterns in the brain which will be necessary for the future successful task of reading and learning. If they regularly miss out on these types of activities, their intellectual growth may be irreparably stunted. One of the most tragic examples of a child being completely deprived of human language during the sensitive period was that of Victor, the Wild Boy of Aveyon. In 1797, Victor was found wandering the forests at the estimated age of 12 in France. It was a mystery as to how it came to be, but Victor apparently had lived most of his life in the forest. He could not talk, his food preferences were not typical, and his body was covered in scars that indicated he had been living in the wild. Despite the fact that Victor could hear, he was never able to speak fully, only learning the words, lait (milk) and Oh Dieu (Oh God). Fortunately, this type of example is not common, but does clearly indicate that once someone has been deprived of the sensitive period for acquiring human language, the opportunity to obtain it is forever lost.

SENSITIVE PERIODS

Children, from birth to three years of age, go through very specific sensitive periods. Children at this age will want to explore their environments. They want to touch things, look at things, and they will want to do it over and over again. As a child gets closer to two years of age, you will see that they want to explore everything! They do not want to hear the word *no* when they are intensely interested in their exploration of the world, and the result of hearing that word can send them into screaming tantrums as many parents have experienced. Even though it can be frustrating for parents at times, the child is actually trying to learn about the world and everything in it. It is that inner force guiding them to discover what has come across their path. It is important not to constantly stifle this need to explore. If that occurs, there will be multiple tantrums as a message to the parent that they are too frequently getting in the way of their learning! We would also not want to stunt that natural desire to explore and learn. This need to explore the environment is another example of a sensitive period. Dr. Montessori actually identified six sensitive periods:

- Sensitivity to language
- Order
- Small objects
- Walking
- The social aspects of life
- Learning through the senses

From the moment of birth, children begin to categorize their world. It is very important for them to have confidence in their world and this can be accomplished by giving them an order to it. They want to be in a familiar environment with familiar caregivers who treat them with love and gentleness on a regular basis. This consistency is comforting to them and meets their sensitive need for order. It makes them feel secure to know that they can depend on that order in their world: their room, their parents, their treatment, and their routines. Children at this age may become upset if their parents change something in their rooms or routine as this disturbs their sense of world order. Dr. Montessori described how an infant was frantically crying and the poor mother tried everything she could think of to calm her baby, to no avail. It was only after the mother removed a kerchief from her head that the child suddenly stopped crying. It was the unfamiliar head covering on her mother that so greatly disturbed the child's sense of order.

Children at this age will also be drawn to objects in his or her environment and will want to explore them. It takes time for them to realize that those objects can be moved to another place; for when they are moved, it can cause disorientation. Their world as they know it is actually being rocked! As the child grows and interacts with those objects and moves them on their own, they begin to have a broader sense of the world. Their world order is expanding.

At around the age of one, children are also drawn to very small objects. They are fascinated with anything tiny. Insects, grass, pebbles, beans, etc., are all objects to smell, touch, and put in their mouths! They are paying close attention to detail in their world.

A child usually begins to walk between the ages of twelve to fifteen months. Here is where the child's world really expands. Movement! They are able to explore more territory and everything in it. They are on a mission to perfect their walking. They will walk and walk just for the love of walking. That inner guidance is helping them to perfect the skill of movement at this sensitive period. Most adults do not realize that these very young children can actually walk very long distances as long as it is at their own pace and rate of interest. Two year olds have actually walked for miles when the adult walks with them and allows them to stop and explore objects along the way. They will tire much more easily when the adult is in charge of the walk, with the usual purpose of getting to a destination, not for the sheer enjoyment of the walk, which is the only motivation for the child.

Dr. Montessori noted that at around the age of two and a half or three, children begin to focus more on other children, rather than their immediate world. Children have been observing the social grouping of the family and other people in the world and they now begin to model that behavior. There is the internal drive during this sensitive period to become part of a group and cooperate with others. They begin to imitate the behavior of others around them. Once again, their world begins to expand a bit more.

We know that everyone learns through their senses, and of course, for children this ability is magnified. At the moment a child opens his or her eyes and takes that first breath, all of the senses are wide open and absorbing the world. They see, touch, taste, hear, and smell the world around them. Dr. Montessori recommended that the parent keep their infant with them as much as possible in order to allow the child to be exposed to everything going on around them. She also encouraged parents to allow the child to explore the world in every safe way. Constantly putting them in a playpen or high chair does not give them the same kind of freedom to explore their world. Of course, they need to be safe as well, and this is what Dr. Montessori also referred to: the prepared environment. At every stage of development, children need safe environments that are specially prepared for them in order to develop in the optimal way. At this stage, the more the parent can provide a variety of safe places to explore, the more the child's learning capacity will grow. This is not as daunting as it would seem. Just a trip to the beach, the park, the grocery store, can become a sensorial wonderland. At home, the kitchen is one of the best places to allow the child to explore; let them take out the pots and pans and find the correct lids. Allow them to squeeze a sponge in water to watch what happens. Don't forget to name everything. The experiences are unlimited, but what makes all of them safe is the adult's presence and observation of the environment the entire time. Preparing the environment means removing anything that is unsafe and making sure any exploration the child may be experiencing remains safe.

MONTESSORI INFANT AND TODDLER ENVIRONMENTS

Today, many Montessori schools offer infant and toddler environments. As is true of all levels, Montessori classrooms are specifically designed for the developmental needs of the specific age and stage. Those schools offering infant/toddler (I/T) programs follow the same method that Dr. Montessori introduced in terms of allowing these very young children the freedom to explore their physical environments while providing a safe place for the needs of the sensitive periods to be met. Consistent loving and nurturing caregivers, consistent routines, consistent classroom environment, multiple experiences for exploration of their world, language development, building independence, and varied opportunities for movement and moving objects are the main pillars of the Montessori I/T program. These environments are calm, loving places where children are free to safely explore their world and build their language development as well as independence.

I/T environments are not watered-down early childhood classrooms. You should not see simpler versions of the early childhood Montessori materials on the shelves, but rather, open space with many different types of materials for exploration. The exception would be practical life because many of those activities are appropriate for infants and toddlers as well. Generally speaking, because infants and toddlers are not in the same stage of development as students in the three to six age range, their classrooms are not equipped in exactly the same way, but designed strictly for the needs of that age. Like every other level, teachers must go through intensive training to become nationally certified Montessori I/T teachers.

In a Montessori I/T environment, real-life experiences, rather than lessons, are the focus in practical life. The children learn how to feed themselves, drink from a cup, prepare meals, and acquire daily living skills. As their skills increase, so too, does their independence. This is very important to them. Their love to touch is not inhibited, but encouraged. There are multiple experiences for them to improve gross and fine motor coordination—grasping, pouring, carrying, dumping, climbing, i.e., constant movement of some sort!

Music is a vital experience at this very formative stage for many reasons. Brain research has shown that allowing children to listen to music and singing enhances the development of the brain in multiple areas. It helps in all other types of learning. Children love to move to music as well. Dance and joyful movement are staples of the Montessori experience for infants and toddlers. They will begin to use simple musical instruments as they physically react to rhythms and sound patterns. There is always dedicated space for movement in I/T Montessori environments.

These young children love the outdoors! Outside play is a must and you will see children sweeping, digging, gardening (and eating their harvest), climbing, running, and exploring nature. They also love water play so there will be areas for children to pour, splash, and just interact with water in a safe way.

Due to the fact that the acquisition of language is a sensitive period at this time, language is constantly used in the I/T environment. It is important at this age that the native tongue is used first, then secondary languages can be introduced. Everything has a name and the students are constantly given those names. Adults often think these children are too young to understand proper nomenclature, and will use baby talk when speaking with them. This is a lack of understanding of the power of this age and will rob the child of an immense opportunity to acquire more of their language. We also introduce proper etiquette at this time, teaching children to say please, excuse me, and thank you.

Children are keen observers, so it is imperative to model the behavior you would like the children to adopt. I once had a toddler teacher tell me that all of a sudden she noticed the children pushing their chairs in with their feet and she was befuddled as to how that habit was forming. This was until she observed the new assistant in the class doing it! The children were imitating her behavior and of course, stopped when the assistant did. Many adults underestimate the observational powers of children. Children know and sense what is going on in their environments and they are definitely affected by it. Parents and all adults must be very mindful of their behavior and conversations when children can view and hear them. I can't even recall how many times parents have told me that they never speak about the conflict or emotions that they may be experiencing in front of their child, yet there is no doubt that the child is aware and has been affected by it. This is because they can hear conversations in another room when you are on the phone or discussing it with another family member. They can also sense it in your emotional state and read your body language. They will know when you are upset or disturbed by something. That energy is real and it is transferable. Children are like receivers and catch it all. They notice and absorb everything even though they do not appear to be doing so.

I would encourage you to visit a Montessori I/T community near you. It is absolutely amazing to see these very little people operating in very independent ways. I am often astounded by the intelligence and amazing abilities demonstrated by such young children and you most definitely will be as well. It is an inspiring sight to behold.

CONFESSION:

It took me a while to feel comfortable providing a toddler environment when it was first requested by parents at our school. My anxiety was due to the fact that I had never worked at a school that had an I/T program and I was inexperienced with that age and stage. In addition, I felt torn about providing it because I still had beliefs that infants and toddlers were best served in the arms of their mothers or consistent caregivers, rather than in a group. After visiting other Montessori toddler programs, I was convinced that the Montessori approach could provide a much more appropriate and better quality of environment for the children, as opposed to traditional day care facilities and nurseries. I sent teachers for I/T training, and we opened a toddler program. It immediately filled—and I watched in awe as these children once again humbled me with their beautiful and intelligent spirits.

Web Added Value™

This book has free material available for download from the Web Added Value™ resource center at *www.jrosspub.com*

9

Montessori Materials in the Early Childhood Curriculum (3-6 Years of Age)

Dr. Montessori began her work with normally developing children at this age level—3 to 6 years of age. She called her first school, Casa dei Bambini, or Children's House, specifically because she did not want an *institutional* feel to her school, but rather a home-like, natural setting where a family of classmates within a three-year age span grow up together. Dr. Montessori wrote a book called *The Absorbent Mind*, referring to the sponge-like capacity of children's brains to absorb everything from their environment.

"Before three, the functions are being created; after three, they develop."[3]

Children at this age go through very specific *sensitive periods* and the Montessori environment, once again, is designed to meet the distinct needs of the children at this age and stage.

The following is a general overview of the sensitive periods from birth through six years of age (these time frames can vary depending upon the individual child):

- Birth throughout life   language
- Birth–3 years   sensory experiences and learning through movement

- 1½–3 years   development of oral language
- 1½–5 years   development of muscular
                                        coordination
- 2–5 years   sense of order in their environment
                                        and need for routines
- 2–6 years   affinity for music
- 2½–6 years   refinement of the senses and
                                        development of social graces
- 3–6 years   highly sensitive to adult influences
- 3½–5 years   writing
- 3–4½ years   most sensitive to touch
- 4½–6 years   reading and math

Parents should be aware that children at this time are highly attuned to a sense of order and independence. They need a dependable routine to their day and to do things for themselves! This strong sense of independence is what allows children to develop a feeling of competency which builds their self-esteem. These children are learning through all of their senses which is why it is imperative to have a multisensory-rich environment. Dr. Montessori developed hundreds of hands-on learning materials in order to meet the needs of this age group: to touch, feel, see, hear, communicate, smell, and even taste. These *concrete* or hands-on learning materials are what set the Montessori experience apart from any other early childhood learning program or philosophy. With today's advantage of technology and research, we can see that Dr. Montessori was absolutely correct with her interpretation of how important her interactive and hands-on environment was to the developing brain. Children will learn effortlessly at this age because of their interaction with the materials, observation of others, and uninterrupted learning time. What makes the Montessori experience unique is that it balances freedom of choice, exploration of the environment, and responsibility to the community. Children happily make choices in their work and contribute to the care of the environment, themselves, and others. This well-rounded experience builds a strong foundation for children to be life-long learners, responsible community members, and happy, self-aware, fulfilled young adults.

Montessori materials are designed to be *self-correcting*—that is, when the child makes an error, the materials will allow the child to discover it on their own, which minimizes the need for adults to correct a child's work. These adult corrections can affect self-esteem and confidence at this age. Even beyond that, children are actually refining their observation and thinking skills as they continue to self-correct and explore what happens as a result of their interaction with the materials. It becomes a game of observation to them and the process will hold their fascination and problem-solving skills for long periods of time. A great sense of satisfaction emerges when the child successfully completes the lesson through his or her own powers of observation and thinking. In the Montessori environment, the teacher knows not to interfere with this process. This is so unlike a traditional approach, where the teacher, although well-intentioned, would be jumping in to correct the child's errors, thereby interrupting the child's train of thought, eliminating the opportunity for the child to discover it on his or her own, and sending the message that the teacher needs to provide the answers—an approach which does nothing to build the child's self-confidence. In addition, the constant interruptions on the part of the teacher will also inhibit the child's ability to stay focused on a task. Dr. Montessori stated that it was the child who needed to *"perfect himself through his own efforts."*[2]

> *"It might be said that the same thing is true of every form of education; a man is not what he is because of the teachers he has had, but because of what he has done."*
> —Maria Montessori, *The Montessori Method*

Another wonderful outcome for the child working in a Montessori environment is the natural development of self-discipline. A child learns to be patient when he or she needs to wait for a favored lesson to become available. This is done by design and why there is only one of most lessons in the classroom. Children learn that they need to wait their turn and to make another choice until their desired lesson is available. This is the direct opposite experience of instant gratification, and it builds patience, a sense of sharing, the ability to make different choices, and anticipation in waiting for something they want. This also results in a sense of satisfaction once it is attained and completed. Children begin to learn to control their own will as a means of becoming a respectful community member. Many adult observers are amazed to see children between the ages of three and six working harmoniously with each other, sharing, and cooperating. In some traditional settings, it is thought that adults must actually *break the child's will* in order to get them to be cooperative and conform. In the Montessori environment, children freely and joyfully work together for the common good of the community all while meeting their own individual needs.

PRACTICAL LIFE

There are core areas in all authentic Montessori classrooms. The first is *practical life*. Practical life gives students of all ages, and most particularly the youngest children, the opportunity to work with a variety of everyday household tools. Typically, children are not allowed to work with many of these types of tools at home, such as glass, ceramic, metal, knives, etc., and it is very appealing to young children to be given the opportunity to use them. The goals in practical life are many. We want the children to learn how to take care of themselves and the environment for many different reasons. It is an opportunity to learn the practical application of the tools that they use, adding to their self-confidence and independence. As important, it is giving the child practice with fine and gross motor coordination, a sense of order (lessons are done in a specific, step-by-step process), including left to right and top to bottom movement. All of this prepares the child for reading and writing at a later time. In addition, the child's concentration span and focus is being exercised and expanded as that child sits for longer and longer periods of time with more complicated practical life lessons. Children will handle the materials with more care because they may be breakable. The children enjoy these types of lessons so it does not seem like drudgery to them to focus for long periods of time while they scrub a table or polish every leaf on a plant. They enjoy it so much that quite often they will finish the task and then do it all over again because the process was more enjoyable to them, not the end product! Children at this age learn by repetition and are working for the joy of the experience, not the end result, unlike adults. This builds not only their attention span but their sense of order as some of these lessons may have hundreds of steps before completion. Practical life in general allows the children to care for their environment and themselves and this builds a sense of accomplishment and pride, not only for themselves, but for the state of the community as well. They will learn how to navigate through the classroom, walking carefully and respectfully. This also includes how to push in their chairs properly, carry lessons and trays correctly, and put things back in their proper place when they are finished. The lessons will include many skills such as learning how to pour, polish, sweep, spoon, garden, sort, and clean in an effort to maintain a beautiful, orderly, and clean environment. In addition, the children will learn how to care for themselves in many ways. They practice how to dress themselves by using the dressing frames (buttons, snaps, zippers, laces, buckles, hooks and eyes, and bow-ties) and aprons. There are lessons covering proper hand-washing, nail and hair care, food preparation, and baby-washing, to name a few. These very important experiences build the children's self-confidence, independence, concentration, physical coordination, and sense of order. All of these are prerequisites to the learning that will come later in language, reading, handwriting, and math. In Illustration 9.1, the artistic rendering focuses on the importance of the hand in the development of the mind.

In addition, the *grace and courtesy* lessons introduce the children to good manners and proper social behaviors; all of which build their self-confidence in the growth of their social skills. Children begin their day by properly greeting the teacher and each other in the morning, along with any visitors who may come into their classroom. In my years of teaching experience in classrooms for children ages three to six, I discovered that the students who spent the most time in practical life developed the strongest set of skills for later success in the more academic areas. My message to the parents who think practical life is not important and try to push their young children

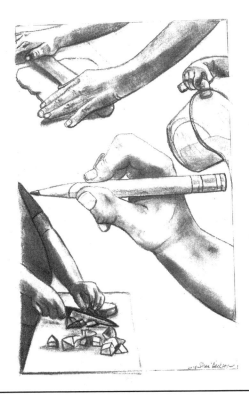

Illustration 9.1   The hand is the chief teacher of the mind

into the math and language lessons too quickly is that practical life is actually the best preparation for success in those later academic lessons as well as in their social development.

In an effort to further educate Montessori parents, I will list in further detail, many of the practical life elements and a sampling of additional activities found in Montessori classrooms. In summary, children learn real-life skills including lessons in care of the environment, care of self, and care of others. The children learn to control their fine and large muscle movement, respond to the orderliness of the environment and the materials, build their independence and self-confidence as they care for themselves and the environment, and improve eye-hand coordination as well as their concentration and communication.

- Food prep lessons: There may be a wide variety of food prep lessons such as: banana cutting, apple coring, nut cracking, bread cutting, orange juicing, etc. Children then serve the food snacks to their classmates using good serving manners. This is limited only by the amount of food available and allergies.
- Sorting, pouring, transferring objects: There are hundreds of options for reinforcing these skills.
- Weaving and lacing activities
- Art activities: gluing, clay work, cutting, painting, drawing
- Woodworking
- Care of the environment: Polishing—wood, glass, silver, plants, shoes (again only limited by the available amount of items that can be polished); Cleaning—correct use of brooms, dustpans, dusters, mops, table scrubbing, floor washing, window washing, dish washing, baby washing, ironing, flower arranging, watering plants, and caring for the classroom animals.
- Care of self: Hand washing; learning how to dress and undress using the dressing frames—buttoning, bow tying, zipping, Velcro fastening, lacing, snapping, belt fastening, buckling, fastening safety pins; hand and nail care; grace and courtesy lessons—children will learn to properly set the table and eat with a knife, fork, and spoon.
- Movement: Children practice careful heel-to-toe walking, tip-toeing, marching, skipping, and hopping on the line and outside, as well as moving gracefully through the classroom, and carrying and placing objects with care. They learn how to push in chairs, carry chairs and tables, roll rugs, and carefully inspect the classroom environment. They also learn how to be completely still during silence time on the line.

SENSORIAL

The next important area is *sensorial*. We know that children learn through their senses. The sensorial materials allow the child's senses to be stimulated and educated through their exploration of these materials. Dr. Montessori discovered that even beyond that, the materials "provoke auto-education".[1] They actually allow children to teach themselves. There are very iconic, recognizable sensorial Montessori materials such as the pink tower, brown stair, or red rods. There are many more but they all have one thing in common, they allow the child to explore and discover through their senses: dimensions, concepts, discrimination of shape, size, color, texture, smell, and taste through different materials and experiences with those materials. Their language development is also enhanced as the children learn the correct terminology for every piece of material, shape, concept, etc. They do not learn that the pink tower is composed of blocks, they learn that they are cubes, and that the brown stair is composed of rectangular prisms, and so on. Here is where they are introduced to geometry both in language and concrete concepts. Illustration 9.2 shows a child working with the geometric solids.

Illustration 9.2 Exploration of the geometric solids

Children learn the names of these solids, such as sphere, cone, ovoid, cube, rectangular prism, square-based pyramid, and of geometric shapes such as a pentagon, decagon, octagon, hexagon, etc. Because children are in a sensitive period for language, they can effortlessly learn these exact terms.

The *binomial cube* is a brilliant concrete representation of the abstract algebraic expression: $(a + b)^3$. Obviously, understanding this abstract algebraic expression is not what we are usually teaching at this age, however the concrete representation of it is like a three dimensional puzzle to the child. The challenge to the child is to find patterns and relationships. The pieces of the cube are organized in a very carefully ordered and mathematical way, and the children enjoy mastering the puzzle. The next level is the *trinomial cube* which is the concrete representation of the algebraic expression: $(a + b + c)^3$. It is very exciting to see older Montessori children, when they are actually working with the abstract version of these expressions, rediscover the connection to the early childhood material. They will sometimes return to an early childhood classroom and revel in the discovery all over again!

Here is a list of names and a brief description of some of the sensorial materials:

> **Cylinder blocks**: There are four blocks with ten cylinders inserted in each block. The cylinders vary by height and diameter and the child's visual discrimination is exercised in trying to find the proper hole for insertion. In addition, the child's finger muscles and eye-hand coordination are being strengthened for writing.
>
> **Knobless cylinders**: These are color-coded cylinders that actually correspond exactly to the ten cylinders in each of the cylinder blocks.
>
> **Pink tower**: The iconic Montessori pink tower gives the child the opportunity to discriminate size differences and understand the concept and language of large, larger, largest, and small, smaller, smallest. There are ten pink cubes built into a tower from biggest to smallest (see Illustration 9.3).
>
> **Red rods**: These are ten red rods built into a stair that allow the child to discriminate differences in length and understand the concept and language of short, shorter, shortest and long,

Illustration 9.3   The iconic pink tower

longer, longest. In Illustration 9.4, a child has built a maze with the red rods and carefully walks to the center and back.

Brown stair: These ten brown rectangular prisms build a stair that allows the child to discriminate differences in two dimensions and understand the concept and language of thin, thinner, thinnest and thick, thicker, thickest.

Color tablets: There are three sets of color tablets. The first set consists of the three primary colors to be matched to a corresponding set. The second set consists of eleven colors for matching in a similar fashion to the first. The third set consists of eight different colors that are graded by shade. The tablets teach the child the name of the colors and sharpen the visual senses in distinguishing between different tones of color.

Illustration 9.4 Building a maze with the red rods

Geometric solids: These are a series of geometric solids that the child handles, learns the names of, and then identifies by touch alone while wearing a blindfold. The solids usually presented are: cube, cone, sphere, ellipsoid, ovoid, square-based pyramid, rectangular-based prism, triangular-based prism, and triangular-based pyramid.

Geometric trays: This is a cabinet of six trays, each containing wooden insets of different geometric shapes such as squares, rectangles, circles, rhomboid, trapezoid, polygons, and curved figures such as an ellipse and oval. The children must discriminate among the different variations and match them to their corresponding frames. This exercise moves on to more abstract work with corresponding geometric cards that match the actual wooden shapes.

> **Sound boxes/cylinders:** These are a series of cylinders filled with varying amounts of sand or pebbles. The child shakes and listens to the sound made by each cylinder and then finds the corresponding cylinder with the matching sound.

There are many other sensorial activities in a Montessori classroom, however, these are some of the most commonly recognized. It is important to note how many of the sensorial materials consist of ten pieces. This was Dr. Montessori's way of ingeniously giving the students the sensory experience of *ten-ness*. It was an indirect preparation for the children moving into our numerical base 10 system.

In summary, children learn to organize, categorize, and understand their world through use of their senses: visual, auditory, tactile, thermic, baric, chromatic, musical, gustatory, and olfactory discrimination are the foundation of this area. The following are the basic sensorial materials designed by Dr. Montessori:

Pink tower	Brown stair	Red rods
Knobbed cylinder blocks	Knobless cylinders	Constructive triangles
Geometric cabinet	Color boxes 1, 2, 3	Binomial cube
Trinomial cube	Geometric solids	Sound cylinders
Thermic tablets	Smelling bottles	Geometric cabinet
Touch boards	Geometric cards	Bells

MATHEMATICS

This leads us into the next important area in the Montessori early childhood classroom—*mathematics*. Even though Dr. Montessori's brilliant insight and approach leads children to a much higher level of understanding and performance across the entire curriculum, the concrete Montessori math materials are without a doubt one of the most unique gifts given to children. It is fair to say that a great percentage of adults either fear or dislike math. The reason may be that most of us as adults were pushed into math in a totally abstract way far sooner than our brains were ready for it; rote memorization of facts and formulas was the approach. If you were mathematically inclined, then the process was predictable and you were successful. If you were not, you were left behind because there was no real education as to why we practiced those rote formulas. For example, in the traditional approach to teaching multiplication, we simply had to memorize our multiplication tables and the formula and we would be successful. If we forgot the tables or the formula, we were out of luck. In Montessori, before the child even moves on to the memorization of multiplication tables, they have learned to build those multiplication tables with math materials. They know *why* $2 \times 2 = 4$ long before they begin to memorize the tables. So if a student forgets the tables at some point in the future, they can actually figure out the answer because they understand the concept. There is no doubt that if those same traditionally educated adults who dislike math had experienced the Montessori approach to learning math, that negatively high percentage would be decreased significantly.

It is a tribute to Dr. Montessori's brilliance that she was able to take very abstract mathematical concepts and make them concrete with the hands-on math materials. Montessori students are given the opportunity to explore mathematical concepts with these materials at a time that the brain needs concrete experiences rather than abstract ones. As the child's exploration of the math materials grows and expands, the understanding of the concepts follows a similar upward spiral. It is not unusual to see children in the early childhood classrooms doing all four operations—addition, subtraction, multiplication, and division—with a variety of the math materials and completely understanding the concepts as they grow in knowledge. This is possible because it is a concrete experience, not an abstract one. It *would not* be developmentally appropriate to have four- and five-year-old children doing the four operations in workbooks and on paper at this time in their development, as it is too abstract. It certainly *is* developmentally appropriate however to have them building the decimal system with golden beads as they watch the base 10 system in which we work, grow, and expand in value. The golden beads allow the children to add, subtract, multiply, and divide into the hundreds, thousands, millions, and even beyond. And then, to experience why we need to exchange and borrow from different place values as they concretely see the need to do so. The golden bead material is the first introduction to the decimal system, however, there are many other materials that lead up to that, and many that follow. All of the materials will grow in complexity and abstraction until the point where the child will automatically move away from the materials because they have, on their own, reached an abstract point of understanding. This usually occurs naturally at the elementary levels.

I will share a story that has stayed with me because it represents how some adults can misinterpret what is going on with Montessori materials.

I had a five-year-old student who was very excited about his division work with the division board. He was in, what we call in Montessori, an *explosion* into division. This refers to a phenomenon where children will literally repeat a lesson, concept, or skill, over and over again until they are satisfied. These repetitions can go on quite long, for days, weeks, or longer in some cases; the length of time is very particular to each child. This young boy was repeating the division board multiple times and he had progressed to a point where he would ask for equations on paper and would find the answers with the board. He would proudly take home dozens and dozens of these division equations by the end of each week. After the third week, his grandfather came in to the classroom and in an agitated manner said to me, "I don't understand why you are telling his parents that he can divide, when clearly he cannot do it! I quizzed him last night on his equations and he could not give me one correct answer; he was guessing! I told his parents that he was too young to be doing division, that you apparently are trying to pull the wool over their eyes, and obviously, I was right." Rather than going into an explanation right there, I asked his grandson to go and get the division board and show his grandfather how he does it. After watching his grandson so confidently and successfully find the correct quotients to each division equation, he looked at me with understanding and a new appreciation for the Montessori experience his grandson was having. At that point, it was very easy to explain to him why his grandson was successful with the materials, but was not yet ready to move to the abstract. He totally understood that after seeing it in action. It is so important for the adults in the children's lives to have a basic understanding of what we do in the Montessori classroom and why we do it in order to fully support and encourage the child on their journey. This is one of the primary reasons I felt compelled to write this book. It is the child who will benefit the most by having informed and supportive Montessori parents (and grandparents).

The following are some of the Montessori math materials that you will see in all authentic Montessori schools:

> **Red and blue rods:** These ten rods look exactly like the red rods except now they are equally divided into sections of red and blue (see Illustration 9.5). They are used to introduce the concept of counting and associating a numeral symbol with a quantity. The child starts with the one red rod, places it on the left-hand bottom of the rug, counts one, and labels it with the numeral one. The child then selects the two rod which is

Illustration 9.5   A child associates numerals and quantity with the number rods

red and blue, and places it above the one rod, aligning the red above the red from the left, and then counts, one, two, and labels the blue section with the numeral two. The child then places the three rod which continues with the red and blue pattern (red, blue, red) and places it above the number two rod, again aligning on the left with the red, and counts, one, two, three, and labels it with the numeral three. The child continues to build the entire stair to ten following the same process. There is also a smaller, table-top set of red and blue rods.

Spindle boxes: These are two boxes that are divided by compartments. Each compartment is labeled from 0 through 9. The spindles are wooden sticks used for placing the correct quantity in each compartment.

Golden beads: These beads provide a very concrete representation of the decimal system. It introduces and reinforces many concepts of counting, quantity, place value, exchanging, and work in all four operations (addition, subtraction, multiplication, and division). See Illustration 9.6.

Color bead bars: These are color beads that have a specific color assigned to each quantity. They are used as the students move on to reinforce numeration, concepts, and operations after introductory work with the golden bead materials.

Multiplication board: A board with 100 indentations for red beads, each row is labeled from 1–10. Children continue to build their understanding of multiplication by building the multiplication tables with the beads and the board.

Division board: This board is used for furthering understanding of division after introduction with the golden beads. It also has indentations for green beads where the child shares a certain amount of beads with each skittle placed on the top of the board. It is another concrete representation that shows how division is sharing.

Illustration 9.6   The 45 layout with the golden bead material—the child builds the decimal system!

Squaring and cubing chains: These are multipurpose numerical chains that allow children to expand their understanding of counting, patterns, multiplication, skip counting, and the concept of squaring and cubing.

Fraction skittles: Skittles are objects similar to a bowling pin but smaller. Each skittle is divided into fractional parts that can be taken apart and then placed back to make it whole. Children understand the concept of a whole and its parts by exploring the skittles.

There are many other lessons with the Montessori math materials that come before and after those just introduced to you. Lessons are given in a step-by-step, sequential way in order to enhance the concrete understanding of the concepts being introduced. Many materials have multiple lessons that are introduced to the child over a period of time, and as they master each concept, they will move up to the next level of presentation and understanding. It is very much a spiral-like journey, circling the concepts with reinforcing materials until the child travels to the next higher level of understanding. For example, some parents are confused when they read in a Montessori progress report that their child has mastered the concept of multiplication that they have been working on and then all of a sudden, they are back to having multiplication presented again and they are not at the mastery level. Hopefully this explanation will help them to understand that the child mastered one level of multiplication, but now is moving on to the next level, hence the change in the comment from mastery to presentation of new material that the child continues to practice until they once again, reach mastery. The cycle just continues. Montessori teachers are specially trained in how to use the materials, when to make introductions, and how to direct them on this ever-upward, spiraling path of knowledge and understanding.

To give a general overview, children will work with hands-on Montessori math materials to understand abstract mathematical concepts. They learn, in concrete ways, that number symbols have a quantitative meaning. They move on to simple counting, 0–9; linear counting to 100, 1000; skip counting, understanding odd and even; working with the golden beads to understand the decimal system and place value; working with all four operations—addition, subtraction, multiplication, division—with the golden beads and other Montessori materials through the process of exchanging;

and working with fractions. The following are some of the core Montessori math materials generally available in an early childhood classroom:

Red and blue number rods	Sandpaper numerals	Spindle box
Golden bead materials	Cards and counters	Color bead bars
Bead chains	Addition strip board	Multiplication board
Division board	Snake games	Subtraction strip board
Fraction skittles	Small bead frame	Large bead frame
Squaring chains	Cubing chains	

LANGUAGE

The next core area in all Montessori classrooms is *language*. The acquisition of language skills, which includes learning to read, write, spell, and mastering all of the intricate rules of grammar in the English language, is once again, a concrete, step-by-step approach. The beginning of the language experience is sensory and begins at age three. The following are some of the core Montessori language lessons:

> **Sandpaper letters:** These are individually mounted, cut-out sandpaper letters. The very first experience is tracing the sandpaper letters in order to imprint the tactile impression of the shape of that letter on the brain. The phonetic sound of each letter is introduced initially, not the names of the letters. This allows the children to see an orderly pattern to how sounds can be blended and formed into words (see Illustration 9.7).
>
> **Moveable alphabet:** Once the children have learned the sounds of the letters, they can then move on to the moveable alphabet. The moveable alphabet consists of a large box with compartments for each letter of the alphabet (see Illustration 9.8). There are multiple wooden letters in each compartment to allow for spelling many words. The beauty of the moveable alphabet is that it allows young children to spell words and read them even before they are ready to write them. This is a very exciting process for the young child and they take great pride in their growing abilities with words. It is very common to see an *explosion* into spelling words as their confidence and joy grows. I

Illustration 9.7   Tracing the sandpaper letters

can remember Justin, a five-year-old boy in my classroom, who exemplified the concept of an *explosion* into spelling. Justin had mastered all of his short vowel sounds and was focused on spelling as many short vowel words as he could. Well, he filled up one entire floor mat with his words and then went on to get another floor mat and filled up that one, then another and another until he had used every floor mat and moveable alphabet box in the classroom! He never lost his focus and drive. After running out of mats and rugs, he then wanted to write them in word booklets, which he did by the end of the day! When children are driven by that inner force, there is no stopping them, or distracting them from their purpose. This whole process was completely internally driven on Justin's part. I never asked him

Illustration 9.8 Spelling short vowel words with the moveable alphabet

to do it or pushed him to keep going. I just stepped back and got out of his way. Once a child's need is satisfied, they move on to the next one.

Metal insets: The metal insets are ten geometric cut-out shapes in metal with a knob for lifting and replacing them. This exercise begins with the child tracing each shape with their fingers in order to refine their small muscle control and eye-hand coordination for future writing. Dr. Montessori believed that when children's fine motor skills are prepared through the many practical life and sensorial lessons and they draw with the metal insets, they will naturally be ready to write. As a result, many of our lessons across the curriculum are designed to refine the small muscle control needed for correct finger placement on the pencil and then subsequent writing. After tracing the metal inset shapes with their fingers, they then move on to using colored pencils to trace, color, and eventually form beautiful patterns with the geometric shapes, which they then color. There are many exercises across the curriculum that lead up to mastery with a pencil and once again, Montessori teachers are specially trained to present all of those exercises.

Sound and reading lessons: Once the child has mastered the initial sounds of the alphabet, the journey begins with the varied language lessons. There are many hands-on lessons that the children are presented in order to build their reading comprehension and writing skills. The exercises are too numerous to list but if you walk into a Montessori classroom, you will see the progression of language lessons on the shelves. You will also see short vowel readers that the children delight in reading, once they have mastered reading sentences. Once again, it takes the trained Montessori teacher to present these lessons in an appropriately sequenced way in order to allow the child to experience optimal success and the resulting confidence in their language and writing skills.

To give an overview, children will initially be presented the short vowel sounds and consonant sounds of the alphabet as they correspond to the letter symbols. Once they are able to associate the sounds with the letters, they can begin to form words and begin to read those words. This excitement with learning to read, fuels the student's own internal desire to continue learning more sounds and rules of the English language to become better and better at reading. This step-by-step approach builds a strong foundation in understanding the structure of the English language which leads to greater proficiency in reading and writing. Children can begin spelling words with the moveable alphabet even before they are able to write them. The children are prepared for handwriting through use of all of the manipulative Montessori materials, and then progress through pre-handwriting activities and use of the metal insets for tracing to further build the eye-hand coordination for a successful pencil grip and handwriting skills. The following are the basic materials used in a Montessori classroom for language:

Sandpaper letters	Moveable alphabet	Metal insets
Green boards for pre-writing	Classification lessons	Sound lessons
Sound lessons with objects	Sound lessons with cards	Words with objects
Short vowel spelling	Long vowel spelling	Parts of speech
Grammar symbols	Short vowel readers	Long vowel readers rhyming
Sight words	Spelling lists	

GEOGRAPHY, HISTORY, AND SOCIAL STUDIES (CULTURAL AREAS)

Introduction to these areas continues with concrete materials such as the *sandpaper globe of land and water*, and the color *globe of the world*. The first globe is strictly tactile; the child traces and feels the difference between the land and water. The color globe of the world introduces them to the concept of the globe and the continents, which are all different colors. The next experience would be the *puzzle maps*. These are wooden maps of the continents, countries, and the United States. Each piece in the map has a knob in order to allow the child to remove and replace each individual part of the map, just as in a puzzle. The children learn the names and locations of the particular continents, countries, or states. At a later time, the children will actually trace the maps onto paper, then color and label all parts of the map, which results in a very complex task that is proudly completed by the child. If the child progresses to a higher level of understanding, they could also include the flags of each nation or state. It is actually an open-ended activity. As is true of all Montessori materials, the only limitation is that of the interests of the child.

Another concrete geography lesson is the *land and water forms*—a set of trays that will have a representation of a land form, such as an island, in the center of the tray (some of these trays will be commercially produced, but some will use a simple piece of clay that has been placed to represent the land). The child will pour water into the tray and will see that the water naturally surrounds the island. The definition is given to the child that an island is a piece of land surrounded by water, a concept that they just engaged in creating! The opposite concept of a lake would also be introduced, whereby the clay would frame an opening for the child to pour water in to form the lake and the resulting definition: a lake is a body of water surrounded by land. There are quite a few other land and water forms that the children work with in a similar fashion, such as: cape, bay; peninsula, gulf; strait, isthmus; and archipelago, chain or system of lakes. Remember that because children are in a sensitive period for language, these words are not too difficult for them to learn. This is one example of why Montessori children have such outstanding vocabularies. We give them the correct language of the entire world and they easily and joyfully absorb it!

Children will also be introduced to the geography of their own body—right and left—and awareness of ourselves and others in the geography of the classroom. They will be introduced to directions—east, west, north, south—as well as directions on maps. In addition, the element of time and history are introduced. The students learn the days of the week, the calendar, months of the year, and time. This leads to discussions about time passing, history, and the events that have happened in our community and in history.

There will be many other related stories, searches, experiences, art, music, and cultural lessons that will reinforce the children's understanding of their world, other parts of the world and their inhabitants, and history in general: personal, community, national, and global.

SCIENCE

Children will learn facts about life, the earth, and the universe. There will be an area in the classroom with concrete materials in the following areas: botany, zoology, human anatomy, chemistry, life cycles, models, physics, space, and rocks and minerals. The materials will be puzzles, objects to manipulate and explore, picture cards, and books. For example, in botany, there will be trays of different leaf shapes, similar to the trays of geometric shapes. These wooden cut-out leaf shapes, like a puzzle, can be removed and replaced, traced on paper, colored, and labeled with the correct name. There are matching cards that would follow that lesson. There are dozens of *parts of…*puzzles and cards such as parts of a tree, parts of a horse, parts of a bird, parts of a flower, parts of the body, and so on. The variety of subjects is as unlimited as nature! Children acquire knowledge of, and respect for, all walks of life. Their vocabulary grows as they learn the correct nomenclature for anything they work with because they are in a sensitive period for language at this time and can absorb all of the scientific terms easily. Of course, the goal is to instill in the child an awe of nature and the phenomena of life itself. Some of the areas in the curriculum are: the study of living and nonliving things, animals, classification of vertebrates and invertebrates, plants, nutrition and health, earth science including rocks and minerals, magnets, seashells, weather, the atmosphere, the solar system, and experiments. The materials are only the reinforcement of what children should be exposed to outside in the real world. Children should have numerous opportunities to observe nature in action, to engage in gardening and the care of animals. Dr. Montessori believed children should be immersed in nature as much as possible. Taking a simple nature walk with the children to observe, and then doing the silence game to listen to all of the sounds of nature, is one example of a constructive use of outdoor time in building their sense of respect and appreciation of the natural world.

MUSIC

Musical variety should also be an important part of the early childhood classroom. The *bells* are a series of standing bells that produce different tones when struck with a small hammer. This initially is a sensorial lesson designed to allow the child to match sounds but can be used later on to teach the fundamentals of music—scale, composition, and playing very simple melodies. Beyond that, children at this age should be exposed to a variety of music. I loved to focus a great deal on classical music, as again, their senses will be trained to appreciate and enjoy the music. It is beneficial to have classical music playing very softly in the background of the classroom and in addition, during walking activities on the line, different composers could be used to provide a rhythm for our gait. It helps to introduce the composer being listened to, along with the name of their composition. One morning, a mother of a four-year-old girl in my class came to me and said, "I could not believe my ears when we were driving in the car yesterday afternoon and I was surfing the radio channels. All of the sudden, my daughter shouted for me to leave it on *that* channel. She said that she loved Beethoven's Moonlight Sonata! I was astounded and asked her where she had heard it, and she said that, in class, they walk on line to it." I must mention that years later, that same mother called me to share that her daughter had become a classical music lover because of her early exposure to it in our Montessori classroom.

Children should be exposed to a variety of musical experiences and songs at this age, including children's songs, cultural songs, and musical instruments. Stimulating the musical parts of the brain enhances its growth and development which contributes to other types of learning as well. Combining walking, marching, skipping, tip-toeing, general movement, and dancing with different musical songs and sounds not only enhances brain development, but the physical development of the child as well.

ART

Most Montessori classrooms will have an art area—either as a separate area, or incorporated into practical life. As Dr. Montessori believed that the hand is the main teacher of the mind, she encouraged us to provide a variety of experiences to help children acquire an appreciation of art and beauty. It is typical to see trays on a shelf with the following: clay for the children to sculpt with, paint, cutting materials, glue, weaving supplies, sewing materials, colored pencils, paper, mosaic materials, and recycled materials. The children are free to explore with them. Students at this age should also be introduced to classical artists and their work. It is appropriate to see fine art reproductions framed and hanging in a classroom; once again, this is a way to train and refine the child's fine art sense.

LINE TIME OR CIRCLE TIME

Most Montessori classrooms will have a taped circle or rectangle on the floor of the classroom for when the class is brought together as a whole. There are many different activities that will take place during this time. Typically, we do not keep the entire class sitting together for long periods of time (15–20 minutes maximum), no more than that once or twice a day. Appropriate activities would be: *walking on the line*, which are exercises in balance and coordination that are practiced in a variety of ways such as I described previously with music. Sometimes children will walk blindfolded or carry a glass of water or balance materials to enhance careful movement. *The silence game* is played where the children become completely silent for a period of time and listen for certain sounds, such as the teacher whispering their names. Stories are usually read at line time along with finger plays, nursery rhymes, and songs (all very important experiences for the development of their language and reading skills). Role-playing is done during this time where older students may model appropriate ways to roll a rug or navigate the classroom, or interrupt a teacher. Finally, appropriate group discussions would also take place at this time. Typically, anything that would be appropriate for the entire class would be done at line time.

OUTDOOR TIME/MOVEMENT

Giving children outdoor time is absolutely necessary for their overall development. They need to have opportunities to run, play, climb, explore, and just be children. Montessori schools will usually have developmentally appropriate playground apparatus and activities to promote gross motor development. Students will also tend their gardens, and have opportunities to explore nature in a variety of ways.

CONFESSION:

When I first discovered Montessori as an assistant in a Montessori lower elementary classroom, I was so eager to take the training to become an elementary teacher. I then discovered, to my horror, that I would be required to train first in the three to six age range because that was the foundation of the entire method. The reason I say I was horrified was that in the course of my traditional educational training, I had to complete a required observation of a nursery school. This observation was in a traditional preschool/nursery, and it was one of the most unpleasant times I ever spent in the presence of children. Based on this observation, I was convinced that I was not cut out to be a nursery school teacher. The children in this traditional setting were screaming and crying and throwing toys. The teachers were doing their best to control the behaviors, but it was plain that they were frustrated and tired. The physical environment was so over-stimulating, with every inch of wall space plastered with pictures, colors, designs, art work, etc. My head was spinning from the visual assault. No, preschool was not for me. So I pleaded for an exception—but, to no avail. I soldiered ahead because I was so enamored with Montessori elementary. I thought to myself that I would just go ahead, put the time in, get out as soon as possible, and move on to elementary. Well, needless to say, once I arrived at the three to six environment, I was astounded at the difference. I absolutely loved my students and ended up staying at that level for 12 years before moving on to elementary training!

REFERENCES

1. Montessori, Maria. *The Montessori Method*. New York: Schocken Books, 1964, p. 169.
2. *Ibid.*, p. 172.
3. Montessori, Maria. *The Absorbent Mind*. Wheaton, Ill.: Theosophical Press, p. 165.

10

Materials for the Montessori Elementary Curriculum (6-12 Years of Age)

"Education is a natural process carried out by the child and is not acquired by listening to words but by experiences in the environment."

—Maria Montessori

Cosmic education—this term refers to what is actually the foundation of the Montessori elementary curriculum: an awe for, and study of the cosmos, more commonly known as the universe. This curriculum, which may sound as if it has something to do with mysticism or astrology, actually has its foundation in hard science. It revolves around *great stories* or *great lessons*, based on scientific facts, that were intended to spark the child's imagination and interest in the universe and everything within it. Examples of great stories would be the Coming of the Universe and the Earth, the Coming of Life, the Coming of Human Beings, and the Story of Numbers. (To give you a flavor of the very first story, the Coming of the Universe, the classroom would be darkened as much as possible by blacking out windows and turning off lights. Once this atmosphere is created, an engaging accurate scientific story would ensue that leads up to a balloon popping which showers confetti on the students along with a flash of light. This dramatic presentation gives the children a rendering of the Big Bang theory which they will never forget.)

Dr. Montessori believed that we need to give what is the equivalent of a high school curriculum to the elementary students because she knew that adolescents are in such a social state of development (i.e., distracted) that the concepts only needed a review once they went on to high school. She felt it was far more relevant and successful to present these abstract high school concepts to younger students in a very concrete, developmentally appropriate way because younger students are much more interested in learning it at that time of development. So students continue their studies of geometry, physics, botany, zoology, and chemistry through the hands-on Montessori elementary materials, experiments, and research designed to revolve around the great stories and the interests of the students.

In terms of educating the child, Dr. Montessori always looked at the big picture. She started with the universe; she wanted children to be in awe of the big, big picture. She believed that sparking the child's imagination, sparking their interest, and fostering the WOW factor was the secret to creating life-long learners at this age. What starts as the study of the big picture of the universe can be broken down to its smaller parts, and eventually, the parts lead right back to the whole, and to the big picture. That exploration and those discoveries are what makes a cosmic curriculum so exciting and so chock-full of information and revelations to the child. The children love it and as a result, they discover everything has a cosmic task—every creature on earth, including us—and even though we do not always understand the task, there indeed is one. This type of approach leads to all kinds of discussions and epiphanies about the interconnectedness of life. What about plants that are eaten? What about their task? The revelation may emerge that perhaps that is what their task is—to provide food and medicine for other creatures on the planet. And so they begin to make all of these beautiful connections—connections that will lead to unlimited studies and unlimited interest in how everything is interrelated.

> *"The essential thing is to arouse such an inter-*
> *est that it engages the child's whole personality."*
>
> —Maria Montessori

The Montessori elementary curriculum builds upon the early childhood experience and continues to integrate all subject areas: fine arts, history, geography, sciences, practical life, math, and language. In addition, the prepared environment continues to offer social and moral development as well. Elementary students begin to become more aware of their role as a social being. If we return for a moment to the early childhood stage, children will focus primarily on their own internal development through one-on-one use of the Montessori material. Due to the nature of intense concentration on the materials, it is not unusual in early childhood classrooms to have complete silence at times when the students are entirely engaged in their work. Conversely, in elementary, children now move on to a stage where their place in the social setting becomes a primary focus. If we use learning to read as an example, in early childhood the child is learning how to individually navigate the English language and all of the rules necessary to become proficient readers. The next step in elementary is to use the skill of reading to discover everything about life and the universe. The students now want to work in groups and collaborate with others on their work and discoveries. There is a *busy-ness* with students discussing their findings. Students will be sprawled out on the floor with all of their research materials, excitedly sharing them with others. Here is where the children will begin to explore what it means to be a member of society. What is wrong and what is right? What are the rules? What is fair? In the first stage of the elementary years (6–9 years), it often appears as if students are constantly tattling, but in reality, they are trying to clarify their moral compass. This clarification eventually leads to the birth of their sense of justice.

Students at this age want answers to all of their questions, both socially and intellectually. They are literally discovering and trying to interpret the world. This is the age of reason where they will explore the relationships between things. It is important to spark this fascination with life and learning, which is why she encouraged the use of stories and the arts and drama in inspiring the students to research their interests. *Spark the imagination* is the mantra. Through the use of Montessori materials, timelines, charts, books, and other visual aids (other than textbooks and traditional worksheets), the children are encouraged to do research and in-depth studies of their own interests. We respect each child's intelligence and areas of personal interest.

The Montessori elementary teacher will also present accurate information through the concrete Montessori materials and curriculum to build a strong foundation in understanding the origins of the universe, the earth, life, history, language, culture, and the arts. Children continue to use the Montessori materials in math to develop a deeper understanding of the concepts on their journey to abstraction. The journey now is from concrete to abstract, simple to complex thought.

The children continue to be grouped in three-year age groupings: 6–9 years of age (some schools will refer to this level as lower or junior elementary) and 9–12 years of age (upper or senior elementary). The multi-age groupings continue to be an important element in the development of the whole child: socially, emotionally, physically, intellectually, and in terms of leadership skills.

Students at this age will further develop their public speaking skills as students continue to present their research to their classmates, and in some cases, to other age levels in the community. There will be special events, such as international fairs, or history and science fairs, where the students will share their research with the entire school community and parents.

There is another element of the elementary experience that is very unique to Montessori, and that is *going out*. Dr. Montessori believed that students should not always be confined by classroom walls. She felt that children needed to go out into the world in order to refine their learning and to continue their enjoyment of it. This applies to not only spending time in nature, but also in continuing their research of a topic or area of interest. Local libraries, museums, government buildings, businesses, etc., may be the destination for a student or group of students interested in furthering their understanding. This does not apply only to field trips that the whole class takes, but also to individual research. Students are encouraged and guided by their Montessori teachers to think about all of the steps involved in taking their research to the next level. Having the students do this independently is what continues their growth in independence, critical thinking, and self-esteem. For example, if a few students are researching ocean life, they may decide to visit the local aquarium and spend time with an expert at the site. The Montessori teacher would then guide them through the steps of what they need to do in order to make that happen. First of all, research where the closest aquarium is and contact them about a visit. Next, how will they get there? They need to find adult volunteers to take them. How much money will they need? What about lunch? They need to formulate a list of questions that they wish to ask the expert to aid in their research and provide those answers to their questions. Do they need any other materials? What if it rains? How are they to behave at the museum? This experience builds their reasoning and thinking skills and self-confidence. The students are entirely responsible for planning and coordinating every aspect of their going out into the community.

Of course, this level of responsibility grows over a course of time. Students who are able to *go out* must have shown responsibility in other *going-out* experiences within the school community; whether it is going out of the classroom or out of the building onto school grounds. The students earn their freedom by exhibiting their responsibility and how they handle the freedom.

Students in the elementary stage are not only focused on their personal social aspects of life, they are very attuned and interested in society as a whole. They are passionate and compassionate about the world and the issues that affect those in need. Community service, therefore, is a very important experience for these students to participate in and to become involved in finding solutions to some of society's needs. This is the best time to involve the students in helping others; for in going through the process, they will begin to see how they can make an impact on the world and others. This helps them to discover who they are and what their contributions can do to help others. Some of the most common situations where the students can be of service to others are by helping: children who are sick or impoverished, the elderly, the homeless, the handicapped, rescue animals, and in areas of the country or the world that are suffering through some kind of disaster or environmental situation. Dr. Montessori felt that education should not be limited to merely the intellectual development of the child, but the moral, social, ethical, and spiritual aspects as well. Community service is the way to allow students to fulfill this deep need to feel connected to society and realize their ability to make a difference for the good of all. They discover that they have the power to create change and they do not need adults to make it happen. This builds a strong inner core of their personality, which will certainly be important to them in the future as they enter adolescence. They can use that inner core to steady them when they begin the tumultuous ride through the next stage.

To help parents better understand the core Montessori curriculum and all that is included, I will list a summary of what is typically covered, or at the least, available for students in the Montessori elementary experience, starting with the 6–9 overview and then the 9–12.

LANGUAGE

Students continue to move through the available Montessori open-ended curriculum at their own individual level and pace.

6–9 Years

Children learn to read with proficiency, expanding upon the phonetic approach to reading that started in early childhood (3–6), working with short and long vowels, phonograms, and sight words. They will work on writing sentences, paragraphs, book reports, proper use of punctuation, grammar activities, parts of speech, synonyms, homonyms, antonyms, prefixes, suffixes, and root words.

They will work on handwriting, both print and cursive, use of the dictionary, spelling and dictation, reading comprehension, creative writing, expository writing, and general composition. Students will work extensively in researching topics and writing about their findings, and giving oral presentations to their classmates.

9–12 Years

Students continue to refine their understanding and performance with sentence analysis, word study, grammar analysis, spelling, dictionary skills, reading comprehension, higher levels of reading in both fiction and nonfiction genres, research skills, all forms of writing, punctuation, handwriting, and sentence diagramming.

MATHEMATICS

Children continue to develop a solid concrete understanding of math concepts through use of Montessori materials. The process is one of moving from the concrete to eventually, abstract understanding.

6–9 Years

Students continue to move through the curriculum at their own individual level and pace. They learn static and dynamic addition, multiplication, subtraction, and division with Montessori materials that lead to memorization; simple and complex operations with fractions; powers with beads, squares, and cubes; fraction equivalents, and concepts of divisor, square root, multiples, lowest common multiplier, money and time, estimation, algebra, products of binomials, highest common divisor, binomial operations, word problems, and measurements.

Geometry

Students learn about types of angles, polygons, identification of geometric shapes, Montessori protractor, types of lines, classification of triangles, study of equivalence, computation of area, measuring angles, classification of lines, study of similarity, classification of angles, and study of congruency.

9–12 Years

The students continue to refine their understanding and performance with Montessori materials. They work on higher levels of addition, division, multiplication, and subtraction with the materials provided. They also explore fraction equivalencies, multiples and factors, prime numbers, operations with fractions, binomials and polynomials, study of powers, square root, decimals, metric system, algebra, trigonometry, estimation, cubing, ratio and proportions, computation of average, percentage, highest common divisor, lowest common multiple, word problems, and problem solving.

Geometry

Students learn about the use of the protractor, study of perimeters, congruency, similarity, equivalence, volume, theorems of Pythagoras and Euclid, measuring angles, and construction of figures with a compass.

SCIENCE

The sciences are integrated into Montessori cosmic curriculum presentations and the students engage in being inspired by the great stories, experiments, hands-on interaction with the Montessori materials, and their own personal research, which would have been sparked by one of the great stories or Montessori material presentation.

6–9 Years

The following sciences are a part of lower elementary Montessori curriculum: botany, zoology, chemistry, earth, physical science, cosmology, environmental awareness, and scientific inquiry. The students will learn to classify animals, plant life, rocks, invertebrates and vertebrates, and learn about atomic structure. Students will research a wide variety of these topics and others, according to their personal interests and as part of our cosmic curriculum. Students love to share their research findings with their classmates.

9–12 Years

The following sciences continue to be a part of upper elementary Montessori curriculum: botany, zoology, chemistry, earth science, physical science, cosmology, environmental awareness, and scientific inquiry. The upper students will refine their work and move on to higher levels of understanding and engagement with classifying animals, plant life, rocks, invertebrates and vertebrates, and learning about atomic structure. Students will research a wide variety of these topics, and others, according to their personal interests and as part of the curriculum. Students continue to love to share their research findings with their classmates and become more adept at doing so. In our school, the upper elementary students put on an annual science fair, where they research a particular interest in science, write a formal research paper on it, and present it to the entire school through an oral presentation and a display board created by them and based on their findings.

SOCIAL STUDIES

Once again, the Montessori cosmic curriculum plays a tremendous role in integrating studies about the world, continents, countries, states, politics, and all aspects of the history of life and man on the planet. Through continued use of the great stories and dramatic presentations to inspire and spark their interests, as well as Montessori materials such as timelines, charts, and other hands-on activities, the students develop an awareness and appreciation of the interconnectedness of all life and people.

6–9 Years

Students continue with their individual research interests in a variety of areas: geography—which would include the study of continents, countries, flags, capitals; and history—which would include studying the timeline of the development of life, history of the needs of man, history of one's country and state, and civic responsibilities.

9–12 Years

Upper elementary students continue to refine and develop their skills through their individual research of capitals, socioeconomic geography, and history—which would include studying the timeline of the development of life, history of the needs of man, timeline of civilizations, history of one's country and state, and civic responsibilities.

FINE ARTS

Typically, the fine arts are integrated into the cosmic curriculum studies. For example, when studying a place in the world, students would also study the music, dance, and art of that country. Montessori classrooms would typically have art and music areas within the classroom available to the students at any time. The students can use these areas to incorporate into their cosmic studies or to just create a work of art or music. Some Montessori schools may have music or art specialists that will teach specific techniques in art, music, or dance.

MOVEMENT

The Montessori approach values development of the whole child, so it is imperative to add movement to the student's day to allow for optimal brain development and subsequent learning. The forms of movement activity will vary according to the school and its facilities. At a minimum, the students should be engaging in free play, formal games, sports, climbing, running, or jumping on a daily basis within the school day.

PRACTICAL LIFE

Practical life continues to be an important part of the Montessori experience for elementary students as well. The practical life experiences, such as sewing, knitting, cooking, woodworking, building projects, personal care, bicycle care, pitching a tent, doing the laundry, just to name a few, will eventually become more realistic and useful to the student in real life. The areas are as unlimited as life itself, and should only be limited according to the safety of the students.

In a further effort to aid parents in the area of communication with their Montessori children and teachers, here are the names of many core Montessori materials.

ELEMENTARY MONTESSORI LANGUAGE MATERIALS

Grammar symbols	Grammar boxes	Grammar solids
Grammar symbol stamps	Parts of speech grammar	Symbol chart
Sentence analysis charts and boxes	Grammar symbol and sentence analysis	Templates
Skyscrapers	Nomenclature cards	Arrows and circles for sentence analysis
Grammar command cards	Function of words	The farm
Detective adjective exercise	Sight words	Word study materials
Command cards	Language classification cards	

ELEMENTARY MONTESSORI MATH MATERIALS

Golden bead material

Stamp game

Ten boards

Bead cabinet

Addition working charts

Negative subtraction snake game

Multiplication working charts

Decanomial bead box

Large bead frame

Long division material

Metal squares and rectangles

Trinomial cube

Algebraic trinomial cube

Geometric stick material

Geometric cabinet

Square root chart

Geometric hierarchy of numbers

Cubing materials

Centesimal circle and protractor

Bank game

Color bead stair

Negative bead stair

Addition snake game

Subtraction snake game

Subtraction working charts

Division working charts

Algebraic (square root) peg board

Flat bead frame

Fraction skittles

Triangle fractions

Power of 2 cube

Pythagoras board

Decimal fraction board

Short bead chains and squares

Small square root board

Equivalent figure material

Multi-base material

Constructive triangles

45 layout

Teen boards

Hundred board

Addition strip board

Subtraction strip board

Multiplication board

Division board

Small bead frame

Checker board

Fraction circles

Binomial cube

Power of 3 cube

Decimal stamp game

Geometric solid stamps

Table of Pythagoras

Volume material

Area material

Theorem of Pythagoras

ELEMENTARY MONTESSORI SCIENCE MATERIALS

The five kingdoms chart	Protoctista kingdom chart	Animal kingdom chart
Plant kingdom chart	Fungus kingdom chart	Leaf chart
Nomenclature charts	Botany cards	Zoology cards

In addition, there are numerous experiments and different types of hands-on activities too numerous to mention.

GEOGRAPHY AND HISTORY

Flag stand of all continents	Maps of all continents	Parts of cards
Geography nomenclature cards	Maps of countries, states	Timelines
Charts	Clock of era	Globes
Land and water forms	Architectural blocks	Rocks and minerals
Biome studies	Space and astronomy materials	

Once again, there are numerous studies, visuals and hands-on materials, timelines, and charts depicting all areas of geography and history. Students use them for research and make their own timelines and charts based on their individual interests.

CONFESSION:

I admit that when I embarked upon my Montessori elementary training, I was taken aback at how much I did not know about the universe. Most of us went through traditional education, and the interconnectedness of life was never the focus. Everything we learned was so compartmentalized and departmentalized. It never appeared as if one thing had anything to do with another. We just studied a set of facts, memorized them, and gave it back on a test. Of course, certain things that were of interest to me seemed to stick in my mind. Unfortunately, it was never presented in a way that stirred much interest. So even though I had had a very fine traditional education, I don't think I really learned much; and since I have been in Montessori training, I am certain of it. I realized that I was learning right along with my students, and it was easy for me to answer them honestly when I would say, "I don't know, but let's find out!" I was a 6–12 elementary student in an adult's body! I do admit that I was just as excited about learning about the universe as my students were—which is why it was so rewarding for all of us.

11

Adolescent Years in Montessori

"Education should no longer be mostly imparting knowledge, but must take a new path, seeking the release of human potential."

—Maria Montessori

In no other time in human development, with the exception of infancy, does the human being change so drastically in a relatively short period of time. The adolescent stage is very misunderstood by most adults. Adolescents have the reputation of being rude, thoughtless, disorganized, daring, and rebellious (to name a few), and they have earned that reputation with good reason in many cases. On the flip side, they are also full of magnificent potential energy, and if we look back at history, they have achieved great things! Through their hard work and high intensity, they helped to build the pyramids and some of the world's greatest structures. They have the inspiration and idealistic view of the world to ask the big questions and passionately seek answers to them. Many of the soldiers who fought in the American Revolution were adolescents. It is only in our modern culture that this *in-between* stage has been created. If we travel back a hundred years or so, adolescents typically entered the adult world at this age. They married, had children, worked, apprenticed, and prepared directly for their adult role. In many other cultures around the world, this direct progression into the adult world still exists. In today's society, they have been placed in this *waiting stage*—no longer children, but not yet adults. So just imagine how these young people cope with all of this new energy. Their hormones are raging and even though they are not emotionally or socially mature enough in our culture to reproduce, their bodies are giving them a very different message. This powerful energy can be very difficult to contain for many young people. Their new thinking skills are forcing them to view life in a very different way; they want answers to the big questions in life. Why are we here? What is our purpose? Who are we? What matters? Do I fit in? I want to belong! They become very idealistic and start to see inconsistencies in not only the bigger world, but in their immediate world as well. They begin to question societies' values, their families, their schools, their parents, their teachers, and even their friends. They only see *black and white*—it is either right or wrong, acceptable or unacceptable—there is no middle ground. Therefore, life seems so unfair to them at this stage because no one ever lives up to these idealistic expectations. Add to that their *egocentric* tendencies, where they see the world only through their own lens and their own world view. They truly believe that every word, action, or emotion from others in their lives is directed solely at them; the world literally revolves around them. They become hyper-sensitive, which only compounds their feelings. This stage is often likened to a *roller-coaster ride* and I often advise parents not to ride that roller coaster!

As much as we may think that the problems that we have with adolescents are worse today, historical notes show otherwise:

> *"Our youth love luxury. They have bad manners, contempt for authority; they show disrespect for their elders and love chatter in place of exercise; they no longer rise when elders enter the room; they contradict their parents, chatter before company; gobble up their food and tyrannize their teachers."*
>
> —Socrates, Middle School Educator,
> The Republic of Athens, Fifth Century BC

If we look at what is happening in the development of the brain at this time, it is very telling. The brain is still growing, there is abundant cell growth from approximately 11 through the age of 17. It is a peak time for making connections and after the age of 20, there is less flexibility. Early adolescence is an excellent time for the brain to reorganize, therefore, the prepared environment is critical. Positive experiences at this time will have a long-lasting effect. The frontal lobe of the brain (prefrontal cortex or PFC), the portion that allows us to think ahead, set priorities, logically understand the consequences of our actions, control impulses, have healthy fears, and plan and organize is not fully developed yet because of this rapid growth. This portion of our brain is what allows us to apply *the brakes* when we are feeling daring or reckless, frustrated, or just full of energy. As a result of it not being fully developed yet, adolescents don't entirely see the consequences of their actions, which is why it is such a potentially dangerous state and why parents are often ready to pull out their hair over the seemingly thoughtless, carefree, careless, and defiant attitude of adolescents.

I like to refer to this stage as *The Land of the Lizards*. The amygdala is the ancient area of the brain, our reptilian counterpart, the fight-or-flight response to danger. Being in the midst of adolescents is like living in a land of lizards where at any given moment, that button can be pushed and we instantly revert into that emotional state of survival: fight-or-flight. This part of our brain was, and is, absolutely essential to our survival as human beings. If this part of our brain was not in operation, we would probably not have survived as a species. The difficulty that comes with adolescents operating more out of this portion of their brain rather than the frontal lobe is that they perceive things as some sort of threat or attack most of the time and they react defensively. Their brains fire to a lower level, the survival fight-or-flight reaction kicks in, and the adolescents see negative emotions (anger, disdain, etc.) in those around them.

"When this area fires up, a child may instantaneously interpret just about anything you do or say as hostile—and react accordingly. The problem is, middle school students don't have the maturity to know when they've crossed the line," explains Steven C. Atkins, associate professor of child and adolescent psychiatry at the Dartmouth Medical School. So they will immediately accuse others of behavior that may or may not have been intended. "Mom, why are you yelling at me?" "Dad, I can tell from the expression on your face that you don't approve of my friends; you are so judgmental!" "Ms. Judy, you just embarrassed me in front of the whole class when you asked me to come speak with you." These impulse reactions can be very extreme. At some point they will usually storm off and slam their bedroom door or if at school, rush to the restroom to be comforted by their friends. There is always a great deal of drama with adolescents because they feel so emotional about everything and they have a hard time controlling those emotions. They will read facial expressions from this fight-or-flight place rather than the frontal lobe/reasoning/logical area. If you are the parent or teacher of an adolescent, I am sure you could provide endless lists of examples of how young people at this age will often react in very defensive ways because of perceived threats—some are valid and some are not. This is why it is such a difficult stage for everyone—not only the students, but for the adults in their lives as well, most particularly their parents and their teachers. To add to the difficulty, it is often a problematic time for parents as well, for their own challenges in

life will often take dramatic turns while their children are in the throes of adolescence. This only compounds the situation for everyone. In years past, before we had the technology to study the brain, hormones were primarily accused of being the main culprit as to why adolescence is such a difficult stage. We now know that one of the reasons most adolescents don't see cause and effect consequences is because, in many cases, their brains are just not firing.

I often name a lecture that I give to parents about adolescents, *Who Is This Stranger in Our Home?* They become masters of button-pushing because they are keen observers and will quickly point out where any of the adults in their lives have not been consistent with rules or behavior. What I discuss with parents is that knowing why these behaviors are going on in the adolescent is helpful because it allows everyone to understand the reason, but it does not excuse the behavior, or mean that these young people do not have consequences for their inappropriate actions. It is probably one of the most important stages in development where young people need *more* structure and guidance from the adults in their lives even though they will insist otherwise. Here is where compassion must enter the equation. When we are aware of how difficult this stage can be for many young people, then it makes it easier to address their behaviors with caring and compassion. I have often told a middle school student who has just done something foolish, "*I love you but I do not like the behavior you just used with your friends. Tell me about what happened and then you need to let me know what you intend to do to make it right.*"

Young people at this age need to be empowered by having a say in whatever event occurs in their lives, good and bad. Just having a voice is what empowers them, not necessarily getting what they want. That is where the adult needs to provide the structure and the guidelines. Give them options in coming up with solutions when something doesn't work. So to follow up with the conversation that I just started with the student in my previous example, it might go something like this:

> "*Okay, I see that you are upset. Once you are calm, we can start the conversation.*"

This is also a very important piece of the equation because when anyone is upset, their brain function slows down, so it is not an ideal time to jump into a conversation (remember the lizard brain). The thinking part of the brain is actually not working when someone is emotional. This will often lead to shouting matches between parents and their adolescents because both parties tend to be in an emotional state when something happens that may be frightening or frustrating. Give everyone the opportunity to calm down and come back to the table. My conversation with the middle school student continues as such:

> *"So, what I understand is that your friend was making fun of what you were eating at lunch and continued to tease you in front of the other students; and as a result, you picked up your friend's lunch and threw it at him. Is that correct? You also feel that your friend and the other students often tease you because you are a vegetarian. I can understand why you might feel that way, but where did you make the wrong choice? What could you have done differently instead of reacting with anger and physical aggression? Could that food have caused a freak accident if it had hit your friend's eye? How would you have felt if that had happened?"*

Going through the process of discussion and giving students the example of following through with their thinking and coming up with other solutions and perceptions helps the students strengthen that frontal lobe development. Metacognition—thinking about thinking—is important. They need time to think about the choices they make in their lives. *What worked? What didn't work? How did you feel? What did you learn?* Usually, once the student calms down, he or she will actually come up with very valid solutions and will then be ready to take responsibility for their part in the exchange. It is very important that young people take responsibility for their actions. When parents unwisely defend their children when they are in the wrong and constantly blame others for their child's mistakes, they are creating a young person who will expect the world to drop everything in order to meet their needs alone. I think most people would agree that this kind of behavior does not lead to success anywhere in life. So typically, I would receive an answer to my question of, "how do you make this right?":

> *"I need to apologize and offer to buy my friend another lunch."* My response would be, *"That is a very appropriate solution. Do we also need to have a discussion with your friend about how you are feeling when he makes fun of your diet? That needs to take place at some point in order to get to the bottom of the problem. Are you willing to do that?"*

Involving all parties engaged in the conflict in a discussion is an absolute necessity in order to get to the bottom of what happened, and to come up with fair and appropriate consequences. It builds their communication and conflict resolution experience which are necessary real-life skills. When students or their parents tell me that they do not want the student to talk to anyone about it, I sadly state that we cannot really find good solutions, nor help the students acquire proficiency in handling real-life problems, by giving into the student's fear of communication. This also hinders the developing self-esteem as students get the message that they are not able to, or should be afraid of, solving problems on their own.

It is also so important to inject the fairness element of speaking to all concerned because of how sensitive adolescents are at this time. Interestingly enough, after the discussion between the two friends, it was once again evident that adolescent angst played a tremendous part in the exchange. His friend responding to the student who threw the food at him:

> *"I am really sorry that you thought I was teasing you. I was only commenting on the things that you said to us last week about you being a vegetarian. You were joking about it and I thought I was joining in on the joke also. I did not mean to hurt your feelings and I am sorry if I did. I won't joke about it anymore, in fact, I admire you for being a vegetarian."*

So, a few things happened with this communication. One, the students were able to hear each other's perception of what occurred. If they had not had this discussion, most likely the anger and resentment on both sides would have led to another altercation that could have been more serious the next time. In addition, they went through the frontal lobe exercise of seeing another's perception of a situation. In the end, they parted as friends and it was over.

I confess my buttons have been pushed by adolescents many times. My particular challenge is that I have had to learn to control my fiery Irish temperament over the years. I have worked with adolescents for approximately 20 years and, in that time, it has often taken feats of grand power and might on my part to control my emotions. A middle school student may roll their eyes at me or throw out a whispered derogatory statement and my reptilian response begins: I get light-headed, my heart starts to pound, I feel flush, and I want to strike out. Thankfully, I have learned to step back, take deep breaths, count to 10, and sometimes just walk away; whatever it takes to not react emotionally and from that ancient part of the brain. Those types of reactions rarely work out well. Things are said or done that can cause more hurt feelings and damaged relationships. I would not be honest if I told you that I never lost control or yelled when I got to that point with our adolescents. As I mentioned earlier, they are masters of button-pushing and, at times, I humbly confess I succumbed in my early years of working with them. When that occurs, the only positive thing that can come out of it is to humbly ask for forgiveness. I have apologized to the students when I reacted emotionally, asked them to forgive me for being human, and to also reflect upon why I, or any other adult, may react that way when the adolescent behaves in a certain way. Once again, the discussion about each other's perceptions of the situation will allow the adolescent to see another person's point of view—another frontal lobe exercise.

I confess that I have had my buttons pushed by not only adolescents, but by adolescent parents, who often will defend their children in an emotional fashion as well. Subsequently, I reacted in a way in which I try not to react, that is emotionally and lizard like. But, I will say it again, when our emotional buttons are pushed, we mortal beings often retaliate in a like fashion. There was an adolescent parent in a conference with a middle school teacher and myself, and this parent was angry at how a situation was handled by the teacher. In the course of the conversation, the parent looked at me and said, "Well, do you have children?" in a tone that implied that if I didn't have children, I couldn't possibly understand how they were feeling.

Well...that's a hot button for me. The reason is that when I was younger, I was diagnosed with Hodgkin's Disease, which is a cancer of the lymphatic system. Obviously that was shocking news and certainly gave me a completely different perspective on life at the age of 32. I actually took it as a challenge, however, and I was fortunate enough to have a young, upbeat oncologist who taught me something very powerful. He told me, "Your survival rate is about 50% and what I can do for you will be 50% of your recovery—but what you do for yourself will be the other 50%." Those words changed my life because I was forced to look at how powerful our attitude is in the course of our lives. In my case, I was very fortunate that with the help of my oncologist, and with a renewed vision of life, I was in the 50% that was cured.

In the interim however, the chemotherapy destroyed my ovaries among other effects, but it allowed me to live. It was a trade off. The result was that I was not able to have children, and I had wanted children. My husband and I had planned to start a family in our 30's and ironically, I had wanted to wait because of my passion for Montessori and knowing that I would most likely need to take a few years off once I started to have children. We considered adoption after learning the news, however, when I returned to Montessori after my healing, I was approaching it with a renewed vigor and passion that I had for really being alive. In retrospect, I do not think that I would have accomplished what I have accomplished today in terms of building my school and career if I had had a family. Knowing my personality, I would have been with family first, and probably would have simply taught and not gone on the odyssey that led me to where I am today. Now, I look at it that I have hundreds of children and I get to spend the better portion of every day with them! I look at this whole experience as an incredible opportunity that was provided for me, a gift for me to give back and provide something special for children in the world. I believe I would not have been able to do this if I had had children; my life would have taken another course. And that has been my attitude in life, that everything is an opportunity.

Now, back to the story and my lizard moment…my button was pushed! I confess that I still can get very upset when people make that kind of statement because I think it is very disrespectful. Most people wouldn't dream of sitting and telling an oncologist or a surgeon, "Well, if you have not undergone surgery or fought cancer, you can't *possibly* know what it is that I am going through or how you can help me." It pushes my buttons that teachers' and educators' formal training is often minimized, they are sometimes second-guessed and not treated with the respect that they deserve. I fully admit it hasn't always been easy for me to put my emotions aside. I have fiery Irish roots and it has taken me 40 years in the Montessori world to really assimilate how to choose to be peaceful rather than reactive. Losing my temper with this parent taught me another valuable lesson, that if I can react that way—so overly emotionally—so too, can parents. It reminded me that finding common ground and having common respect for each other is what allows us to work together as a productive team, and be partners for their children. We all want the same thing, although it is not always easy getting there.

THE ORIGIN OF THE MONTESSORI ADOLESCENT PROGRAM

Dr. Montessori had envisioned an environment, the Erdkinder, or Children of the Earth, as the optimal experience for adolescents. She recognized that because of the rapid physical changes going on during puberty, to expect students at this age to focus solely on academic studies is not productive, nor does it meet the developmental needs at this stage. She recommended that young people live close to nature, be involved in all aspects of practical work in relation to their lives on a farm, and be away from their parents. They would be totally self-sufficient, learn to be independent, and acquire the practical skills of living and working together based on the needs of the community: food, shelter, transportation, communication, economics, and positive, supportive relationships. Hershey Montessori Farm School, located in Huntsburg, Ohio, opened in 2000 and is one of the most successful Erdkinder-inspired adolescent programs in this country. It is a day and boarding school, and consists of a large working farm, a main house, and numerous barns and buildings housing a variety of activities. The students work alongside the adults in fully running the farm, the finances, and a bed and breakfast for visitors; they are involved in every aspect of the care of the land and the community. The students also participate in multiple workshops where they will learn different skills, such as woodworking, or participate in environmental labs. There are art shows presented to the community and the students have 90 acres surrounding the farm where they are able to hike, explore, horseback ride, and swim. The academic classes that would traditionally take place in most middle and high school classrooms are integrated into their everyday life and workshops.

Unlike all previous stages, Dr. Montessori did not leave a clearly outlined curriculum for adolescents other than her general reflections on the *Erdkinder*. This is one reason why we have not seen a growth in Erdkinder in comparison to the growth of younger Montessori environments. In addition, many parents are not ready to send their children away at this age, no matter how developmentally appropriate it may be. Additionally, many Montessori schools do not have the physical or financial resources to establish such an environment.

The Montessori adolescent program designed by Dr. Betsy Coe, former American Montessori Society (AMS) president, and world-renowned Montessori teacher-trainer and expert on adolescent development, is the program I chose to use at my school. Dr. Coe created the early adolescent program that originated at the School of the Woods, Houston, Texas. Today, Dr. Coe's program includes a very successful high school as well. I have worked with Dr. Coe's program for the past 20 years and, as with all Montessori prepared environments, it was designed specifically for this stage.

Dr. Coe's program has combined the known developmental needs of the adolescent, what the current knowledge and brain research tells us about how people learn, and the leading ideas of the Erdkinder, into the adolescent program. The program includes working on the land through gardening and environmental projects, caring for animals, both farm and domestic, week-long overnight trips, day trips, week-long internships in the general public and business world, student-run businesses, long-term projects, student-directed and group activities and studies, daily community meetings run by the students, refined time-management and organizational skills, and an enriched academic program focusing on integration of studies, Socratic discussion, literature, and the humanities. The students are also given varied opportunities to develop more personal and social awareness in order to learn more about themselves, as well as how to get along with others.

Over the past 20 years I have learned a tremendous amount about adolescents by being with them on a daily basis. As a service to adolescents and their parents, I would like to provide you with a summary of what we do in Dr. Coe's AMS Montessori adolescent program, and why we do it.

Adolescents consider academic goals as a secondary priority. They put personal and social concerns above all others and those concerns dominate their thoughts and activities. To help them refocus at school we provide dependable systems: we set very clear daily routines, goals, and time frames; we establish a structure conducive to helping them achieve their goals and there are natural consequences to inappropriate behavior. We provide cooperative learning activities to support their need to be social and to learn how to get along with others. At home, parents can help by consistently supporting the school structure, providing a home structure, and allowing the student to experience the consequences of their choices. Establishing routines at home and school helps the adolescent to refocus and not be constantly distracted by all of the social pulls.

Adolescents are moving from concrete to formal (abstract) thinking and they need pictures and other visual stimuli to help bridge their thinking. In Montessori we will provide concrete materials to the adolescent by using pictures, videos, charts, and other graphic organizers. Sometimes having a student draw a problem will help with their understanding of it. They can only handle one direction per instructor at a time; their memory is not proficient at this time, so planners, and the use of them, are essential! Exposure to multiple points of view, and multiple ways of doing things, are valuable preparation for formal thinking, and studies have shown that the number of years in a Montessori environment creates earlier formal thinkers. The Montessori experience teaches the students that there is never just one way to solve *any* problem. It is very interesting to note that in general, the brain begins to be ready for formal or abstract thinking around 12 years of age, however, research has shown that only a small percentage of college freshmen are formal thinkers! I would venture to guess that a good majority of those that are have a Montessori background.

The adolescent is egocentric; seemingly, the world revolves around them. They feel that they are the center of attention of an imaginary audience. The worrisome aspect of this stage is their *Personal Fable*, that is, that nothing bad will ever happen to them; hence their urge to do daring things without thought of any negative consequences. They lack seeing other options at times, and then lack the skills to apply them. They want to learn about things that are relevant to real life, and they are curious about anything having to do with their lives. At school, we provide stimulating experiences that are real and empowering, such as: participation in a *ropes* course, a safe way to feed that need for daring activities; week-long internships in the outside world, which gives them an entirely different perception of life; participating in student businesses, land and environmental projects, and fund-raising for community causes. When adolescents participate in these types of real-life activities, they experience firsthand that other people depend upon them to fulfill their responsibilities, and if for some reason they do not follow through, people are impacted. Our middle school students participate in the Montessori Model United Nations. This impactful and transformational experience shows them how they can have a very real effect on others around the world and they can actually facilitate change. An additional advantage is that they are working with other students from around the world on common causes. What a wonderful way to experience the celebration of diversity and a world view of problem solving.

Physically, we want them to be personally aware of what is happening to their bodies and why they are feeling the way that they feel. Their bodies are gaining physical strength rapidly and they are not aware of it. They will often break things or seem careless, but in actuality, they are not cognizant of their own strength and therefore, are not able to regulate it. We educate them about how important good nutrition and sleep are to the healthy development of their brains and body. We explain why they become *night owls*. The developing adolescent needs 9.25 hours of sleep a day and in general, their sleep pattern is two hours later than adults. Add to that the additional stimuli: 24-hour TV, computers, iPads, social networking, etc., and we have adolescents who are sleep deprived. They then have a hard time getting up in the morning and end up trying to fix it with caffeine. This becomes an unhealthy and vicious cycle. If we look at the symptoms of lack of sleep, we see many adolescent behaviors that are exacerbated by it:

- More emotional
- Lack of memory
- Poor school work
- Fatigue and falling asleep
- Weaker immune system
- More prone to accidents and injuries
- Less control
- More drama
- Sadness, and/or hopelessness
- Brains that cannot recharge

We also want them to be aware of how important it is not to put anything into their bodies that can be dangerous, such as alcohol and drugs. The brain is very vulnerable to both of these and the impact can be much more severe during this period of brain reorganization. Depression and anxiety can also be heightened at this time.

On the positive side, we want them to become aware of what kind of learner and thinker they are. Cognitively, in order for them to make connections as we integrate curriculum, we have themes that dominate each learning cycle and through Socratic discussion and application of learning, they begin to see connections that make sense to them.

This is the age of constant complaining! They are idealistic dreamers and they want everything to be *perfect*. They notice every inconsistency and nothing is fair. In order to survive this stage, the adults in their lives cannot take the constant complaining too seriously; just listen nonjudgmentally, acknowledge, but don't rescue! One of my favorite statements that I learned from Dr. Coe was, "Do you want to blame and complain, or do you want to solve the problem?" Sometimes they responded, "I just want to blame and complain!" Once again, my advice to parents and teachers of adolescents: Do not get on the roller coaster with them!

One of the elements that can be very distracting for all concerned is the adolescents' *pseudo-stupidity*. Students at this stage really do feel like their heads are in the clouds sometimes, if not always! We have heard, "*I want to pay attention, but I can't.*" They have described themselves as *being in a fog*. Remember that there are many chemical changes going on and brain functions slow down at this time. There is either too much, or too little, dopamine in the brain, and it is constantly trying to balance itself. They forget and lose things, can't make decisions, worry, and may lose all organizational skills. They have challenges with time management. At school and home we can help them by giving them different strategies and tools to stay organized and make decisions. They need planners and weekly feedback so that they can improve their time-management skills. If there are consequences that need to occur, they should be handled in a timely fashion. Help them to develop possibility thinking; what are the pros and cons of a decision? Use many *what-if* scenarios. They are more interested in conceptual ideas at this time, not details. We don't want to give them answers, we want to provide opportunities for discussion and let them come to conclusions on their own. Give them feedback, structure, organizational strategies, and tools, and let them know it is a safe place to make mistakes. In addition, let them experience the consequences of their mistakes. Oftentimes, parents will think that now that they are older, they should be completely on their own. Although that is the future goal, at this particular stage, they absolutely need the support and structure that the adults in their lives can provide. It is a mistake to *expect* them to do what needs to be done. They need the *support* of caring, compassionate, and trusting adults to do it. Parents should not be rescuing them from their responsibilities, rather providing them with the time, tools, space, conversations, and monitoring for the students to successfully meet those responsibilities.

Our peaceful, respectful elementary Montessori students now become argumentative, and at times, downright rude. This is where you cannot let it get emotional. Be matter of fact, *"Do you realize that what you said can be interpreted as extremely rude?"* I can attest to the fact that most of the time they have no clue that they were being rude. In their mind, they were passionately righting a wrong! It is important to engage in intellectual talks after the emotions pass. Talk about different points of view. At school, we will have them engage in debates, role play, stage dramatic presentations, or write editorials, poetry, or creative writings as ways to express their passionate views. They are very sensitive to hypocrisy about what we say and do at this time. It is best to ask open-ended questions, *"Tell me about it." "How are you feeling right now?" "Why do you think that might have occurred?" "How could things have ended differently?"*

In terms of their psychosocial development, they are in a stage where they are seeking their identity, not only individually, but within their peer group as well. At school we will have them engage in many different roles and work with different peers and genders in groups. On week-long field trips, they may not be in groups that include their close friends. These trips are not meant to be vacations, but real-life experiences where they need to be independent and responsible as a group member. We work on building a sense of community on a daily basis so that friendships will be built with a variety of students of the same and opposite sex. Daily community meetings are led by the students, where they will have discussions as well as acknowledge one another for kind and positive behavior toward each other. Students continue to mentor each other, with peer and cross-age teaching and support. The influence of their peers is very powerful. It will drive their choices on fashion, music, clothing, hair, and behavior. Even though they want to express their individuality, they also want to look and be like everyone else.

Adolescents usually have a challenging time in their relationships with adults during this time. They fluctuate between wanting independence and dependency on adults and others around them. Parents and teachers need to develop opportunities for independence and also aid them in learning to ask for help when they need it. These young people can feel very insecure inside so it is important for them to receive affirmations from the adults in their lives. Teachers and parents should be caring and consistent in their values and beliefs and in sharing them with the adolescent. Trust is a very big issue for adolescents and it is imperative that they are able to trust the adult mentors in their lives. Parents still have the most powerful impact on the adolescent in terms of major decisions. Only make promises you can keep, and provide routines (structure), and clear expectations of the adolescent based on your value system. Be secure in your values. Allow the adolescent to talk and share his or her opinion without belittling or judgment, but the adult should still hold the position of making important decisions that can impact the safety or the future of the adolescent. Keep in mind that this idealistic stage is driving them; they have a strong sense of fairness and often get caught up in big, unanswerable questions. Just by empowering adolescents with the right to voice their opinions or ask their questions in a calm and respectful way will go a long way in their view of fairness. This does not mean that they should always get what they want. The adults in their lives need to make unpopular decisions at times based on family/school values in order to keep them safe. One example would be when parents think that middle school students are mature enough to hang out at a mall on their own, or throw a party without parental supervision. These decisions are recipes for disaster. They will complain and cry that all other adolescents are allowed to do it (keep in mind, every other parent is hearing the same argument), and will rage at the unfairness of it and the adults, but in the end, parents need to always monitor adolescents at this time…remember that they have no brakes! They need a *surrogate* frontal lobe, that is, an adult ally who will apply those brakes for them. They need a parent who is not afraid to say no when needed.

In conclusion, I must say that some of my most rewarding years have been spent with the middle school students. Although it can be one of the most challenging stages to deal with, it also allows us to experience the transformation of the child into the adult that they will become. When I see such well-rounded, genuinely nice young people, who have so many skills and qualities that will lead to their success in life, I am humbled to have been a part of their journey. Our graduates have gone on to higher learning and into the professional domain with a multitude of talents, following their passions and strengths, and making their own positive imprint on the world.

I will share another example of this from one of our Summit-Questa graduates. Kali graduated from our middle school program in 2009. She is now a junior at the Massachusetts Institute of Technology (MIT) and is thriving. She traveled to Hawaii this past January to work on a project for Traveling Research Environmental Experience (TREX). While there, Kali was given this question to answer: "How does your Course 1 (Civil and Environmental Engineering) embody big engineering at MIT?" Kali made a video about her findings and submitted the video to the MIT CEE Annual Video Competition. There were ten submissions; two were undergraduate students and eight were either MIT professors or graduates. Kali's video won 1st place! She is already making her own imprint on the world.

Many parents have asked me to go to the next level, high school. At this point of my career, I will probably encourage a younger Montessorian to step up and take on that challenge. There are not many Montessori high schools in the U.S., however I am sure that will eventually change. Today, two of the most well-known AMS Montessori high schools in the country are the School of the Woods, in Houston, Texas, and the first public Montessori Middle and High School in Cincinnati, Ohio. Internationally, there are Montessori high schools in Europe (an interesting historical fact is that Ann Frank, famous for her diaries during WWII, was a student in the first Montessori high school in Amsterdam before it was closed by the Nazis).

Based upon what we know of how the brain works, what adolescents need, and how we learn, it is evident that the Montessori approach will continue to grow and expand as a viable method through high school, and maybe even beyond!

> *"If education is always to be conceived along the same an-*
> *tiquated lines of a mere transmission of knowledge, there*
> *is little to be hoped from it in the bettering of man's fu-*
> *ture. For what is the use of transmitting knowledge if*
> *the individual's total development lags behind?"*

—Maria Montessori

CONFESSION:

Although I have probably confessed more in this chapter than any other; confession is still good for the soul. I think one of the most challenging elements in creating a strong adolescent program, and certainly a source of frustration for me, is finding the right teachers for the program. This is much more difficult than merely sending someone off for training. I have had Montessori-trained middle school teachers who in the end, really did not accept, or enjoy, the behavior of adolescents. I have come to the conclusion that I will not send anyone for training in middle school UNTIL I am sure that they truly understand the adolescent and enjoy working with this age group. Therefore, I usually only consider experienced middle school teachers looking for a new way to teach, as candidates for middle school training when there is a need to send someone. Or, as Dr. Coe so wisely advised, send a toddler teacher for middle school training, since the stages are very similar, and the adult working with both groups needs the same qualities to be effective: patience, love, compassion, and a passion for seeing the child's potential emerge, and an ability to not take anything personally!

This book has free material available for download from the
Web Added Value™ resource center at *www.jrosspub.com*

Section III:
Spirituality
and Montessori

12

Spirituality in the Montessori Philosophy

A typical question that comes up when introducing the Montessori philosophy to a parent is, "How is religion handled in a Montessori school?" Unless a Montessori school is faith-based, then generally it will have a very diverse population of varying cultures and religions. In fact, many parents seek out a Montessori experience for their child specifically because it is not affiliated with any one religion. It is the nature of the Montessori approach to be respectful of everyone and to celebrate differences. I tell parents that although the Montessori philosophy is not generally based in any religion, it is however, very spiritual. I have discovered that the roots of most religions can be narrowed down to some very basic spiritual elements: treat others the way you want to be treated (The Golden Rule), love others, love yourself, help others, respect all life, be grateful, forgive, and love our Creator. These spiritual elements are the seeds, or roots, of almost every religion on our planet. Most of the challenges we face and paths we take in life can be guided by these basic principles. In a Montessori community, they are our *ground rules*. The beautiful thing about the philosophy is that children actually learn *to live* these principles in a Montessori classroom. When children are able to live principles, they become a part of who they are to their very core.

In Aline Wolf's book, *Nurturing the Spirit*, she quotes a few people on their definition of spirituality. I will share them with you.

The late Dr. Beverly-Colleene Galyean: *"We all have spiritual experiences such as the feeling of being uplifted, transported beyond ordinary sensory experiences...the awesome sense of oneness with the universe that comes from contemplating the stars or from climbing a high mountain and surveying the vast panorama beneath us, or the ecstatic sense of wonder at the birth of a child...*"[1]

The Faithkeeper of the Onondaga Nation of Native Americans, states: "*Spirituality is the essence of our lives. It's what makes a tree grow and what makes a bird sing. What makes a human smile. Spirituality has its own force and has its own being, something you can't see. It's the power of the universe.*"[2]

Albert Einstein, as quoted by Beverly-Colleene Galyean: "*A spirit is involved in the Laws of the universe—a spirit vastly superior to that of man, and one in the face of which we, with our modest powers, must feel humble.*"[3]

Aboriginal woman: "*To understand us, you have to understand our spirituality. It makes us unique. It shows respect to Mother Earth in thankfulness to God...Our spirituality begins from the day we are born, and continues in how we live, how we care for our brothers and sisters, how we deal with our extended family, and how we care for God's creation. It is all balanced and cannot be divided.*"[4]

Albert Schweitzer: "*Life affirmation is the spiritual act in which man ceases to live unreflectively and begins to devote himself to his life with reverence, in order to raise it to its true value.*"[5]

Leo Buscaglia: "*Fully functioning persons have a deep sense of spirituality. They know that the world in which they live cannot be explained or understood through human experience alone. They must go beyond themselves, beyond their limited reality. They have an inexplicable sense of something more. They feel a greater operative intellect than their own, even if they are at a loss to give it a name.*"[6]

It is clear that thinkers beyond the ages and cultures have contemplated spirituality. We have been doing so from the start of human existence. It is also evident that everything mentioned in these quotes are the roots and tree of our Montessori philosophy.

Most Montessori schools will attract a wide variety of families. In my school in South Florida, there have been many families from all around the world with many religions represented: Christianity, Buddhism, Hinduism, Islam, Judaism, Baha'i, and Confucianism to name a few, and not to mention, the atheists and agnostics. I have had some lively discussions with parents who are atheists in the respect that even though they may not believe there is a God, it is very hard to dispute that there is some kind of intelligence or creative force at work that has been instrumental in creating our universe. The mathematical precision and layer upon layer of interconnecting relationships that move life forward are not by chance, but by design. Even with all of our differences in perception and point of view, everyone has been able to live together harmoniously in our Montessori community because we are mutually respectful of our differences. We enjoy learning about each other by sharing what we value in our culture and traditions. It is a rare occurrence when a student does not discover on his or her own, that as different as we may seem, there are many common traditions that we all share. If only the world would become more Montessori-like! The truth of the matter is, Dr. Montessori did indeed have a larger, universal goal for her philosophy—that the Montessori children would go out into the world and transform it.

> *"Establishing a lasting peace is the work of education; all politics can do is keep us out of war."*
> —Maria Montessori

Dr. Montessori wrote and spoke a great deal about her vision of peace for the world. She clarified that true peace is not the absence of war, nor is it the end of a war where one side wins and one side loses. When that occurs, the losing side certainly does not experience a peaceful existence. In fact, throughout the history of mankind, the losing side often becomes the captives, the slaves; they lose their property, belongings, and in many cases, their social and professional status, or even their lives. There is no peace in this situation. Dr. Montessori had hopes for the spiritual element in mankind to overcome this attitude of winner and loser.

She saw the beautiful spirit inherent in her young students. Her vision was one of collaboration, conflict-resolution, respect for all, and allowing man's greatness within to fully emerge and rise above humankind's lower consciousness of the past. She believed in the innate goodness present in the child. Lofty ideals to be sure, however we see it happening everyday in Montessori classrooms, so it is possible. In fact, the reality of our philosophy is that these children growing up in our environments can certainly go into the world and evoke change—and they have. You will get a glimpse of that inner spirit in a sampling of some of our student's writings, which I have included in this chapter. That is the hope for the future that Dr. Montessori had, and her followers continue to believe. This hope of a better life for mankind cannot exist without believing in some kind of inner spirit or intelligence that guides us along life's path. This inner force is there for our use and it is our choice whether we use it or not. Dr. Montessori saw that this force was very powerful and if tapped and allowed to emerge, would transform the child and the world. Once again, we speak of how this spiritual development, like intellectual development, is most effective and long-lasting when it is from the inside-out; an internal journey rather than one forced upon us externally. That was the ultimate goal; turning the process of education and development inside-out! It needs to come from within to be transformative. This is the beautiful and brilliant paradox: Dr. Montessori had the sharp and systematic mind of the scientist yet also the intuitive, spiritual approach of a visionary.

The spiritual theories that I share now are mine alone and certainly not representative of Dr. Montessori's philosophy or method. I do feel, however, that my theories have emerged as a direct result of my personal experiences while working with children in Montessori environments for 40 years. It is an area that I have reflected upon, and experimented with, in many different ways in my own spiritual growth and journey as a person, and as a Montessori teacher and principal.

I was raised as a Roman Catholic and went to all-girl Catholic schools from 1st through 12th grade. This experience certainly shaped me in both positive and negative ways as I grew and developed. I loved the rituals of the Catholic mass and the kindness and gentleness of many of the nuns who taught us. I received the message that there was an awesome God who loved us, which was comforting. I also experienced some negative interactions because not all of the nuns and priests were kind or patient. I did not grow in self-esteem because I was more fearful than confident in a very strict, traditional classroom setting where we were not to question, only listen. Students who were not strong students or did not memorize their class work in some classes were often punished. There was no discussion, negotiation, or collaboration, only conformity and strict obedience. This type of learning atmosphere taught me to be quiet, do what was asked of me without question, and to not have an opinion. I was a fairly good student so I wasn't punished very often, but fearfully observed how others were so I anxiously learned how to conform. It took many years to overcome the apprehension of questioning and expressing an opinion.

Socially, one would think that a religious school would create a strong culture of kindness and respect, but some of my most vivid and frightening memories are those of the social relationships that went on among the girls. Here in the midst of a religious school, there was a culture of insecurity. I can remember thinking to myself, "Why do I have to be mean to others to be liked?" In fact, that was an indication of how *cool* you were. Could you come out with zingers that would strike at someone's weakness or directed at someone that was different. I was conflicted for many years with this type of social setting. In retrospect, I have a better understanding today of why that occurred. I realize that the school was like every other traditionally structured school, where the smart students and auditory learners excelled. Although religion was the foundation for the philosophy of the school, the traditional educational approach still separated the smart students from the not-so-smart ones; thereby resulting in a group to be targeted. One would think that the religious approach would have created a kinder, more accepting atmosphere, but that was not always the case. I compare it to going to mass every Sunday where you saw your neighbors praying and receiving communion, only to spend the rest of the week gossiping and fighting with each other. It didn't make sense to me at that time, and the school experience was a microcosm of the larger community experience. Even though we memorized our prayers and received religious instruction, learning it and doing it seemed like two entirely separate experiences.

As soon as I graduated from high school, I told my parents that I was not interested in continuing to practice Catholicism because of the hypocrisy I experienced. My journey then began in exploring many different types of religions and spiritual experiences, as I was still very drawn to my inner spiritual growth. My immersion into my art also fed the strong creative spirit that had been stifled in my earlier years. I have spent many years reflecting upon my spiritual growth and journey. Without a doubt, when I discovered Montessori, I could feel the spiritual hum within me. Dr. Montessori's writings spoke to me like no other, and my spiritual development began to steadily climb as I lived with my students on a daily basis in the Montessori classroom. They were my teachers, and their beautiful spirits quenched my spiritual thirst. I could not verbalize this feeling at that time, or put words to the awareness of experiencing something very profound. I only knew that it was very important and I needed to be a part of it. I began to understand why some people saw Montessori teachers as being *cult-like.* I became so passionate about this philosophy that it did occupy most of my time and thoughts. To me, however, that cult-like passion was *positive* because I felt I was part of a movement much larger than myself or my classroom. The Montessori philosophy was based in love for the child, humanity, and the planet, and I was a part of it. That deep connection to this day can still bring tears to my eyes and gives me such an inspiring sense of purpose and fulfillment.

So, what makes the Montessori experience a spiritual one? The classroom is a community of students on a journey to the adults they are to become. Human nature is such an interesting phenomenon. What I have observed is that all human beings have a dual nature. There is the dark side and the light side. It seems that our Creator has given us free choice to decide toward which side we will gravitate. Every choice we make has a consequence. In general, the positive choices usually lead to positive consequences and the negative choices tend to lead to negative consequences. I like to talk to my students about creating energy. Since we know from our scientific studies that everything in existence is some form of energy, I make the association to our thoughts as well. When we think positive thoughts, we create positive energy and vice versa. Positive energy attracts and builds more positive energy.

Sometimes adults think that a Montessori community is some sort of paradise, where conflict should not exist. There is conflict in our Montessori classrooms, like anywhere else, because we are human beings. It is how we handle the conflict that sets us apart. So in our Montessori communities, we are always trying to focus on the positive in every situation—positive thoughts, positive words, and positive actions to overcome conflict and create positive energy. This cycle helps children form positive patterns and habits when learning to navigate life and the challenges that go along with it. This is not a Pollyanna approach. This is a transformative process that will lead children to become happy, healthy, and successful in all areas of development. How so? Let me give you an example of a very common interaction in the Montessori classroom:

Sarah: "Ms. Judy, Johnny just pushed me."

Ms. Judy: "I am so sorry, are you all right?"

Sarah: "Yes, but he shouldn't have pushed me."

Ms. Judy: "You are right, we agree not to invade each other's personal space. Let's go talk to Johnny."

Ms. Judy: "Johnny, Sarah told me that you pushed her. What happened?"

Johnny: "I kept asking her to stop touching my work but she wouldn't listen to me, so I pushed her."

Ms. Judy: "Sarah, did Johnny ask you to stop touching his work?"

Sarah: "Yes, but I wanted to work with that lesson and he wouldn't let me join him."

Ms. Judy: "Let's talk about the agreements we all made in our classroom. One agreement is that we respect everyone's personal space. Another agreement is that we listen to each other and respect one another. Another agreement is that we use our hands to help, not hurt…and, that we use words to solve our problems. So,

Johnny, what agreements did you choose not to follow? And Sarah, what agreements did you choose not to follow?"

Johnny: "I used my hands to push Sarah and I didn't use my words."

Sarah: "I did not listen to Johnny and I invaded his space."

Ms. Judy: "You are both correct, and how did you feel?"

Sarah: "I was mad that Johnny wouldn't let me work with him. So I didn't listen to Johnny and I touched his work and then he got mad and pushed me."

Johnny: "When Sarah wouldn't listen to me, I did get mad, and then I pushed her."

Ms. Judy: "So I am hearing that when both of you chose to break our class agreements, there was anger, and pushing, that could have led to an injury, correct?"

Sarah and Johnny: "Yes."

Ms. Judy: "So, how do we make this right and go forward?"

Johnny: "I need to say I am sorry for pushing her."

Sarah: "And I need to say I am sorry for not listening to Johnny and touching his work."

Ms. Judy: "Those are good choices. We all make mistakes and the good thing about mistakes is that we can learn from them. It sounds as if both of you learned that when you choose to make a wrong choice, unpleasant things can happen. Let's think about how you can handle it the next time something similar happens. Johnny, what will you do differently next time someone does not listen to you and invades your personal space?"

Johnny: "I will ask them to stop and if they don't listen, I will get help from a teacher."

Ms. Judy: "That would be a great choice."

Sarah: "I will ask if I can work with him, and if he says no, I will listen to him."

Ms. Judy: "Another great choice! Is there anything else you would like to say to each other?"

Sarah: "I am sorry, Johnny."

Johnny: "I am sorry too, Sarah. Do you want to work with me now?"

Sarah: "Yes, thanks!"

Ms. Judy: "The next time something happens, you can also go to the Peace Table and see if you can use the Peace Rose to work it out on your own."

These types of interactions are very common and can go on a dozen times a day with different students in the beginning of the school year. Children begin to experience that conflict is most often caused by how someone perceives and interprets something that they, or someone else, does or doesn't do. In our interactive communities, they see this happening on a daily basis. As the year progresses, however, and the communication skills of the children improve, it is amazing to watch how successful the children become at handling the little conflicts that emerge just because they are in an interactive community, and human beings have emotions. In addition, there are the third-year students in the community who have become adept at helping the younger students develop their problem-solving skills in an appropriate way. There are usually *Peace Tables* in most Montessori classrooms that help the students acquire the process of successfully coming to a peaceful solution on their own. A few things I would like to point out about the exchange between Sarah and Johnny is that they both were involved in discussing the problem, communicating how they felt, and they both took responsibility for their part in the exchange. This helped them to see both sides of the situation. Notice there was no punishment involved—rather a process took place that allowed the students to come to their own conclusion as to the appropriate consequence to their actions. When punishment is the only discipline approach used with children, it leads to humiliation, resentment, and revenge. When students go through this process over and over again, they begin to understand that they have the power to make the choices that will benefit them, not hurt them. Students will learn to go to the Peace Table on their own, not necessarily needing the adult to guide them through all of the conflicts that they may encounter in the community. This is the ultimate goal; that they learn to do it on their own, thereby building their self-esteem and communication and social skills. Day after day, we see the goodness in children overcome the dark side of their nature when this approach is used. With every positive choice, the light grows within them and in the community. What else is this but the growth of the spiritual nature of the child? The children choose to make good decisions for the right reasons, not because of rewards or punishments. They care greatly for each other, the environment, and the world. They reflect upon their own place in the world and their role in it. When they look at each other as friends, they understand each other and create a unity that is the goal of all peacemakers. Even when there is conflict, the goal is to make better choices for everyone involved so that we all grow in self-discipline and self-respect. This light within us is the energy of love. Love is the energy that drives spiritual development. It is the love of the child, humanity, and the universe that fuels every Montessori teacher.

This loving energy is transformative. I have seen many children come to us deflated, defeated, unhappy, and angry. They came from traditional settings where they did not quite fit in for one reason or another. When they entered our Montessori classrooms, they were welcomed and given the opportunity to learn from their classmates and teachers that they were accepted just as they were. They discovered that as long as they were willing and able to live by the agreements that make our Montessori classrooms safe, nurturing, and stimulating learning environments, they were free to be themselves and learn in the way that was best for them. The vast majority of those students were transformed. They began to believe in themselves again and became confident young people. Some still had learning challenges but the difference was that they began to realize that everyone else in their community had some sort of challenge as well because we all do to some degree. Very few of us are good at everything. In our communities, we share our strengths and help each other with our weaknesses. This accepting, giving, and forgiving atmosphere has healed many wounds. Those students learned to love themselves again. I point out to our children and the parents that there is no Utopia anywhere because human beings are not perfect. We all make mistakes, but what makes the Montessori experience so different is that we believe those mistakes are opportunities to try again. Our character, spiritual and otherwise, is not built only upon the mistakes we make, but on how we handle those mistakes and move on for the better. If we can genuinely seek to come up with positive solutions to our conflicts, take responsibility for our part in the situation, and be willing to forgive each other and ourselves, then we are on a strong course for deeper self-growth and spiritual development, as well as creating more peaceful communities. These skills that they acquire have resulted in our young people going out into the world with positive conflict resolution experiences that make them stand out. Imagine if our conflict-ridden society, organizations, and countries were to adopt this type of loving conflict resolution; the world would be transformed. "Love is an act of endless forgiveness"[7]—this is a quote we can all live by, if we truly want to be loving human beings.

To return to the belief that spiritual development is rooted in love, forgiveness, and the values of helping others, the Montessori community is a very powerful tool for developing the spiritual nature of all, children and adults alike. Interestingly enough, it was through my spiritual development in the Montessori philosophy that I actually evolved to a place of acceptance and forgiveness, and returned to my religious roots, Catholicism. I realized that the church was an institution composed of people, people who make mistakes because they are human. I returned to the church because of my relationship with God, not the people who are members of the church. The same philosophy of forgiveness and moving on that I learned and live by in our Montessori community taught me to apply it to my relationship with the people in the church. My circuitous path led me back to the spiritual rituals of the Church that I love so much, and fulfilled a deeper spiritual need. In no way do I intend to imply that all of my experiences were negative in my Catholic upbringing. In fact, one of my fondest memories of a teacher is that of Sister Jerome, a loving, nurturing nun, who so inspired me with her words, "Judy, I so enjoy your writing that I fully expect to be reading one of your books one day." Thank you, Sr. Jerome, for inspiring me, as all teachers should. Your words gave me the confidence to put writing a book on my bucket list and here I am. Those words stuck with me. This is a good reminder to adults of how powerful our words can be for children in both a positive and negative way. It is very important to take great care with the messages we give our children.

Dr. Montessori saw the child as the purest form of our Creator's love and because of their spiritual purity, we should be following the child as our teacher. Have no doubt that their light is alive and burning, and can lead us out of the darkness.

> *"We see the figure of the child who stands before us with*
> *his arms held open, beckoning humanity to follow."*
>
> —Maria Montessori, *Education and Peace*

A wonderful by-product of the freedom and respect experienced by the students in a Montessori environment is that they feel safe enough to express their creativity. Creativity comes directly from the spirit. I will share some of our elementary students' poetry with you here and in the following section on Peace. It is in the writings of the students that one can see the passionate spiritual inner call that these children so deeply feel to make a difference in the world for themselves and others.

Lights

by Sophie, upper elementary student, age 11
They surround me, enveloping me in a warmth, and they whisper:
All who see the lights have pure hearts,
All who touch the lights receive a renewed spirit,
He who accepts the lights has prepared for everlasting life.
And he who accepts the lights should send outward that same
comforting warmth.

****

One cannot doubt, when you read these words from an elementary age child, that there is such wisdom within them and all of us. Sophie actually expresses her close relationship with light and how she experiences and understands it. It expresses the understanding that accepting the light within is a choice that we make and notes that there is a responsibility to share it with others. This spiritual writing is as eloquently written as any prayer I have ever read.

****

Love

By Ethan, upper elementary student, age 10
Love is as sweet as a bee's fresh autumn honey.
Love is as kind as a child changing the world.
Love is as powerful as a leader speaking up.
Love is as peaceful as a pure white dove sitting in a perfect Olive tree.
Love is as strong as a lion's loud roar.
Love is as fast as a cheetah at full speed.
Love is as fragile as a thin shard of glass.
Love is as graceful as a butterfly in a garden.
Love is as forgiving as a pure kind heart.
Love is as beautiful as a large red rose.
Love is as soft as a small white pillow.
But most importantly, Love is as contagious as
an old common cold.

****

Once again, our Montessori children express themselves so stirringly. Ethan talks about the power and beauty of love, the most powerful spiritual energy in the world.

* * * * * * *

Talking to God

by Adam, upper elementary student, age 9
Mother Teresa said, "We need to find God, and he
cannot be found in noise and restlessness. God is the
friend of silence. See how nature—trees, flowers, grass—
grows in silence; see the stars, the moon and the sun,
how they move in silence…We need silence to touch souls."
This inspires me because I feel that we cannot have
a spiritual connection with heaven if there is chaos, or
if everyone is being restless and in need of help. You
can only talk to God when he knows you're trying your
best to help out and when he knows you're trying to be
peaceful; only then you may talk to God and be able
to help others.

* * * * * * *

Living Religious

by Daniel, upper elementary student, age 10
"You cannot love me and hate your neighbor."
Why do people worship Jesus but not live like He did?
Why do they end up being cruel to friends?
They worship someone honest and become tyrants to others.
They worship one who was a very good spirited man and
became the destroyers of the land and people.
People must learn one day not to worship Jesus, but
to live like Him.

* * * * * * *

Deep

by Tai, upper elementary student, age 11
Is the deepness of life what makes it exciting,
Or is it the excitement that makes it deep?

* * * * * * *

A Second Chance

by Luciana, upper elementary student, age 10
A second chance means to be able to redo a mistake,

To be able to do something twice, to make it better,
So make your second chance count.
I have been given a second chance, a blessing, to be able to start over,
I have been blessed, purified, to have a better life than the first one,
I have been purified, welcomed, to make this second chance count.

* * * * * * *

We can hear how Ethan, Daniel, Tai, and Luciana are questioning the world and how it works. They are reflecting upon their own spiritual development within the midst of this earthly existence. Anyone who works with children in our Montessori communities knows and respects that the children have this inner life and we encourage them to reflect upon it and express it. You can see how their spiritual awareness and questioning is reflected in their writings.

I will share one more memorable spiritual experience that we do with our adolescents. I created a special ceremony for our graduating 8th grade students called the *Spirit Naming Ceremony*. It is a tradition that is always done at school on the morning of their graduation. It is a Native American inspired ceremony that is meant to give the students one last parting gift—a *Spirit Name*. The middle school teachers and I look at each student. We reflect upon who they are, what their gifts are, what their challenges are, and their core essence that reflects their unique spirit. We then research native names that represent those individual's qualities. I will often come up with a combination of indigenous names or just symbols from nature in finalizing each student's own *Spirit Name*. The student's have come to love this tradition and look forward to receiving their own name. An example might be something like *Soaring Eagle* for someone who may have lofty dreams and who works hard to accomplish them, or perhaps *Dakota* for a person who is a friend to all. I will elaborate on each name and the meaning behind it and as we sit in a circle and talk about the beautiful essence or spirit of each student, you can see and feel the emotional impact this experience has on each student. This is about showing the students love, respect, acknowledging them for their gifts, and encouraging them to use those gifts as they move on to their next level of education. I also discuss the nature of the spirit and the different theories that mankind has had about it since the beginning of human existence. I try to transport them through time to think about how the same type of ceremony they are experiencing now could have also gone on thousands of years ago. We, as human beings, are connected in more ways than we understand. As far as we have come today in terms of technology and lifestyle, some things of the spirit remain exactly the same. Our final communal sharing is a discussion about the spirit and its importance in our growth and development, not to mention for the health of our communities and the world in general; a very fitting discussion based upon our Montessori principles and goals.

This special ceremony is one of many *markers* that we have created in our school community. I was introduced to the concept of markers by reading a book by David Elkind, called, *All Grown Up and No Place to Go.* His book is about adolescence, and should be required reading for every parent of an adolescent. He encourages families and schools to create markers for children that literally mark their arrival at a certain time or age. These markers are privileges or events that are earned by a child just for arriving at a certain point in time. When I was growing up, my family actually did use a few markers. I was only allowed certain privileges at marked ages. I was given two markers when I turned 13. I was allowed to wear hose and have one cup of coffee on Sunday mornings after church. I could not wait for those two privileges! My first cup of coffee, however, wasn't what I anticipated. In fact, it made me sick. Despite this fact, I continued to drink that cup once a week because I had earned that privilege and was not about to give it up! I was allowed to get pierced earrings and wear make-up when I turned 16. I can still remember feeling so grown up and excited to enter the realm of grown up activities.

Why are they important?—precisely because our children are growing up in an *instant gratification* type of world. Children want what they want and they want it now! And unfortunately, many parents are giving it to them. This creates children who believe they are entitled to whatever they want immediately—without having to wait, work for, or earn it. This instant gratification also robs children of the anticipation of waiting for something they are looking forward to, the enjoyment of finally getting it, and then the sense of accomplishment of looking back on how far they have come on their journey. I would also add that children need to know that life is not always going to go according to their demands and needs—that learning to navigate and experience disappointment, gaining patience by waiting your turn, and earning the respect of others through celebrating their arrival contributes to their inner spiritual development. They learn that it isn't all about them; that other people have needs and the right to accomplish or acquire something that may not also include them. When families and schools create events or markers in children's lives, something magical happens. Children actually learn to enjoy the waiting and anticipation of what is to come. They feel a part of a community effort to acknowledge those who have *arrived* at a certain place in time and it is very satisfying to them. It touches a chord in their spirit that they are part of something bigger. Our society does not generally do this for children or adolescents. In fact, just the opposite occurs. Out-of-control commercialism drives children to become more materialistic, they want more—the newest, the best—right now, before they are gone! Parents, in an effort to keep their children happy and not disappoint them, succumb. I hope you will read David Elkind's book and consider another approach. I have seen a remarkable shift in our students' willingness to wait for things and showing happiness and support for those who arrive at their marker before them, as well as excitedly awaiting their turn. The following are some examples of the markers used at our school.

The very first marker is when kindergarten students are able to go on field trips. They have arrived at an age that we feel comfortable sending them out into the larger community. The students cannot wait for this and once they arrive at this age, they proudly experience the exciting event of being able to leave campus and ride on a bus!

Another marker is the *Bridging Ceremony*. We have an actual wooden bridge that is brought into our gymnasium. Any students who are moving up to the next level, for example, from lower elementary into upper elementary or from upper elementary into middle school, walk across the bridge in a symbolic gesture of crossing over to the next stage in their education. The students receive a traditional gift for their arrival at this point in their journey. One year I changed that traditional gift because I was told no one uses physical dictionaries anymore because of online dictionaries. Previously, I had always given a very nice dictionary to all of the 3rd grade students who were moving up to upper elementary. Well, when I changed the gift, the students were so disappointed because it wasn't the traditional gift! I learned my lesson and offered to buy them dictionaries as well—and we are now back to our traditional gift. This shows that tradition turned out to be important for the students.

Probably the biggest markers are in middle school. This involves the dress code—or lack of it, I should say. All students in our school must follow a dress code; it is not a strict uniform, just a general policy that everyone must follow. The exception is when students arrive at middle school, they may then choose to follow the dress code or not. It is up to them. This, of course, is one of the most coveted markers! It is also based on the developmental needs of that age. Students in middle school are in a stage that includes a search for identity; they are trying to figure out who they are. They now have the freedom to explore their individuality through their dress as long as they are following appropriate guidelines which were set in place. There are a few other very big markers in middle school—they get to go on week-long trips to very exciting cities like Boston, New York, Philadelphia, and Washington, D.C. They also experience a ropes course which is a very exciting event that centers around team building and personal and group challenges. Finally, they are the ones who get to care for the biggest animals on campus—the pigs, goats, and chickens!

We have quite a few other markers and it has been very successful for students to experience this sense of waiting and their place in the community. I link this with their spiritual development because it is a part of building community, supporting others, and being happy for them, along with feeling a sense of accomplishment and self-worth, and looking forward to what is to come in their lives. These are all qualities that build the inner strength that is so needed for spiritual development.

I have so much hope for the children and the world when I see young people with strong spiritual connections to other people, with nature, with a power beyond ourselves, and our earthly existence. The children's love of self, others, and the environment can, and will, change the course of our future.

REFERENCES

1. Galyean, Beverly-Colleene. Honoring the Spirituality of Our Children Without Teaching Religion in the Schools," *Holistic Education Review*, Summer, 1989, p. 24.
2. Burns, M.C. "Interview with Oren Lyons," *Syracuse Herald Journal*, July 9, 1991.
3. *Holistic Education Review*, Summer, 1989, p. 28.
4. Pattell-Gray, Anne. *Through Aboriginal Eyes*. Geneva: WCC Publications, 1991, pp. 5–6.
5. Burnett, Walt, Editor, *The Human Spirit*. London: George Allen and Unwin Ltd., pp. 308–309.
6. Buscaglia, Leo. *Personhood*. Columbine, NY: Fawcett, 1978, p. 118.
7. Karon, Jan. *Somewhere Safe with Somebody Good*. New York: Berkley Books, 2014, p. 368.

13

Peace Education

As was discussed in the previous chapter on spirituality in the Montessori philosophy, our students become very proficient in positive conflict resolution because of the interactive nature of the Montessori classroom. Although building our students' communication and conflict resolution skills is an on-going process, and certainly contributes to creating more peaceful environments, there are other ways that we build a peaceful community. Peace is not just a result of conflict resolution, but a type of energy created that starts within. We help children learn how to create the peaceful energy that is necessary in all areas of life to maintain health, calm, and happiness. The first step is to seek peace within ourselves. When we learn how to calm ourselves and make choices based on our tranquil inner nature and what we know is right, then we are less prone to react in emotional and irrational ways. We work on helping children to understand that the most important place to create peace is within themselves; in fact, it will rarely happen for anyone if they do not start within. Most of us create the habit of living somewhere else in time. We are either worried about something that might happen in the future, or are still living in the past because of how we feel about something that occurred. One of the healthiest messages we can give our children, and ourselves, is to create the habit of living in the moment. Take a breath, look around, and be grateful for where we are right now. Everything is fine—we have food to eat, water to drink, a home to go to, a family or circle of friends who love and support us—if we choose to focus on what is right in the world and enjoy that feeling right now in the present. Make it a habit of staying there.

"Write in your heart that every day is the best day of the year."
—Ralph Waldo Emerson

I tell students to create a different channel in their minds. When we do not like something that we are watching on television, what do we do? We change the channel. Do the same thing with your thoughts. When something is going on that you may not like or you are worried about, change the channel; find the happy and peaceful place in your mind. This is a way of developing your personal power. Personal power is a strength that will carry all of us through the most difficult challenges that we will face throughout our lives. I explain to our students that when someone says something about them that they know isn't true, and they allow those false words to disturb their peace, then they are giving their power away to that person. Bullies love to find people who do not use their personal power. In fact, they thrive on it. Bullies are usually very insecure people who are trying to steal other peoples' personal power because their own personal power is so weak. It takes work and practice to arrive at a place of strong personal power, but it is worth it. When we realize that other people have their own sad reasons for not being able to be kind, it makes us aware of the fact that we should not take things personally. It is usually always about something else in the other person's life. If a statement made is not true, we can change the channel in our mind and think, "It's very sad that this person is so fearful, hurt, or angry, and needs to hurt others in order to feel stronger. I feel sorry for them." And walk away rather than engage in the negative energy. When we can build this internal power, we are on the path to becoming very healthy, happy, peaceful, and productive individuals. The power of positive thinking can work miracles and lead to a personal peace that will overcome all challenges in life. Peace within; peace without. While students are working on creating their own peaceful inner self, we are simultaneously working on building a community.

Building a community requires a number of things in order to make children feel connected, competent, cooperative, and collaborative. Community means working for the good of all, one member of the community at a time, which ultimately leads to a cohesive, supportive, positive energy that embraces the entire group. A strong community lifts each other up always, even through the daily conflicts. One thing that we try to help children to understand is that we sometimes have to let things go for the right reasons. One of my favorite sayings is, "Do you want to be right, or do you want to have peace?" This is a very powerful question. Having to be right is the path of the ego, and feeding your ego does not usually lead to peace—personally or in a community. It is something I have to remind myself of often when I want to fall back into the mindset of *being right.* Actively working for peace will result in amazing communities.

Let's look at how we make children feel connected, not only to each other, but to a greater cause. Children are given the message that we are all in this together. Each one of them has a gift to share with the world—their cosmic task—and we are here to share our gifts in order to help ourselves and each other. They matter and are needed, not only in the community, but in the world. They are greeted and welcomed every morning with a joyful attitude so that they know they belong and are appreciated. They are respected for being the unique individuals that they are. We will find numerous ways and activities to acknowledge students for the kind and positive contributions that they make to the community, and for the gifts that they each possess. As their roots grow firmly in their community, their self-esteem continues to grow because they see themselves as successful, important, and competent members of their community. As they feel more connected and competent, they naturally become more cooperative and collaborative. They want their community to function smoothly and peacefully so they are willing to work with others to make that happen. They want to contribute to the greater good of the community. They actually lift each other up and celebrate each others' accomplishments. This energy will extend beyond the classroom walls, with the students caring about nature, the environment, and other people who are less fortunate than themselves; arousing a desire to take action to help. We see this over and over again with our Montessori students. There are some months that I need to slow the efforts to help with multiple community service causes because there are just too many to realistically put out into our school community. Even at that, the students will work with me to fairly redistribute their altruistic efforts over an extended period of time. I never discourage them; we collaborate on how to make it work for everyone. This is the energy of love, compassion, and wanting to create more peaceful solutions to the problems in the world through the action of community service and giving back.

The following are some activities that are commonly done in Montessori classrooms to build community and create a more peaceful setting.

In a previous chapter, I explained that the *silence game* was an experience that Dr. Montessori provided for young children in order to learn to be still, listen, and cultivate the state of calm and silence. Becoming silent and still is a habit that leads to further growth, not only in terms of observation, listening, and calmness, but as an exercise for the spirit. No matter what age we are, we all need quiet time; a time to be still and comfortable with silence. There is no way that we can get in touch with our inner spirit if we are constantly bombarded with noise, action, and distractions. It is spiritually and physically healthy for all of us to stop the noise of the world for a brief time and lose ourselves in silence and calm. This is what leads to a peaceful state within. You can find multiple studies today that directly link good physical and mental health to this practice of stopping the world for a time. Some of the greatest minds in the world spoke to us about finding stillness and tranquility for the health of our souls. Stillness, meditation, yoga, quiet places, deep breathing, and escaping to nature are just a few of the things recommended to balance our lives, which ultimately leads to better health in many areas. This is a part of the Montessori philosophy beginning with early childhood and continuing all the way through adolescence. Our hopes are that they will carry this healthy habit into adulthood.

So, we begin this practice at age three, with the *silence game*. Initially this is done as a group experience, both inside the classroom and outside in nature, but can also grow into *individual silence*, where students can go individually to a *quiet place* in the classroom and become silent for a period of time. In this safe quiet place the students can reflect, look at some beautiful things from nature or pictures that may be in that special place, or just be. I have seen miniature rock and sand gardens in a classroom where students may silently reconfigure the sand and rocks into their own interpretation as a meditative exercise. The only ground rule is that they are silent. There may be an outdoor quiet place—perhaps a bench overlooking a garden or a beautiful natural setting. At my school, we actually have a circular wooden bench outside under the trees in a quiet place that is away from the hubbub of the rest of the school. There, the teachers will bring the students to be surrounded by nature and shaded by trees. They will do any number of activities such as silence, have a discussion, sketch, read a book, tell stories, or just be. It is important to note that this outdoor classroom (as the students named it) was given to the school by a previous graduating class. Each year, the graduating class of 8th grade students gives a legacy gift to the school in appreciation for all that they received and also as a way to be remembered. This speaks greatly to the sense of community our students develop and meets the need that they have of leaving a piece of themselves behind so that they are not forgotten in this community—one that means so much to them. The graduating students work hard throughout the school year raising money through various events and fundraisers to pay for their legacy gift.

Many people are astounded when they see that these 8th grade students, who in most cases can't wait to graduate and move on, can be so passionate about leaving behind a legacy of love. Typically most traditional graduates have one foot out the door and wouldn't put in the time or effort to leave something meaningful behind. Their thoughts are typically looking in the direction of where they are going. Here is the power and love of community in action. That loving energy contributes to the peaceful atmosphere of unity in our Montessori communities. I am certain our Montessori school is not alone in this beautiful practice of giving back. The other important point is what the graduating students choose to leave. Typically, it has something to do with nature, love of the environment, art, or a creative aspect of all three. Other legacy gifts have been: a tiled bird bath and garden area with walkways made out of their own clay creations; an art sculpture of the *Eternal Flame of Learning* with all of their names etched in—both their given names and their spirit names (as described in the chapter on spirituality); a large outdoor and beautiful metal sculpted Native American dream catcher—each graduate etched their dreams for themselves, the school, or the world, on their own individual metal feather hanging from the dream catcher; another class left a solar-powered stained glass pyramid with their names etched into it that beautifully illuminates the area at night. These are some examples, but no matter what legacy they have chosen to leave behind, it is always given with love and appreciation; powerful forces that result from building a community.

In many Montessori schools, including my own, there are yoga cards on the shelf and a place where students can choose to do yoga poses on a mat to help calm and center themselves. At times, I was fortunate enough to have a yoga teacher actually sit in a corner of the classroom for any student who might like to partake of yoga with the teacher's guidance. The message given to the students is that this is a habit that needs to be practiced in order to benefit fully. It will not happen automatically; it takes work, like anything else beneficial in life.

> *"Silence predisposes the soul for certain inner experiences. You are not the same after silence as you were before it… It is one of the tragedies of our mechanical age that so many people grow up without ever having discovered the beauty of silence."*
> —E.M. Standing[1]

Another way that the Montessori experience develops and strengthens the child's inner growth is to aid the child in acquiring an awe and wonder for the natural world. Montessori and nature are closely interwoven for many reasons. Dr. Montessori's curriculum introduces the world to the child in such a way that he or she is naturally drawn to explore the wonders of it. Children need to be outside observing and interacting with nature and those observations and interactions are some of the things that create the awe of which we speak. The activities are limitless: nature walks; gardening; journaling and drawing in nature; observing the sky during the day and at night; hunting for rocks, shells, leaves, insects, animal prints, or bird nests; animal care; worm farms; composting; studying water; watching rain—these are just some of the activities that children of all ages should be exposed to for the health of their inner being and to create awe, respect, and wonder for the world.

> *"In an ideal world, every school would be located on several acres of ground with a stand of beautiful trees, a field to explore, a pond to observe, a sunny garden, and even room to care for a few farm animals such as chickens or sheep. Such schools do exist."*
>
> —Aline Wolf[2]

I took Aline Wolf's words to heart and looked for property that would provide these same features as she described in her book, *Nurturing the Spirit*, and was beyond joyful when I found exactly what I was looking for. In a process that I feel without a doubt was divine intervention, I was led to a piece of property that was made for Montessori. I am sharing the story, not only because it is such a moving one, but also because I believe that the spiritual aspects are too powerful to deny its telling.

It was 1997 and as I mentioned previously, I began the search for a piece of property to expand my growing school. We were outgrowing our existing building. I had consistently visualized the new school on a nice plot of land, perhaps a few acres, large enough to have gardens and small farm animals. I have a particular affinity for trees; in fact, our school logo is a tree, so I envisioned a crop of beautiful trees scattered throughout the property. Knowing that visualization is a very powerful tool, I visualized this for months and simultaneously affirmed, "I am being led to the perfect property for our school, a peaceful oasis, and it will be beyond anything I can visualize." I said this every morning and every evening. I had enlisted a group of my passionate Montessori parents on this quest, and we called them the *Vision Committee*. They would help me find possible property listings keeping my vision in mind. One weekend when a member of the committee and I were out looking at possible sites, I happened to notice a small hand-painted wooden sign on the side of the road that said, *For Sale*. It was not a typical real estate sign and there was no property visible from the road but something inside of me told me to stop and check it out. So we did. We turned around and as we approached the sign, there was a small drive that became visible and led into a massive fence of greenery. This massive fence of greenery was the reason that nothing was in sight from the road. As we turned into the drive, the first thing I saw was a huge, old oak tree sitting near the entrance—just like my school's logo. The hair on my arms stood up and an inner knowing stronger than anything I had ever experienced, told me, "This is it." I just *knew* that this was the property I was envisioning. The next thing that occurred was something that went beyond even my wildest dreams and has no earthly explanation. The people who lived on the property were a new-age group of spiritual writers. They wrote nondenominational spiritual writings and sold them to many different religions. They had lived on this property for 20 years and now were being spiritually called to move to the mountains. This commune of writers had a deep reverence for nature and had spent the previous twenty years planting and caring for flora from every continent around the world (except Antarctica obviously) to represent the unity, love, and respect for all of God's creatures. There was one gentleman whose job was exclusively to care for all of the plant life on the property. Much to their chagrin, when they decided to sell the property, the only people interested in buying the ten acres were developers. Of course, this was very upsetting to the commune since they knew that the developers would remove all of their precious plant life in order to build multiple homes. They vehemently turned the developers down. This is what they then told me: "We have been praying and meditating every day for months for someone to come along who has a higher purpose for the property. You have arrived." Even though I could not afford the price they were asking, they told me that they were going to make it work because it was meant to be—and they did.

This property was beyond my wildest imagination. It did not even come close to the picture I had initially envisioned. Here were ten acres of magnificent natural beauty. There were trees, flowers, bushes, grasses, coffee plants, all kinds of unimaginable plant life from around the world. There was a live pond full of fish, turtles, frogs, and water fowl. The animal life was rich: birds, foxes, raccoons, rabbits, insects, worms, snakes, even an occasional alligator in the pond! The one very powerful and intangible energy on the property was one of peace. This commune of spiritual writers had prayed and meditated multiple times during the day for twenty years and the peaceful energy was, and still is, palpable. To this day, almost twenty years later, most visitors will comment on how peaceful and calm it feels on the school grounds. I have no doubt that the peaceful energy is real and being emitted by every plant and creature that was loved and protected on that property. It has been quite a gift to all of us to be blessed with such a setting. The children get to enjoy that peaceful energy every day as they spend time tending the gardens, enjoying the plant and animal life on the grounds, including our pigs, goats, and chickens; not to mention the multiple class pets throughout the school. The live pond is host to beautiful birds, fowl, turtles, fish, snakes, and yes, still the occasional alligator.

This natural setting allows for the peaceful energy of nature to permeate our children's inner state of being. When a child is having a bad day, just a walk with me through the campus can calm their inner emotional turmoil. It is not unusual to find our students out on the grounds sketching something of interest, reading, journaling, testing the waters of the pond or the soil, observing and discussing some aspect of nature, or feeding the goats and pigs. This direct interaction with nature fuels that inner peace so necessary for creating the outer peace in our communities. Nature is healing.

This interaction with nature will naturally lead the child, along with the exposure to Dr. Montessori's cosmic curriculum, to a passionate sense of stewardship toward caring for all creatures and the planet itself. The children become defenders of the environment and feel very strongly about their commitment to helping keep our planet and everyone on it, healthy and thriving. They become avid ecologists. They see that the earth and its creatures also have a right to a peaceful existence and they actively work to make that happen.

> *"Peace will come only when people's hearts are imbued with respect for the Earth, for nature, for all human beings, and when they can transcend personal gain to work cooperatively for universal good."*
>
> —Aline Wolf[3]

A very common practice in most Montessori schools today is the use of the Peace Rose, or the Peace Table. Typically, there is a silk rose in a vase on the Peace Table and it is used for conflict resolution. When two or more students have a conflict, they go to the Peace Table, and each child has a turn speaking while holding the rose. They talk about what happened and how they feel about it. It would not be appropriate for the child holding the Peace Rose to say hurtful things to the other child, only how they feel: "I feel sad that you would not invite me to work with you," for example. Both children take turns talking about how they feel while holding the rose. They then need to come up with solutions, or if there is not a solution agreed upon, just getting over their conflict by talking about it. When that occurs, they both put their hands on the stem of the rose and say, "We declare peace." This is a procedure that the children learn and when used consistently, will empower the children to solve most of their conflicts on their own, thereby building their confidence and self-esteem. The Peace Table may also hold pictures of peace makers or some inspiring verse about peace.

I need to reiterate that building community and creating peaceful communities is not always peaceful in the process! It takes hard work, consistent commitment to peaceful practices in thought, words, and behavior on the part of everyone in the community, children and adults alike. Like everything else in life, hard work and consistency pays off, and we see it on a daily basis in our children and community. When you create an atmosphere where people are encouraged to think, and have opinions, and care about others and the world, when those opinions start to emerge, there can be a great deal of disagreement over their theories and views! Just look at the holy books written over the course of history and how many different interpretations and perceptions emerge from some of the very same roots of spirituality. Human nature is very emotional and passionate and it is an on-going process that we live everyday in our Montessori communities to channel those emotions and passions into constructive and positive thoughts, words, and actions, while not harming others.

I will share some of the poetry and other writings in which our elementary students reflect upon the world, their concerns, their conflicts, and their commitment to the energy of peace, healing, compassion, and love. Please note that this poetry does not whitewash the world; conversely, they see the darkness in themselves, others, and the world. Their quest is to further understand that it is part of human existence to overcome it and rise above it.

****

Amrita's Prayer: Embrace the Trees

By Emma, upper elementary student, age 9
When I stepped on the Earth, I knew something could be done.
I knew I could make it into a wonderful world. I tried
but every time I did,
something bad happened to the Earth.
Mother Nature, Help Me Now.
Is man destroying our world or is he making our world a better place?
Is man helping to rebuild nature or take down nature for once and all?

Is man rebuilding himself or taking down himself?
I think he is taking down his kind.
Since he's taking down his kind, he's also taking down the forests and the animals with him.
Everyone is polluting the air and cutting down trees.
I speak but no one listens.
People just say I'm a little girl in a big world.
But I know, in my heart, I can make a difference.
Mother Nature, Help Me Now.

****

Hope

By Drew and Emma, upper elementary students, age 10
Hope is like a bird that flies from soul to soul.
It is one of the things in the world that comes to all.
It fires up in your heart and then gives you a head start.
The head start gives you more power to reach for hope.
There shall be hope in the world of lights.

****

"Speak"

By Sophie, upper elementary, age, 11
Speak of wisdom, even when you are not very wise.
Speak of courage, even when you fear.
Speak of honesty, even when people around you
aren't being very truthful.
Speak of kindness, even when those you know are not being very kind.
Speak of generosity, even when people around you are being selfish.
Speak of loyalty, even when you've been betrayed.
Speak of harmony, even when there is pandemonium.
Speak of perseverance, even when you've lost hope.
Speak of love, even when you have been uncared for.
Speak of life, especially when your dreams become reality.

****

"Slaves"

By Ethan, upper elementary, age 10
Beaten, hurt, nearly dead, but you can't stop the pain
from flowing through your body.

The pieces of your heart in a stream after being broken by your master,
who was beating you with nothing else but a hard, cold stick.
I won't fight, but I refuse the pain.
If I am killed or if I die,
it will be better than being forced to feel the pain of others.
I won't speak, but will die.
But if I die, answer me this,
What's the joy?
What's the hope in seeing someone die or getting beaten?
It will one day happen to you, because we are no different than you.
We both love hearing the birds chirp, we both love seeing the sunset.
We're no slaves in the end, and we are just people.

****

This is just a sampling of some of the poetry that the students were compelled to write based on their reflections and feelings about life. As you can see, their thoughts cover many aspects of how we react to life in general. These upper elementary students decided to hold a poetry festival to share their thoughts. They planned it, wrote passionately, and then had a collection of their poems printed in a booklet. The following is their introduction to the festival.

"We are questioning the future and expressing our feelings of hope. The poets in this festival believe poetry is a way of preserving the human species. The world is one, now more than ever before. Poetry can contribute to understanding the feelings between people, between people and nature, and between people and the Spirit. Poetry, we have found, has the ability to make a community listen and to establish a dialogue on whatever subject. For that reason, we have called our festival, "Voices of Children.""

I have included the cover of their poetry booklet in this chapter. The cover design was created by one of the students as well (see Illustration 13.1).

In closing, a peaceful community is not just a destination, but also an on-going journey. Due to the dynamic nature of human beings, we must be committed to always redirecting ourselves and others when we step off that path of peace, which does, and will happen. We are all imperfect beings, however, the wonderful news is that we are all also capable of creating a new moment, a new reality, and a new future through this peacemaking process. This is the Peace Education that we refer to in our Montessori world. I invite all of you to join us on this Montessori mission; the only prerequisite is a willingness to commit to it.

Voices of Children

☮ SQMS UPPER ELEMENTARY POETRY FESTIVAL

Illustration 13.1

CONFESSION:

This area, without a doubt, has been the most challenging aspect of my life. Finding peace within took many, many twists and turns on my life journey. Just when I thought I had it mastered, and my sense of internal peace would revel in reaching the summit, boom, another emotional bomb goes off in my world, and I would struggle to find my way out of the disequilibrium. Over and over again, it would be the children in my world who would redirect me back onto the correct path. They have always been my teachers on so many levels. I have learned far more from them than they have ever learned from me.

REFERENCES

1. Standing, E. M. *Maria Montessori, Her Life and Work.* London: Hollis Carter, 1957, 9p. 226–227.
2. Wolf, Aline D. *Nurturing the Spirit.* Hollidaysburg, PA: Parent Child Press, 1996, p. 74.
3. *Ibid.,* p. 110.

Section IV:
Contemporary Issues
in Education

14

A Global Approach for the 21st Century

Today, education needs to have different goals as compared to generations ago. The world is a totally inconsistent place and is continuing to change at a mind-boggling pace. Technology has transformed our world to a state that would be unrecognizable to our ancestors. The extraordinary thing is that it may be unrecognizable to us as well in the near future. Whereas in the past, education looked to prepare students for a familiar and predictable world; the goal was to have students memorize a set of facts or learn specific skills that would serve them well in a variety of career choices. Today, in the Information Age, any fact that a student would need or want is at the tip of their finger, a button-push away. As educators, it is imperative to prepare our students for the very unique demands that the 21st century world will place upon them. It is vital in this age to teach students how to find the appropriate knowledge that they need, and that knowledge may be as varied as the changing times themselves. It is necessary to have students know how to think out-of-the-box and be creative learners and problem-solvers. Students entering the workplace will need to work in the global community so it is imperative for them to know how to communicate well and get along with others. It is necessary to be respectful of other cultures and traditions as it is very likely that in any business transaction, the clients, or even the team that they work with, will be from somewhere else in the world. Therefore it is necessary to be a competent networker by making the right contacts and being a team-player. In an instant, they will be communicating with colleagues around the world. The statistics also indicate that people will be changing jobs much more frequently than ever before. The young people who are able to adapt to new and changing needs and expectations, will be the ones getting and keeping the available jobs in this changing workforce.

In addition, our world is facing a multitude of challenges at different levels: environmentally, socially, ethically, politically, and economically. We need young people who have the skills to face unprecedented situations in the world. These are very different skills necessary for success in the 21st century and for the survival of our culture, planet, and species. When parents ask me, "Will Montessori prepare my child for the real world?", I confidently respond by saying, "Montessori will, without any doubt, prepare your child much better than traditional education ever could for this *new* real world."

If you look at all of the previously mentioned skills necessary for success in the 21st century, they are all inherent in the Montessori experience. Children learn to think—and think differently based on their own unique perception of the world. They learn how to get along with classmates who may be from a different culture, or just a different age or gender, or perhaps a very different type of learner, thinker, and problem solver. The exposure to all of these different personalities, abilities, and individual gifts allows the children to develop very different skills as compared to their traditional counterparts. Their vocabulary, critical thinking, social, and communication skills increase with every year that they are in the Montessori classroom. They learn to explore their own interests and the Montessori materials at their own pace. The Montessori teacher will always guide the students along the path of learning, not by providing the answers, but by constantly asking the child the questions needed to stimulate critical thinking and discovery on the child's part. A Socratic questioning type of approach allows the students to develop and expand their own learning and critical thinking skills.

As much as our world has turned into a machine/technology-dominated society, social skills are still highly important for success. The highest paying jobs today demand people who are not only competent with technology, but also have strong people skills—an important human trait. Social skills are not usually part of the curriculum in traditional schooling. Michael Horn, cofounder of the Clayton Christensen Institute where he studies education, said, "Machines are automating a whole bunch of things so having the softer skills, knowing the human touch and how to complement technology is critical, and our educational system is not set up for that."

Economists Frank Levy and Richard Murnane further state that, "in the new world of work, the most desirable jobs—the ones least likely to be automated or outsourced—are those that require expert thinking and complex communication."[1]

A nobel prize-winning economist, James Heckman, Ph.D., concluded in his research that skills such as character, dependability, and perseverance are as important for future success as cognitive achievements. "These types of skills can be taught," he said, "yet American schools don't necessarily do so. A focus on achievement test scores ignores important noncognitive factors that promote success in school and life."[2]

Although these skills may not be taught in traditional schools, they are a fundamental part of the Montessori experience. In a Montessori interactive and ever-changing classroom, students learn to communicate, adapt, and problem-solve in socially appropriate ways as they navigate the classroom. That classroom is like a sea full of unique and beautiful creatures, all with their own needs and interests. As the day flows, they all learn to share their habitat, enjoy each others' company and beauty, negotiate, and sustain the peaceful atmosphere. In the process, their own gifts grow and flourish, contributing to the overall health of the environment. Contrary to some who believe that Montessori classrooms are chaotic and nonstructured, where students can do whatever they want with no responsibility—nothing could be further from the truth. Students are expected to be responsible community members, finish the work that they choose, and return it to the shelf so that someone else is able to use it. They mentor each other and care about each other. They collaborate with each other, thereby learning to be more productive as a team. They trust each other and work on sharing their strengths with each other for the good of all. Our Montessori students are very well-prepared for the 21st century.

President Obama stated on CBS news, "I'm calling on our nation's governors and state education chiefs to develop standards and assessments that don't simply measure whether students can fill in a bubble on a test, but whether they possess 21st century skills like problem-solving and critical thinking and entrepreneurship and creativity."[3]

Remarkably, the traditional world of education does indeed have this important information, however, implementing a system to actually allow students to incorporate these skills into their classroom still remains a mystery to them. The National Education Association (NEA) has been working for many years to try and bring innovation into the public school systems. Their educational researchers have long recognized that students do need to acquire very different skills for the future and have narrowed the focus to the "Four Cs."[4] They name these Four Cs: communicators, collaborators, creators, and critical thinkers. Sounds very familiar, doesn't it? It is also interesting to note that we have had this Montessori system of education in place worldwide successfully for over 100 years, which includes all of these elements, however very few policy makers or educators seem to take our approach very seriously.

The American Management Association in a 2010 survey on critical skills stated that, "The *Four Cs* will become even more important to organizations in the future. Three out of four (75.7 percent) executives who responded to the survey said they believe these skills and competencies will become even more important to organizations in the next three to five years; additionally, 80 percent of executives believe that reading, writing, and arithmetic are not sufficient if employees are unable to think critically, solve problems, collaborate, or communicate effectively."[5]

Communication skills encompass not only proficiency in oral communication, but written communication as well. Sadly, many traditionally educated high school graduates are unable to write clearly or effectively in their own language, which greatly limits the transference of the same skills to other languages in our global market. In the report *Are They Ready to Work?*, these communication skills are clearly lacking. "High school graduates fare the worst, with 72 percent of employers citing this groups' deficiency in writing in English, and 81 percent citing their deficiency in written communications. Almost half of employers said employees with two-year college degrees were still lacking skills in these two areas, while over a quarter of employers felt four-year college graduates continued to lack these skills."[6]

The importance of collaboration in education is also stressed in an NEA article, "Collaboration is essential in our classrooms because it is inherent in the nature of how work is accomplished in our civic and workforce lives. Fifty years ago, much work was accomplished by individuals working alone, but not today. Much of all significant work is accomplished in teams, and in many cases, global teams."[7]

To further emphasize its importance today, author James Surowiecki, stated, "We use the *wisdom of crowds* in the economy by saying that, under the right circumstances, groups are remarkably intelligent, and are often smarter than the smartest people in them." He continues, "a large group of diverse individuals will come up with better and more robust forecasts and make more intelligent decisions than even the most skilled *decision maker*."[8] This type of collaborative energy affects everyone, increasing the knowledge and skills of all participants.

In addressing how important creativity is today in preparing students for the future, author Daniel Pink stated, "The future belongs to a very different kind of person with a very different kind of mind—creators and empathizers, pattern recognizers, and meaning makers. These people…will now reap society's richest rewards and share its greatest joys."[9]

I share further feedback from other specialists in education, human development, and business; emphasizing how important these skills are for successful adaptation into the future. Keep in mind that the information that I am sharing with you in this chapter is not coming from Montessori educators.

Sir Kenneth Robinson, a specialist on creativity, said, "Creativity is as important in education as literacy and we should treat it with the same status."[10]

Robert Sternberg of Tufts University shares, "Successful individuals are those who have creative skills, to produce a vision for how they intend to make the world a better place for everyone; analytical intellectual skills, to assess their vision and those of others; practical intellectual skills, to carry out their vision and persuade people of its value; and wisdom, to ensure that their vision is not a selfish one."[11]

Further still, Howard Gardner states, "*the creating mind* is one of the five minds necessary in the future." He continues, "We need an education that features exploration, challenging problems, and the tolerance, if not active encouragement, of productive mistakes."[12]

Critical thinking in the past was generally a focus for gifted students in traditional education. Today, this skill will be necessary for all students as they enter a very different adult world. There was research done for the Bill and Melinda Gates Foundation at the University of Oregon by professor David T. Conley, and in it, he found, "that habits of mind, such as, analysis, interpretation, precision and accuracy, problem solving, and reasoning"[13] can be as important as content knowledge in terms of success in college.

I could continue to cite dozens and dozens of additional resources that give the same message as to the importance of many other skills beyond reading, writing, and arithmetic that need to be given to our students today. It should be obvious to anyone who is reading this book and is familiar with the Montessori approach that Montessori has been doing this for the entire time it has been in existence. There is no doubt how timely it is today in preparing our students for the world in which they will find themselves as adults. Dr. Montessori, ever the visionary, was able to understand what our students would need in their future.

CONFESSION:

*I certainly admit that I often shake my head in disbelief when I see tradi-
tional school systems still holding on to many antiquated paradigms despite the research and opinion of experts that show otherwise. What is it
that keeps this system in place? Is it only fear of change, or is it also fear of
losing control of a system that makes billions of dollars in the business of
selling text books and testing materials? Once again, as a society, we need
to ask: What is more important; our children and their future or the profit
margins of big business and powerful policy makers?*

REFERENCES

1. Levy, Frank and Murnane, Richard J. *The New Division of Labor: How Computers Are Creating the Next Job Market.* New York: Russell Sage Foundation, 2004.
2. Heckman, J. J. "The Case for Investing in Disadvantaged Young Children." Big Ideas for Children: Investing in Our Nation's Future. www.heckman equation.org.
3. Obama, Barack. "Obama's Remarks on Education." CBS News, 10 Mar. 2009. Web. 16 May 2011. http://www.cbsnews.com.
4. National Education Association (NEA). *Preparing 21st Century Students for a Global Society: An Educator's Guide to the "Four Cs"*, pp. 19–21.
5. American Management Association (AMA). Critical Skills Survey: Executive Summary: p. 21. American Management Association, 15 April 2010. www.amanet.org.
6. National Education Association (NEA). *Preparing 21st Century Students for a Global Society: An Educator's Guide to the "Four Cs"*, p. 21.
7. *Ibid.*, p. 19.
8. Surowiecki, James. *The Wisdom of Crowds.* New York. Anchor, 2005.
9. Pink, Daniel. *A Whole New Mind.* New York: Riverhead, 2006.
10. Robinson, Ken. "Ken Robinson Says Schools Kill Creativity." Speech. TED Talks. Monterey, CA. *Ted Talks.* Web. 16 May 2011. http://www.ted.com/talks/ken_robinson_says_schools_kill_creativity.html.
11. Sternberg, Robert J. *Wisdom, Intelligence, and Creativity Synthesized.* Cambridge: Cambridge UP, 2007.
12. Gardner, Howard. *Five Minds for the Future.* Boston, MA: Harvard Business School, 2007.
13. Conley, David T. "Toward a More Comprehensive Conception of College Readiness." Educational Policy Improvement Center, 8 Feb. 2008. March 2007. http://epiconline.org.

15

The Education of Boys

There has been a great deal of research done in regard to boys and how the current trends in traditional education are failing them. There is an alarming rate of failure among boys in the school system today. Richard Whitmire, author of *Why Boys Fail*[1], Michael Gurian, author of *The Minds of Boys: Saving Our Sons from Falling Behind in School and Life*[2], Christina Hoff-Sommers author of *The War Against Boys*[3], and a myriad of other educators and researchers are documenting that boys are falling far behind in comparison to girls. Here are some of those alarming statistics as presented in Gurian's book:

- Boys get the majority of Ds and Fs in most schools
- They create 90% of the discipline problems
- They are four times more likely than girls to be diagnosed with ADHD and be medicated
- They account for three out of four children diagnosed with learning disabilities
- They become 80% of the high school dropouts
- They now make up less than 45% of the college population[4]

In addition, according to statistics collected by Hoff-Sommers, women in the United States today earn 62% of associate's degrees, 57% of bachelor's degrees, 60% of master's degrees, and 52% of doctorates. This situation is not limited to the United States. In Great Britain, Australia, and Canada, boys are also falling behind. These countries are very concerned and are looking for ways to change those statistics because they can foresee the impact on their countries and their economy.

Why is this situation an epidemic at this point in time? Many experts will explain that it is because the traditional educational system has been high-jacked by the obsession with judging students' academic success by test scores, along with the resulting reaction of pushing students earlier and earlier into higher levels of work in language, math, and comprehension in an abstract way. Children are being forced to acquire certain skills much earlier than ever before, and the vast majority of boys' brains are just not wired for it this early, or for the way in which it is taught. This results in boys turning away from schooling, losing interest in learning, and eventually dropping out in many cases. Boys need to move; their brains are wired in a way that physical movement is very important to their growth and development. When traditional schooling places too much emphasis on forcing children to learn in a very abstract way before the brain is ready, the result is what we are seeing in this type of approach.

There is a very scientific reason for the differences in boys' and girls' brains. If we look back hundreds of thousands of years ago, our ancient ancestors had to learn to survive. Typically, the ancient hunters and protectors were the men in the tribes. This primitive physical interaction with the environment resulted in a brain that was wired to survive under these circumstances. So as human beings evolved generation after generation, a brain emerged that allowed the species to survive by giving the genders different strengths. Young boys' brains are virtually still operating as hunters and protectors who need physical stimulation to feel safe, happy, and fulfilled, and for their brains to grow and develop normally. The men were the *tinkerers* and builders, creating tools and using their hands to improve their lives and the life of the tribe. Again, if we look back on the tribal way of life, it was typically the women and girls who created the safe, nurturing, and predictable home life—preparing food and cooking, sewing, washing clothing, raising and nurturing the children, etc. These were stable, consistent activities that depended upon communication and cooperative human interaction for the best results in terms of survival of the tribe. It is not surprising that the female brain is very strong in the area of communication and language and that women are strongly drawn to *empathy-centered* work. Typically, women are drawn to working with people, while men are drawn to more physical activities because of how the brain has developed.

I am certainly not suggesting that we need to return to a primitive lifestyle, nor that there are not females who love to work with their hands and men who are nurturers—there certainly are—however, I am referring to the predominant traits that were genetically passed down. Nor does it indicate that only certain genders should be working in certain fields. It is also important to note that women have always been, in one way or another, held back in terms of equal treatment as compared to men. Girls and women to this day, in many cases, have still not been given equal opportunities based on the cultural beliefs of the time. Ironically, this may in part be due to how women have excelled in their past traditional roles, and the power of men in keeping them there. This trend in education at the moment, however, definitely favors girls over boys. It is important that educators and parents understand how boys and girls are wired differently, and to appropriately meet the needs of both.

When schools are eliminating, or minimizing recess and physical education, they are doing a disservice to everyone, both boys and girls, but for boys it can be devastating in terms of how important it is to their learning. In addition, if traditional schools do not incorporate hands-on, interactive, and experiential learning experiences, they are putting boys at a distinct disadvantage. Setting up boys to fail in this system not only hurts the boys, but our society as a whole. Depriving any gender from equal opportunity is wrong. We do, however, need to make sure that we make the right decisions for students based on the knowledge that we have on how they grow, learn, and develop best. How many great achievements or advancements have we missed out on because of turning off a large percentage of students to learning? How many students would still need medication if not strapped to a desk all day? Imagine if we were able to constructively channel all of that natural energy into positive contributions?

It is interesting to note that when schools do offer a *hands-on* curriculum, we see an increase in boys' graduation rates: Georgia Tech is 68% male; Rochester Institute of Technology is 68% male; and the South Dakota School of Mines and Technology is 74% male. This success rate has led to an increase in vocational education, now called Career and Technical Education (CTE). Even the Harvard Graduate School of Education had this to say in their recently published study, *Pathways to Prosperity*, "Our system…clearly does not work well for many, especially young men." The authors cited successful vocational educational systems such as the *Cadillac of Career Training Education* in Massachusetts. In fact, Massachusetts seems to lead the nation in offering vocational-technical high schools to young men and women. *Pathways* reports that these schools have some of the highest graduation and college matriculation rates, and close to 95% of the students pass the state test necessary for graduation.

The most commonsense approach, rather than worrying about which gender should pursue what field, would be to allow all students, without regard to gender, to choose a path of individual interest. When we offer equal opportunity to all genders, races, and socioeconomic groups, only then will we begin to meet the needs of all.

We do not see the same statistics in Montessori education. There are really no large gaps in gender performance because the learning environments have been designed to meet the needs of all developing minds and bodies at the appropriate times. Boys and girls both love all subjects based on their own individual preferences. Movement is a fundamental freedom given to the students and Dr. Montessori understood how important it was for everyone to be able to move, especially the boys. It has been observed however, that girls will typically be drawn to do more *stationary* or *empathy-based* work because of their neurological wiring. As mentioned previously, the language and communication areas of the brain are more dominant in girls, whereas the need for physical movement is more dominant in boys.

Most parents with both boys and girls will know that they can be very different and have different needs. In general, girls will tend to enjoy being the nurturers, the teachers, the helpers, while boys will participate more in being the wildly daring adventurers, barely able to sit still for short periods of time. I can remember growing up with my two brothers; we made more trips to the emergency room for stitches and broken bones before they turned 12 than I have ever had to do to this day. It is no wonder that boys feel trapped in desks all day with no way to channel that energy. By having to focus all of their attention on literary and abstract tasks at such a young age, we have a recipe for the type of failure we are seeing in the traditional world of education today. In many school systems across the country, they have even eliminated recess in order to devote more time to test preparation and drilling skills. This is sheer neglect, or blatant ignorance, of the scientific knowledge of what our students' developing brains need. The brain research is there and it is clear, and until the traditional world of education pays attention to it, they are doomed to provide developmentally inappropriate learning environments for children. Some scholars will argue that when we begin to point out gender differences, then we promote sexism or stereotyping. This type of thinking only allows the situation to continue as is. While it may seem too much of a broad generalization to say that boys and girls are wired totally differently, the facts are there. Of course there are always exceptions to everything, but in general, brain research supports this difference and there is no doubt that the statistics in education are supporting it as well—in terms of academic performance, boys are declining while girls are climbing.

At McGill University in Canada, Sumitra Rajagopalan, an adjunct professor of biomechanics, developed a program for high school boys based on Montreal's staggering statistic that one-in-three boys drops out of school. She discovered that after interviewing many of these bored male students, most of them had never held a tool. She decided to create *hands-on* activities for them, with very successful results. The boys actually built a solar-driven Stirling engine using Coca-Cola cans and straws. She shared her belief, "Boys are born tinkerers; they have a deep-seated need to rip things apart, decode their inner workings, and create stuff." Research is supporting her findings.

Dr. Montessori knew what *all* children needed over 100 years ago—the education of the *whole child* was the best, and only way, to meet the needs of children and their growing and developing brains. She incorporated into her method hands-on, developmentally appropriate learning materials and experiences to meet the needs of all types of learners and stimulate all areas of the brain. She intuitively knew that human beings and all creatures in the universe are *living systems* which are interconnected and dependent upon each other to grow and develop in a healthy way. The brain needs to work along with the entire body and the environment it is exposed to, in order to reach optimal efficiency. She knew that every aspect of the child's life contributed to his or her healthy growth and development. Dr. Montessori never differentiated between genders; to her, all children needed certain things and it was our responsibility, as Montessori educators, to provide the prepared environment to meet all of those needs. Traditional educational systems would do well to follow her lead.

When I think about a student who excelled in Montessori after coming from a traditional setting, I can't help but think of Jay. Jay's mother came to tour the school and explained that her son had been a naturally inquisitive boy who loved to learn. He was always exploring nature and asking questions about the world. That was until he went to 1st grade in a traditional school. "The light has gone out of his eyes," his mother sadly told me as his 1st grade year was coming to an end. I thought perhaps Montessori could help. Fast forward two years and Jay has once again become the inquisitive and impassioned learner that he once was. In fact, even more so, as the Montessori curriculum and interactive learning environment have allowed him to follow his interests and develop skills that allow him to be a life-long learner. Not only has the light in his eyes returned, it shines brightly on everyone and everything in his path. His latest research study as a Montessori elementary student… stellar nucleosynthesis!

CONFESSION:

I will admit that as a Montessorian, I have never isolated my thinking to compartmentalize genders. Even though we would have class discussions about cultural and historical events that certainly centered around gen- der-related issues, I always wanted the students to receive the message that we are individuals first, and a group member second. I never wanted them to think that because they were in a group by birth, that it should hin- der them, or give them special advantages, in any way. This resistance to brand individuals could be taken in different ways; such as not encouraging girls to stand up for their rights, or for boys to feel as if it isn't masculine to feel certain ways or have interest in certain things. My goal was to always encourage our young people to develop their own personal power, which is unique to each person. No matter what gender, race, religion, social or economic class, I want children to know that they have an unlimited power within themselves to rise above any labels or limitations that people or society may try to place upon them.

REFERENCES

1. Whitmire, Richard. *Why Boys Fail: Saving Our Sons from an Educational System That's Leaving Them Behind.* AMACOM Books, January 2010.
2. Gurian, Michael and Kathy Stevens. *The Minds of Boys: Saving Our Sons from Falling Behind in School and Life.* Jossey-Bass. An Imprint at WILEY, 2007.
3. Sommers, Christina Hoff. *The War Against Boys: How Misguided Policies Are Harming Our Young Men.* Simon and Schuster, 2000.
4. Day, Lori. "Why Boys Are Failing in an Educational System Stacked Against Them," on The Huffington Post. Web. Aug. 2011. http://www.huffington post.com/lori-day/why-boys-are-failing-in-a_b_884262.html.

16

Testing, Grades, and Report Cards

As most people who are familiar with the Montessori method would imagine, testing, grades, and traditional types of reporting on the progress of children are as different as what we do in the classroom. In a culture that thrives on competition, it is sometimes difficult for parents to truly embrace a practice that does not give them a definitive label for their child. Is my child on grade level, above grade level, average, gifted? So many people are conditioned to want to label and compare children. It is understandable that most parents have not had a Montessori experience and can only relate to a traditional approach of assessing students and reporting those results to parents. Add to the fact that not only do we not give grades, but we have minimal paperwork going home, and none with grades on them. The vast majority of the work done in Montessori classrooms is with the materials, and of course, parents do not see that part of the process. I remind parents that it truly requires a tremendous amount of trust to be a Montessori parent. There are minimal *external products* to verify learning; it is really an *internal process* for the child and of course, that is much more difficult to measure and quantify. Have no doubt, however, that the internal process is going on. I think parents begin to see the changes in their children rather quickly, and those positive changes are what convince the parents that yes, it is working. They may not understand it, but they definitely see it transforming their children.

One of the reasons that Montessori schools do not give grades is that the development of the child's self-esteem is critical to our approach. How do you explain to any young child that even though he or she did not get an A, that doesn't mean that he or she isn't smart? Children are actually more intelligent than that. When teachers start to assign grades, the children know that if they don't get an A, somehow they are lacking. No matter how we sugar-coat it, they are going to get the message that they are not smart enough to get an A. This, without a doubt, causes young children to feel discouraged about learning and themselves. They begin to believe that they are stupid and can't learn. If I can't learn, why bother? I may as well just give up. How many hundreds of thousands of students get this message because of the traditional grading system? It is a self-fulfilling prophecy; I can't do it, so I don't try. You may have heard of the psychological studies where the researchers will put a group of *slow* students in classrooms and the teachers are told that they are actually gifted. When the teacher treats them as *gifted* students and has higher expectations for them, the students actually perform at a higher level. The expectations of the learning environment have a tremendous impact on the attitude and performance of the students. The expectation that those children were gifted and thus, were treated as such, resulted in the students creating that reality.

Our Montessori approach believes that all children are gifted in one way or another. We want children to understand that all people have their gifts and their challenges. We want them to feel confident enough to jump into learning with their entire being. Children need to be encouraged and excited about learning for the love of learning, not to receive a good grade. Once again, this leads to the discussion about the internal process as compared to the external process of learning. When children are learning and not being judged and compared, they will naturally follow that internal force that guides them to explore things that are meaningful and exciting to them. This internal process has many rewards. Children are now enjoying the learning process and are on a life-long path that will lead them to have a different approach to new experiences, and the self-confidence to follow their own interests. When students discover new things and excitedly share them with their classmates, they receive an acknowledgment of appreciation for sharing something very interesting and expanding everyone's knowledge. This builds their self-confidence because their efforts are appreciated and valued and they realize that they have important contributions to make to the community.

Conversely, when children work only for the acquisition of a good grade, we see many things. One, usually the subject matter is chosen by the teacher and is just a set of facts to memorize and spit back out in order to receive a good grade. Most of the memorized material is quickly forgotten and the focus is on memorizing the next set of facts for the next test. This kind of approach at a young age can actually rob children of the true joy of learning and thinking. Obviously, the students who get As are successful test takers, and their self-esteem is fine. Let's consider everyone else, as noted previously; they are buried in a system that is telling them that they are not smart enough to learn. Their self-esteem slowly erodes. Sadly, I cannot tell you how many times I have seen young students come to us from traditional settings and they have been beaten down by the system. They had very poor self-esteem or were just completely turned off to learning. Upon entering a Montessori community, their transformation is a beautiful thing to behold. No one will ever convince me that children should not enter Montessori classrooms if they do not have previous Montessori experience. I have seen too many transformations take place.

One of the most dramatic transformations I have witnessed is that of Gary. He was highly intelligent, so much so, that he preferred the company of adults because of his keen intellect. The first five years of elementary school in a very exclusive traditional private school was a bit bumpy because Gary never felt as if he fit in. He would rather read or work on his computer than join in the typical boy's banter and, unfortunately, this difference made him a target. Gary was bullied and ostracized; he became anxious, fearful, and lonely. His self-esteem plummeted when he entered middle school because the bullying escalated. He learned to go inward and tried to become invisible.

It came to a head one day when the class was on a field trip and the boys were so cruel to Gary that he actually locked himself in a bathroom and refused to emerge until his parents came to get him. His mother called me and pleaded that I take him into our Montessori middle school community. I agreed and the healing began for Gary. Our students welcomed him warmly and saw nothing unusual in his quiet, intellectual ways. In fact, they embraced those qualities in Gary and saw how it could benefit the community. Gary emerged slowly from his shell as he began to feel safe and appreciated. When he graduated from our program, his transformation was complete. He was a different young man: confident, self-assured, and grateful to his Montessori community. He went on to high school and college and excelled at each stop on the way.

Many parents will ask me how do we know if the children are learning if we don't test them or give them grades. My response is that although we do not test them in a traditional way, there are informal assessments everyday in the constant interaction between the child and the teacher. Since all lessons are given individually or in small groups, Montessori teachers will get immediate feedback as to whether the child grasps a concept. The child will then reinforce the concepts with continued work with that lesson as they practice it. Montessori teachers are trained to be highly observant and meticulous record-keepers. All of the lessons given to children are noted in the child's individual record. This is updated daily. As a result, any parent should be able to be shown their child's entire record of lessons given in the Montessori classroom along with the child's progress with them. So even though we are not giving the child a grade, or a traditional report card, we are carefully observing and noting the child's progress in every area of development. These progress reports should always be made available to parents.

Montessori record-keeping systems are some of the most detailed and complete in their overall snapshot of the child. In fact, some Montessori parents can be overwhelmed with the pages and pages of records kept on their child. The most common request that I get from parents is: "Can't we get something simpler?" Due to the fact that this approach is such a holistic and well-rounded experience for children, it is very difficult to simplify the documentation of the child's experience. Sometimes simplification leads to reverting to just labeling a child with a rating as compared to others. Some things in the Montessori world are always topics of discussion for Montessori educators, and finding efficient and valuable tools for recording children's progress is certainly one of them. Today there are computerized versions available, which have certainly made the lives of Montessorians much easier!

The second most commonly asked question by parents is whether we give standardized tests. The answer to this question is multilayered. The question by the parents is usually related to a need to know how their child is doing in comparison to other students in the nation, especially since they do not receive grades or traditional report cards. Some Montessori schools do not administer standardized tests to their students, however, some certainly do. I will share my journey with standardized tests in my school. When our school was primarily an early childhood school, I did not administer standardized tests and felt no need to do so. As the school expanded into elementary levels, even though many parents requested we do so, I still stayed true to my belief that there was no need to subject the students to the pressure of a standardized test. For some parents, it was one of the reasons that they chose Montessori because their child was traumatized by the pressure of performance on standardized tests in traditional schools, both public and private. When my school grew into middle school, however, my perspective began to broaden on the subject. Remarkably, it was the middle school students who actually asked me to do it. Many of those students had been in Montessori all their life and they wanted to know how they stood in relation to other students in the nation. So, I decided to try it. The way we approached it, however, was that this was a new practical life skill that would be helpful to them as they moved into high school and beyond. I wanted them to learn a new skill, and standardized test taking is certainly a skill that can be learned by understanding how it is formatted. I didn't want the students to feel any pressure; I wanted it to be a learning experience.

The results of the test would just be an interesting by-product and something that the students themselves were interested in learning. As is true with all things in Montessori, the value was in the process, not the end product. We looked at it as a new opportunity to think in a different way. In addition, I further explained to them that because this was a new skill and they had not had practice with it, the results may not be truly indicative of the kind of student that they truly were. It would be a work in progress. So, I purchased some practice test booklets to give them an idea as to what the process would be like. Much of standardized testing is based upon text book learning and language, and that is an unfamiliar arena for Montessori students. So we moved ahead with this new adventure, not quite sure of what to expect. After completing the standardized tests and receiving the results, not surprisingly, our students performed exceptionally well. The students couldn't believe how easy it was. The majority of our students scored in the top quartile of the nation. There were a few average scores (which means at grade level), but very few below average. Even though we made a point of stressing that it was the *process*, not the *product*, which was most valuable, we were all excited with the results, and the students were proud to see how they ranked in comparison to other students in the nation. The parents let out a sigh of relief.

As the school grew, and our first middle school graduating classes went off to high school, our view was forced to expand even further. The high schools had no idea what to do with our students' records, and without proper records, they could not accept them into their schools. We had no grades, and thank goodness, we at least had the standardized tests to pass on to them. Another problem arose however because we were not accredited, and credits for some subject areas, such as algebra and geometry, could not be accepted. As a result, I felt compelled to look into accreditation options. I discovered that accreditation is a very expensive process! We were a very small school and it would be a hardship, but it seemed as if it was necessary to do for the benefit of our students. So, our school became accredited and this accreditation brought us recognition by the high schools; our students' credits were freely accepted. Today, after 18 years of graduating students, many of the local high schools have become familiar with our school's program, and are eager to admit our students because of the consistent qualities and skills that they see in them. The high schools want them as students.

One of the requirements of many accrediting organizations is that all students, from elementary age and up, take standardized tests. Our school complied, however, once again, our view of the whole process was to treat it as a practical life skill—process, not product. Since that is how it is treated, the students are much more relaxed and therefore will tend to do very well. It amazes me, however, that some of our Montessori parents fall into the *labeling* mode so easily when the students receive their results. It prompted me to write this memo to parents whenever we get ready to do standardized testing in order to help them to put it into perspective. I will share it with you:

"Dear Parents,

Integrating a standardized test into the life of Montessori students is considered a practical life skill here at Summit-Questa. Due to the fact that standardized tests are based on textbook learning, Montessori students must be introduced to the different format. Children in traditional classrooms are constantly reinforced with the format, the language, and the mind-numbing repetition of test-taking strategies throughout the year, in place of other learning experiences, and I believe, at the risk of losing true learning and thinking opportunities. Of course, most of you who seek out our school have told me many times that it is precisely for that reason that you want a Montessori experience for your child. With that said, since we are an accredited school, it is a requirement to give standardized tests to our students. We only take a couple of weeks before the actual test to familiarize the students with this practical life skill.

Some students are natural test takers and will excel on every test they take, while some students, due to past negative experiences, are anxiety ridden about tests. This anxiety will actually cause their brain functions to slow down, which may give an inaccurate view of the student's true abilities. Most students will fall somewhere in-between, gradually acquiring these new skills as their experience builds upon itself year after year. Usually, by the middle school years, our students have mastered the test and most score off the charts. Fortunately, this is when test results matter the most because high schools only want to see 7th and 8th grade test results. Fortunately, our school tends to do very well on a cumulative basis because our students perform very well on the nationwide test.

I am writing this note to you to try and help everyone put this type of testing in perspective. If there was a test that truly *measured* the depth of understanding and learning that goes on in a Montessori environment, then it wouldn't be necessary to write this note or to have to explain to parents that standardized testing is only a *snapshot* of a student's true abilities. That *snapshot* is very limited because it is, again, only focusing on a textbook type of approach, and it is very dependent upon how the student felt and performed on that day and in that moment in time. I have literally had children tell me that they were rushing through because they didn't really enjoy this type of work and wanted to get it over with. Another time, a young student told me it was more fun to make a triangle out of the dots, so that is what he did! Of course, as students mature, they understand the more serious nature of the work, but young students don't always feel compelled to give the test their full attention. This is perfectly fine; they understand over time.

I am including a summary of some of the research I have done over the years on standardized testing:

- Children today are tested to an extent that is unprecedented in our history and in the world. Few countries use standardized tests for students below high school age or multiple choice tests for students of any age.
- Standardized test scores often measure superficial thinking. Studies have shown those students who are *actively* engaged in learning, such as asking questions of themselves while they read, or try to connect what they are doing to past learning, do not always test well because it takes extra time to analyze each question rather than skipping through and guessing.
- Measuring the quality of learning or teaching was not the intent of giving norm-referenced tests. These types of tests were designed so that only half of the test takers would respond correctly to most items (hence average). The main objective of these tests is to rank, not to rate; to spread out scores, not to measure the quality of a school or student.
- Student's self-esteem is damaged when adults put too much emphasis on test score results and then compare that student to others.
- Many educational specialists actually condemn the practice of giving standardized tests to children younger than nine years of age.

In summary, I hope that you understand that standardized testing is only one very small piece of our students' experience here. The whole Montessori experience is a deep-thinking, broad exposure to many different levels of learning, creating, communicating, and interacting; it cannot be measured in a superficial, snap-shot way. The truest representation of how the Montessori method works is in the students themselves. When you witness the self-assured, self-motivated, well-rounded graduates that come out of the Montessori program, there isn't any question that this method works. Thank you for your support of our Montessori school and for understanding and seeing the value in what we do for your children."

One more thing to add is that most standardized tests are now being adapted to include Common Core Standards. Common Core is incorporating more critical thinking skills into the standards. Everyone acknowledges that critical thinking is certainly an important goal in education and needed for the future world that the students will be entering. Here is the problem however; the policy makers think that by adding abstract critical thinking problems to the test at younger and younger ages will force children to acquire them earlier. This blatantly disregards how children learn and what their developing brains need. If you speak to any traditional teacher about how developmentally inappropriate the expectations for the young students are, they will not hesitate to tell you how difficult it is for their students and for them, as their teachers.

I just shook my head when I saw the latest version of standardized tests built upon this idea of forcing critical thinking skills on young children. Fortunately, we are not driven by test results. Critical thinking comes when given the correct ingredients in a well-rounded education. Montessori students are known for their high levels of critical thinking and it did not happen by forcing them to do abstract work before the brain was ready for it.

CONFESSION:

I secretly admit that when we were required to administer standardized testing due to accreditation standards, I vacillated between fear that perhaps the students would not do well, and excitement at showing parents that yes, Montessori students can do well on standardized tests. As much as I espoused our belief in the minimal importance of standardized testing as a true indicator of the value of the student, I still recognized that our society places a great deal of value on its importance. So, I admit that it was not only the parents who breathed a sigh of relief after receiving the first results; I also felt a weight lift off of my shoulders. After eighteen plus years of administering standardized testing to our students, I can truly say that our Montessori students, once again, show us that they are multitalented individuals who cannot be defined by one test score. It is just a piece of the pie.

This book has free material available for download from the
Web Added Value™ resource center at *www.jrosspub.com*

17

Special Needs in Montessori

As a Montessori practitioner, I have always tried to be as inclusive as possible without disrupting the Montessori learning environment. Our philosophy certainly speaks to meeting the individual needs of all children, and whenever it has been possible to do so, we have tried to offer the Montessori environment as a means to help children learn and grow. More often than not, children with a variety of needs have not only been helped, but have flourished in many cases. We have had students with stuttering disorders, low IQs, attention deficit disorder (ADD), attention-deficit and hyperactivity disorder (ADHD), Down syndrome, varied processing disorders, and students on the autism spectrum. We weren't always able to accommodate everyone's needs, but we certainly made an effort to do so if we felt there was a chance that the child could succeed in a Montessori environment. In some cases they couldn't without specialized intervention. If the parents were able to supply the specialist for the child, we were willing to try. If parents were not willing or able to supply specialist support, then we would not be able to accommodate some of those needs because our teachers were not trained in those specific areas, or the child required too much one-on-one intervention, which was not possible in our Montessori classrooms. If there was a behavioral issue that might impact the safety of the students in the classroom, then that was a situation where there was nothing further that we could offer. Safety always comes first.

I will share that when all of the pieces fit together, such as a child receiving the specialized support that he or she needs, and the integration into the

Montessori curriculum where children move at their own rate and pace, we have experienced many beautiful success stories. One of the most touching elements is how protective and supportive the fellow classmates are toward anyone who has obvious disabilities, such as Down syndrome or stuttering. Our Montessori community grows stronger in love, compassion, and empathy when they actively work to help and support others with disabilities. Even though the classmates will treat them with respect and acceptance most of the time, if someone happens to be insensitive, unkind, or thoughtless, the backlash is swift and protective. Montessori students will come to their aid.

I remember when a student who had a severe stuttering problem was graduating from 8th grade. It is a tradition that our graduating students give a speech to the audience which typically lasts three to five minutes. When the young man got up to give his speech, encouraged and supported by his classmates, he painfully stuttered while speaking from his heart. His speech took over twenty minutes to complete and you could have heard a pin drop in the theatre, so respectful were the students and the audience. At the conclusion, his classmates gave him a standing ovation. I will never forget the feeling of love that permeated that room at that moment. Everyone cried because of the perseverance of the graduate who felt safe and would not quit, the respect of the audience, and the love and support shown to him by his classmates. It was one of those inspiring moments in life.

Years ago, sadly, a local Montessori school was closing, and there were 25 families seeking to relocate their children to our Montessori school. These families were dedicated to Montessori and the community that had been forged at their previous school. When they approached me about taking in these students, they only had one condition. They explained that they would only transfer all of their children if I would also accept the Down syndrome child that had been a part of their community for so many years. It was all or nothing. I assured them that it was not an issue for me or our school because we had already had Down syndrome students previously as part of our school community. This is another beautiful example of the power of the Montessori community, supporting and protecting every member. These are the types of real-life experiences that shape and form the souls of every member of the community.

I will share yet another story about a young boy who attended our entire Montessori program through 8th grade. This young man would be classified as being very slow, with a very low IQ. As he matured, it became more and more evident to his classmates that learning was difficult for him and he would probably never attain the same levels of learning as everyone else. In a traditional setting, he most likely would have been made fun of, called names, put into special classes, and shunned. In the Montessori community, just the opposite occurred. He was always supported, helped, and protected. No one made fun of him, which would have outraged his Montessori classmates. He was protected and nurtured right up to the time when he walked up on stage to give his speech, which was very short and sweet. He shared how much he loved his school and classmates and would miss all of them. He was not able to earn a standard diploma but nonetheless felt as successful as any of the other graduates because of the climate of acceptance and support that surrounded him as he grew up.

I have seen many students come to us with ADD or ADHD. The symptoms for both disorders can range in severity for every student, therefore the experience in a Montessori environment can also vary widely. I have had some students become transformed learners when they were not required to sit at a desk all day. The freedom of movement can be a healing elixir for so many of these students. On the other hand, I have had students that had such severe focusing issues, that the constant movement and distractions of a Montessori classroom was not what they needed; they could not focus long enough to absorb anything. Parents will often ask me or the teachers if we recommend medication. This is a very difficult question to answer, as we are not health practitioners. All I can share with parents is that in my experience, there have been times when a student seems to not be able to control their focus at all, and when medicated, they can. It comes at a cost, however, as many times there are side-effects such as loss of appetite, fatigue, or depression. Even though as Montessori practitioners we tend to lean strongly toward natural remedies, this is not a call I feel comfortable making for anyone. It is really a family decision to be made by parents and doctors.

Fortunately, we have had success when it comes to helping students with certain language and auditory processing issues because we have found specialists that come into our school and offer the appropriate support to the students. It has been very rewarding to see students' self-esteem and self-confidence return when they are given the tools to overcome their learning difficulties. The beautiful thing is that in the Montessori classroom, students are used to seeing everyone work at a different rate, ability, and pace. There is nothing out of the ordinary for everyone to be in a different place, or to help and support each other. This atmosphere helps many students to overcome the feelings of defeat and failure that may have been a result of their educational experience in the past and at other schools.

Another area where there seems to be an inordinate amount of students coming to us in comparison to years past are those students with autism spectrum disorders (ASD). Some of the statistics are alarmingly high. A new government survey of parents from the 2014 National Health Interview Survey suggests that 1 in 45 children, ages 3 through 17, have been diagnosed with ASD. These figures from the parent survey are higher than the 1 in 68 figure from the Center for Disease Control and Prevention (CDC). The National Health Interview is considered the most in-depth survey of its kind in the United States and is likely a more accurate representation of autism prevalence in the U.S., according to Michael Rosanoff, Autism Speaks director for public health research. According to the Autism Science Foundation (ASF), the numbers have been climbing decade by decade; in the 1980s, autism prevalence was reported as 1 in 10,000; in the 1990s, 1 in 2,500 and later, 1 in 1,000. What has changed in terms of escalating numbers is that the diagnostic criteria have changed over the last three decades. Today, Asperger's syndrome and other forms of autism have been included in those numbers. Further statistics from ASF include: ASDs continue to be almost five times more common among boys (1 in 42) than among girls (1 in 189) and they are reported in all racial, ethnic, and socioeconomic groups.

Autism spectrum disorders are a complex set of neurological disorders that seriously affect social behaviors, communication, and cognitive functioning. Many children with ASD have average or above average intelligence. Typically, the behaviors may include hand-flapping, or body rocking, a demand for sameness, a resistance to change, and in some instances, aggression or self-injury. There may also be a savant type of knowledge or obsession about a certain topic or interest.

In our experience with students on the spectrum, most of the time our dynamic and constantly changing Montessori environments can be very upsetting to some students with ASD. Students with Asperger's have had more success at our school. These students have been able to adapt to the interactive environment and daily changes a bit better than others with autism. We do have a student with autism who is successfully navigating our program with the help of a full-time support person. That support person is able to take the student aside or outside to calm down and refocus on what the student needs to do in order to return to the learning environment. This allows the autistic student's needs to be met without disrupting the entire class or taking the teacher away from the rest of the class for too long of a time. In this case, it is working.

It is very hard to make broad generalizations about any child with or without disabilities. I go back to looking at each child as an individual and determining if our Montessori environments can not only meet his or her needs, but also be allowed to function normally. It also depends upon whether the school has access to specialists that can come into the school to offer the intervention that the child needs. In addition, the parent must be willing and able to provide that support. It will not serve anyone well if a student is placed in a setting where no one is trained to meet their specific needs, and the other students are adversely affected by a student whose needs cannot be met. It also can add a great deal of stress on a Montessori teacher if he or she feels that a student's needs cannot be met. It is an equation that must be looked at very carefully for the good of everyone. There are some Montessori schools that do not accept any students with learning disabilities, just as there are some schools that will not accept students without prior Montessori experience after the age of three or four. I would say that they may be missing out on the addition of some wonderful children and learning opportunities for all in the community. In the stories that I relayed in this chapter, the students with those special needs added a dimension to our classrooms that would never have occurred without them being a part of our community.

CONFESSION:

There have been times when I was tempted to make blanket policies at my school about not accepting any students with special needs, especially when the situation took a negative turn. More often than not, this negative turn resulted in parents becoming so angry with us because we would not put their child's needs ahead of the entire class. I would remind them that at the very onset of our meeting, before they enrolled, we discussed that our school is not a special needs school, nor are all of the teachers trained in that area. I stressed that we would be willing to try if they would provide the needed support as long as the student did not disrupt the learning environment. It would be a probationary period until we knew it was going to work. Obviously the negative behaviors came into play when it did not work. We were the ones who the parents lashed out at, and sadly, sometimes in public ways. It was at those moments that I would think, "Okay, enough. Here we are willing to try and help, and we end up getting slapped in the face. No more." Until the next family comes along that pulls on our heartstrings and we say, "Okay, let's try again."

18

Technology and Montessori Education

There is no doubt that the world today is one in which technology plays a critical role. Montessori education has occasionally been referred to as a *dinosaur* by traditionalists who believe that Montessorians are burying their heads in the sand when it comes to opening up our classrooms to technology. There is some truth to this, but with good reason, if you look at much of the brain research out there. We are not saying that we should turn a blind eye to the need for students to be engaged in technology, we are merely stating that it needs to be done at the appropriate time in the child's development. Research is showing that technology can be harmful if not controlled appropriately for the growing brain. Children's brains will actually be rewired differently if exposed to too much technology at this very critical and formative stage. One of the changes occurring in our frequent use of the Internet is that our brains are being trained to scan information quickly and effectively, instant answers, instant gratification. As discussed throughout the book, children are greatly impacted by the type of environment in which they live, work, and play every day.

When I was growing up, my childhood was very different compared to that of what most children experience today. I do not think I am alone in this. Past generations had a more sheltered, predictable life for many reasons. Living in a semi-rural/suburban environment, after school I would get on my bike and ride off to some adventure with my friends. The standard rule would be, "Be home when the streetlights come on." There was little fear for families in those days in regard to predators and the general safety of the children in the neighborhood. There was usually always a *pack* of us playing. We explored the woods, built forts, played baseball, rode horses, went sleigh riding, or just hung out in each others' bedrooms dreaming of the latest musical heartthrob. We imagined all sorts of worlds and sometimes played them out in theatrical performances for each other. We were exposed to a world that was full of nature, physical movement, social interaction, and imagination. We all had to be home before dark and then were expected to help with the household chores before, during, and after dinner. Most families still had a dinner time where everyone ate together and discussed their day. All of these types of physical, social, and emotional activity played an important role in our developing brains, bodies, and social and emotional relationships.

Fast forward to today and it is actually unusual for most families to be able to juggle their busy lifestyles in order to eat together as a family. The hectic pace results in over-scheduled activities, a lot of on-the-run food, and people connected to their devices constantly, whether it is the computer, television, phones, or musical devices. According to Cris Rowan in her article, *The Impact of Technology on the Developing Child*, "A 2010 Kaiser Foundation study showed that elementary age children use an average of 7.5 hours per day of entertainment technology; 75% of these children have televisions in their bedrooms; and 50% of North American homes have the television on all day. Gone is dining room table conversation—replaced by the *big screen* and take out."[1]

The result of this type of lifestyle is that children are not as physically active, socially connected, or free to just *be*; and because of the dependence upon devices to constantly *entertain* our children, the development of creativity, imagination, and self-control are very limited. The child's attention span is being rewired for excessive speed, which is making it very difficult for these students to adapt to learning environments where they need to focus and pay attention—important prerequisites to learning. Health issues for children such as diabetes and obesity are at an alarming, all-time high due to physical inactivity. There are researchers who are associating many learning disabilities and disorders with overexposure to technology at developmentally inappropriate times. This sensory overload can also result in higher stress levels for young, developing children, which then impacts their immune system.

The child's attention span is determined by their immediate environment. For past generations, children's brains have adapted to the culture of emphasizing the importance of reading. This led to their brains wiring themselves to focus intently on reading with minimal distractions, and this resulted in the emergence of imagination and remembering what they read. Then, a new generation of children was introduced to the television. This provided a very different environment which resulted in children being entertained by visual stimulation, a disjointed, choppy view of the world, and a tendency to allow other factors, other than themselves, to stimulate imagination. Today, in this environment of constant exposure to the Internet, their attention is constantly being splintered, which without a doubt has an impact on memory and in many cases, the development of imagination.

Dr. Jim Taylor, in an article, "How Technology Is Changing the Way Children Think and Focus," in *Psychology Today*, shared, "Technology conditions the brain to pay attention to information very differently than reading... the metaphor...is the difference between scuba diving and jet skiing. Book reading is like scuba diving...submerged in a quiet, slow-paced setting with few distractions and is required to focus narrowly and think deeply on the limited information available to them. In contrast, using the Internet is like jet skiing...skimming along the surface of the water at high speed, exposed to a broad vista, surrounded by many distractions, and only able to focus fleetingly on any one thing."[2]

Limited exposure to technology is not harmful and research has shown that certain skills are certainly improved through its use, such as visual-spatial skills, eye-hand coordination, reaction times, and the ability to find information among the massive sea of stimulation. These are good skills to acquire, but not at the loss of others. Once again, balance in life is very important and knowing when to allow children to delve into the digital world based on their developmental needs is critical information for parents and educators to consider.

This helps us to better understand that if we want our students to develop in healthy ways: physically, neurologically, emotionally, and socially; and to specifically acquire reflective skills, deep-thinking skills, creativity, increased memory, better comprehension, and problem-solving skills it is necessary to provide them with opportunities to develop those skills—and constant use of the Internet will not help that to occur. The ways to help develop these important skills are to expose children to reading, hands-on activities for learning, exploration of their physical environment, interaction with nature, and social interaction. This is exactly what goes on in Montessori classrooms. These are the foundational skills that will allow children to flourish in the 21st century and be able to balance their entrance into the world of technology.

From a Montessori perspective, we are absolutely connected to what Dr. Montessori told us over 100 years ago, and what the current research states; that is, that from birth through the elementary years, children must be allowed to physically interact with their environments, using their hands to build their knowledge. They need to interact with others in the environment to learn from them and with them. The need to spend time in nature, observing and interacting, is paramount to their healthy development. Technology cannot replicate this, nor should it. The developing brains need something other than a device. Therefore, in most Montessori schools you will not see any technical devices in infant-toddler environments, and very few in early childhood environments since the brain needs something very different, and this type of technology is actually proving to be somewhat harmful at many levels to the young, developing brain. Infants and toddlers need to hear their parents and caregivers speaking to them; not language coming from a device. The brain will not process that type of language activity in the same way as when it is coming from a human being. We are already seeing an increase in language processing issues in young children because of too much exposure to devices as compared to the human voice and interaction.

At my school, and some other Montessori schools that I have observed, the use of technology will begin to be introduced in lower elementary. Students are taught keyboarding skills and may use the computers for research. In fourth grade, we introduce Rosetta Stone, a foreign language program that is accessed on the computer. When technology is introduced into the lower elementary classroom for developmentally appropriate activities and it is balanced so that the majority of the child's work is with Montessori materials, we have seen a successful integration. Recent studies at Princeton University and the University of California have shown that even in college, those students who still wrote notes by hand actually retained more than the students who used their laptops. When tested, "the longhand note-takers did significantly better than laptop note-takers, despite the fact that laptop note-takers had more notes to look at."[3] This has been linked, once again, to the fact that the hand is the main facilitator of the brain's interaction with learning. The information is processed differently when the hands are directly involved in an activity.

As the children grow and mature in our Montessori classrooms, their computer use will also increase. In middle school, much of the students' work is directly linked to technology. They will become much more proficient in the appropriate and exciting use of technology in learning.

The truth of the matter is that this is their world. Children will become proficient in the use of technological devices whether we introduce them into our classrooms or not because they are surrounded by it. The best that we can do as educators and parents is to make sure to balance the child's world with a variety of activities that will allow the entire child to develop in a healthy and holistic way. Cris Rowan clarifies, "It's important to come together as parents, teachers, and therapists to help society *wake up*. Rather than hugging, playing, roughhousing, and conversing with children, parents are increasingly resorting to providing their children with more television, video games, and the latest iPads and cell phone devices, creating a deep and irreversible chasm between parent and child."

I will state one very strong belief that I have developed over the past ten years as I have watched students be given by their parents (against my advice) what I consider to be not only an inappropriate device, but what I have come to call a *weapon*…the cell phone. Of course, as we know, these smart phones are not just used to phone parents in an emergency, which is the excuse used for purchasing them, but are able to be used to gain access to social networking sites and the Internet. These devices, and the subsequent access to the Internet, are very dangerous territory for young students. I have often asked parents, "Would you just drop off your child in the middle of Times Square and allow them to fend for themselves?" I tell them that they are doing something just as potentially dangerous when they hand their child a cell phone. I have listened to too many lectures and presentations by experts in this field and even law enforcement officers who try to warn young people about the danger of using these devices, for me to not take a strong stand on it. Parents succumb to the pressure of their child not wanting to be *the only one who doesn't have one*! Yet, those same parents are the first ones in my office when their child receives a mean text, which of course, hurts the child's feelings.

These are devices that allow the child's darker nature to be fed because it is so easy to do. You don't even have to be in the same room or look at the person with whom you are angry. Those angry emotions often lead to an impulsive act of sending a mean message to someone. This is not a healthy release of emotions. What will ultimately occur is that the child receiving the angry text will then respond with another angry reaction and so on, until finally either someone steps so far over the line that parents are pulled in or the nasty messages are shared with all of their friends. This compounds the problem and it escalates to a whole different level. We have all seen too many news reports where young people actually kill themselves because of the messages or pictures broadcast to the whole school about them. If this is not a weapon, I don't know what is.

In addition, sexual predators have free reign over these types of sites. It is very frightening to realize that they can gain access to your child through this device and actually determine where they physically are through tracking devices built into the phone. Parents have a false sense of security because they believe that their children are highly responsible and have common sense. Unfortunately, young people entering adolescence do not look ahead to what might happen, they live in the moment, and they have no brakes; even the highly responsible ones with common sense.

The best advice I can give parents is to always remain hyper-vigilant about knowing what your child is doing with his or her device, have rules, and check the device constantly if you are going to allow your child to use it. The Internet world truly is today's version of the *wild west*, and parents must be the guardians of their child's safety at all times.

REFERENCES

1. Rowan, Cris. "The Impact of Technology on the Developing Child." Web blog. 2013. www.huffingtonpost.com/cris-rowan/technology-children-negative-impact_b_3343245.html
2. Taylor, Jim. Psychology Today, Web, "How Technology is Changing the Way Children Think and Focus." Posted Dec. 04, 2012. www.psychologytoday.com/blog/the-power-prime/201212/how-technology-is-changing-the-way-children-think-and-focus.
3. Holtz, Robert Lee. "The Power of Handwriting." The Wall Street Journal. April 5, 2016.

19

Emotional Intelligence

Emotional intelligence (EI), also referred to as emotional quotient (EQ), is a term created by two researchers—Peter Salavoy and John Mayer—and popularized by Dan Goleman in his 1996 book of the same name. The Institute for Health and Human Potential defines EI as the ability to:

- Recognize, understand, and manage our own emotions
- Recognize, understand, and influence the emotions of others[1]

Society is now recognizing how important EI is in relation to being successful in all aspects of our lives. Previous to this emerging field of study, it was assumed that real success depended primarily upon intellectual intelligence or intelligence quotient (IQ). As I would hope that by now, anyone reading this book would be much more aware of how Dr. Montessori incorporated the development of a healthy EI into her method. I will briefly expand on the science of this relatively new field.

The chapter describing adolescents and the stage that their brain is in, is a good preview to the discussion about EI. Let's go back to the review of the amygdala, the source in our brain for all emotional memory. This is the site where our *fight or flight* instinct kicks in when we feel threatened. All of the emotions that we need in order to survive will take precedence over other parts of our brain; in particular, the neo-cortex, or *working memory* part of our brain. When there is a perceived, or real threat to us, we need to act, not think about it. To give an example, if we are walking down a deserted city street and all of a sudden, a knife-wielding attacker jumps out at us, our amygdala immediately goes into action, flooding our brain with chemicals that actually slow down our neo-cortex (or thinking aspects of our brain) to give power to our response to fight or flee. Our heart will start pounding, our palms will start sweating, and we will feel light headed as the blood rushes to our extremities to allow us to run or fight. The adrenaline is kicking in because of the threat. Scientists once thought that a person's intelligence was what would first respond successfully to a threat. Today, we know that the amygdala reacts 1000 times faster to a threat. We go into survival mode. If we think about it logically, in the face of that kind of a threat, it would not serve us well to begin thinking about what kind of knife the attacker was holding, or how this event is going to change your plans for the evening. If we were to survive, other rapid processes would need to take place in order to overcome the situation.

If we look at another scenario much more common for most of us, it may involve a time when we became emotionally upset or angry about something someone said or did to us. Typically, very similar side effects would begin to occur; the chemicals would start to flood your brain so that you are not thinking clearly. Literally, your thinking brain is held hostage so that *it cannot* think clearly. Have you ever said or done something in the height of this emotional state, and then afterwards deeply regretted saying or doing it? You literally ask yourself, "What was I thinking?" Well, literally, you weren't thinking because your amygdala kicked in as a response to feeling threatened in some way. Today, consequences can be even farther reaching when we have email and social networking sites at our disposal. In the height of this emotional state, you respond in an angry or agitated way without thinking, and the damage is done, permanently, and for everyone to see. Peoples' lives, jobs, and reputations have been severely impacted by this with far worse consequences in some cases.

So, how do we get a handle on our emotions, thereby strengthening our EI levels? The first step toward making healthy choices is to learn more about you. Your perceptions of people, situations, and life itself determine your reactions to all of it. This requires some self-reflection and self-observation on our part. It is a very valuable life exercise to think about who we are. What is important to us? What are our values in life? Is there anything worth getting that angry over? And if so, would it make any difference other than hurting ourselves? We need to pay attention to those things or people who push our buttons. Why are those buttons being pushed? If we step back when we are aware of ourselves in the process of becoming upset, it will serve us to reflect, rather than respond. Easier said than done, you may be thinking—and yes, that truism is very accurate. The real truth, however, is that if we sincerely want to change a habit that is not working for us, it takes work. In addition, is this reaction in line with your values, your mission in life? The old adage, "Stop, and count to 10," is a very wise one because we know now that our brain is in the process of turning off the thinking mode, and we need to give it time to return to a normal state. The first rule of thumb is to not respond in any way when emotions are at their peak, whether you are with an adult, a child, or have your finger on the key of your computer or smart phone. Sometimes counting to 10 will not be enough; there have been many times that I am getting close to 100 before my heart starts to return to beating at a normal rate. A very important point to note here is that we must give children the same opportunity to calm down when something has occurred that puts them in an emotional state. They are experiencing exactly the same thing. When we ask a child, or even an adult, "Why did you do that?" chances are they have no idea why they did it. Remember the thinking part of the brain is not functioning in the same way when we feel threatened. This is another reason why it is so important to let children know that they are not their behavior. Children can be very upset and do something wrong or foolish, and the message to them needs to be, "We love you, but we do not like this behavior. When you are calm, we can talk about it." It is critical that both the adult and the child are in a calm state of mind before any discussion or consequences occur. We can then resume the discussion which should include thoughts about whether the behavior exhibited supports our community and personal values, and how we can help ourselves make a different choice in the future when, undoubtedly, our buttons will be pushed again.

In addition to counting to 10, most people do not realize how important it is to breathe deeply in order to restore our brain and body to a normal state. In general, most people breathe in a very shallow way. It is vital to take slow, deep breaths when we are emotionally upset. Slowly inhale through your nose, count to five, hold, and exhale slowly through your mouth to the count of five. This exercise will help to restore a sense of calm almost immediately. Do it as many times as necessary in order to restore a peaceful state of mind and body. It is an excellent habit to acquire and repeat throughout your day, whether you are emotionally upset or not, it is very good for us. I have taught many of our students this same exercise in an effort to help them acquire this habit at an early age.

I will share a story with you about how I am learning to overcome one of my triggers. I have discovered that my patience is always stretched when I am driving. I try playing classical or spa music to help, but all it takes is one driver to cut me off. I feel the rush of chemicals. Instead of reacting, I immediately change the channel in my head. I imagine that the poor person in front of me must be in dire need to have just done something so unsafe. Perhaps a loved one is in the hospital, and they are rushing to their side. I breathe deeply and my calm is restored. This is a good example of how our perceptions determine our reactions. In addition, the calm reaction is in line with my values in life, and to my sincere desire to contribute to peaceful energy in the world. I like to use the metaphor of changing the channel in your head with our students. It is a good visual for all of us; get the remote and change it! What we perceive creates our reality. When we control our perceptions, we create a new reality. So instead of me feeling irritated or angry that someone was a careless and unsafe driver, I created the perception that there was a critical need and my response was one of sympathy and patience. Many of our students have responded very well to this metaphor...changing the channel is something to which they can relate. Students have asked me, "What channel do I change it to?" I tell them that they need to create the different channel choices in their heads because everyone is very different and may need different channels. Some suggestions I have given them to think about are: favorite music, a favorite setting, a place where they feel safe or that they love, a favorite time with their family or parents, a sport, their pets, their friends, or to God, if they are religious, etc. I also like to suggest a gratitude channel. What are you grateful for? I want them to create the habit of switching their thoughts to something positive. The more we train ourselves to focus on positive images and things for which we are grateful, we create a habit that will help us deal with our emotions and life in general. Think about things you do have in your life, rather than what you don't. A very amazing thing will happen, the more you are grateful for what you do have, the more you will receive for which to be grateful. This healthier state of mind leads to a healthier physical state.

> *"We can complain because rose bushes have thorns,*
> *or rejoice because thorn bushes have roses."*
>
> —Abraham Lincoln

Once we are aware of how important EI is to us as individuals, the next step is understanding that it is important to everyone else as well. Everyone else is going through the same challenges as we are. They have their perceptions, and they may be very different from ours. To return for a moment to my example, when I am in the car with my husband, and someone cuts him off, he will react in a very angry manner. I have tried sharing my perception and he looks at me as if I have two heads. He chooses to stay in an angry place, and of course, the results are unpleasant. We have to make the choice to change a habit. If we are all willing to look at our individual perceptions as being unique to our own lens and view of the world, then we need to understand and accept the same about others. We have to be willing to step into the shoes of another and view life from their lens, even if it is momentarily. I have discovered that almost everyone who comes across our path is some sort of a teacher for us. Sometimes those teachers are obviously positive influences and other times, they are like thorns in our side. If there is a person who always pushes your buttons, I would suggest you reflect upon why that is so. What is it that we need to do in order to grow as a more tolerant, compassionate, or patient person? In order to build relationships, we must find common ground and communicate from there. The common ground is that we are all in this life together, and it is in everyone's best interest to learn how to not only get along, but work at understanding each other and contribute to the good of all.

Our Montessori classrooms nurture the development of EI for every member of the community, children and adults alike. We experience on a daily basis social and emotional interaction among everyone there. It is not easy building community, but it is certainly worth the effort. When we experience children helping each other, caring about each other, looking for positive solutions to the daily challenges that arise, and the willingness to forgive and move on, we are getting a glimpse of how the world could be. Our hope is that these children will go out into the world and create the change we want to see for them and every person on this planet.

CONFESSION:

Here is an area in which I have been challenged for most of my childhood and early adult life. It seemed like such a peripheral area of life; not something that anyone ever seemed to give a name to, or initiated any kind of serious study. I always felt as if I was on the outside looking in; it seemed to me as if everyone else had figured this out and somehow, I was lacking. Everyone else seemed to naturally know how to speak to each other in a way that was effective; and seemingly able to handle their emotions in a socially respectable way. I had a temper, was quick to anger and judgment, and was highly critical of myself and others; I tended to be a perfectionist who had a hard time being wrong, I liked to control things, and I was always fearful that someone would think I was not good enough or smart enough. I was fearful that they would discover my inadequacies; therefore I put on a mask of not caring what others thought. I would remain silent more often than I should have, believing that it was better to remain silent and appear less than intelligent, than to speak and confirm it. Fortunately, as my life experiences and challenges grew, I was able to find my way through them by my work with children in Montessori classrooms, and my spiritual growth. It was only recently that I discovered there is actually some serious study of this facet of life and development. I am intrigued by it and am acquiring a new passion to discover more about it. A new teacher emerges.

REFERENCE

1. Institute for Health and Human Potential, "What is Emotional Intelligence?" WEB http://www.ihhp.com/meaning-of-emotional-intelligence.

Photo Gallery

Figure 1 Practical life leads to the joy of discovery on the face of an early childhood student

Figure 2 A lower elementary student doing skip counting and squaring with the short bead chains

Figure 3   A lower elementary class in action

Figure 4   Elementary students tending to their gardens

Figure 5   Students working in the Peace Garden

Figure 6 Upper elementary classroom

Figure 7 Middle school students in New York City participating in Montessori Model United Nations

Figure 8   Middle school students in group work

Figure 9   Middle school students caring for the barn animals

Figure 10 Middle school students experiencing a Civil War reenactment in Charleston, SC

Section V:
Reflections on the Montessori Experience

Reflections on the Montessori Experience from Students, Alumni, Alumnae, Parents, Montessori Educators, and Specialists

As one reads the passionate and sincere words from these Montessori students, we cannot help but hear in their own words how Montessori has impacted their lives so deeply and permanently. Their words should be more powerful than any of mine for the reader because they are coming directly from the children's hearts and souls. I have hoped to tell you how and why Montessori works, but their words show you how Montessori has actually transformed their lives. I did not grow up in it, I have merely studied and practiced this philosophy; but for the students, they have lived it, it is part of their being. Starting with the very youngest students to the oldest, they recognize the intangible elements that make them feel safe, free to be themselves, and eager to learn: the freedom, the peaceful setting, open-mindedness, creativity, compassion, love, acceptance, respect, and kindness. The overwhelming message from all of them was one of gratitude for the Montessori environment and the ability to learn in their own way, at their own pace, and for the support and guidance of their teachers. Their innate goodness resonates with the loving, caring, and positive energy generated in Montessori environments. Their words say it so eloquently. To me, these are the most inspiring words in this book.

I also want to mention that even though these reflections are from my school to ease the collection process, I in no way feel that the children's thoughts are indicative of the experience the children are having *only* at our school. These reflections could be from any authentic Montessori school anywhere because of the similar experiences the children would be having.

Earlier in this book, I talked about the importance of field trips. One of the field trips our upper elementary students get to take is to Sea Camp. Sea Camp is located in Florida's Big Pine Key where the students go to experience hands-on interaction with marine life and related environmental studies. The students spend three days immersed in marine biology studies, and two nights learning to be a cooperative and supportive community member on the road. Some of the upper elementary students mention Sea Camp in their reflections.

EARLY CHILDHOOD STUDENTS (3–6 YEARS OF AGE)

"Montessori is when you water the tomatoes and beans everyday and you look at them for ten minutes because our teacher told us that plants need love." (Rocco, age 3)

"Montessori means when you do not go home without hugging your teachers." (Arielle, age 4)

"When I'm home sick I know that my friends will wish me well during our morning circle time. That is helping me to get better faster." (Antonia, age 5)

"Montessori is when you have meetings like grownups and talk about serious problems like life cycles." (Ellie, age 6)

"To learn and include everybody and be nice and to listen to the teachers." (Tallulah, age 5)

"Montessori is when you help to take care of Mother Nature and save animals in danger. We worked very hard to keep the Monarch butterfly and to make a bond in our school garden. When I see a butterfly now, I'm a little proud." (Gianna, age 6)

"Love and peace and working together in kindness." (Layla, age 6)

"To be kind and have love in your heart and respect the other children's wishes." (Lydia, age 5)

"Be kind to the lessons because they are one of a kind." (Charlotte, age 5)

"What I love about my classroom is we are exploring everyday something in nature. We found dinosaur fossils, snake skin, and special rocks in our own playground. Our teacher is not always sure about it, but she is helping us to do research about our treasures." (Jun, age 6)

"Montessori has a lot of lessons and it's a lot of fun." (Marcos, age 4)

"In a Montessori school we plant seeds and go to the garden to observe our plants and water them." (Katie, age 4)

"In Montessori you get to help your friends and teach them." (Ray, age 6)

"I love being in a Montessori school because I get to do science, math, read books, and build things." (Marco, age 5)

"Montessori is when you come to school in a bad mood and your friends and your teachers make you laugh." (Nicholas, age 6)

"It is the best school ever in my life. I didn't learn in my old school. Thank you for this school. It is fun." (Jacob, age 6)

LOWER ELEMENTARY STUDENTS (6–9 YEARS OF AGE)

"Montessori teaches you to be a problem solver and a peacemaker. I have been in Montessori for six years. My favorite lesson in Cultural is the Puzzle Maps that you trace, color, and label. I have done all of the maps." (Isabella, age 9)

"I feel great about Montessori because you do not need to sit in your desk all day. My brother is in public school and his teachers are not the same as the teachers here. I feel smart because when I was at my last school, I wasn't like myself how I am today, but when I attended SQ, it felt amazing, I felt like I was a new child." (Noah, age 9)

"Montessori has taught me how to be a peacemaker and it has changed me by showing me how to be a better person, swimmer, and most of all, a good writer. It has also taught me how to be a better friend. I wish even when I am an adult I could still be here." (Selene, age 8)

"I love Montessori because you don't have to sit and look at a board all day. I've been in Montessori for almost three years. My mom always had trouble helping me to read. Montessori taught me how to read and now I read chapter books. Montessori has helped me improve so much. My favorite Montessori lessons are the Checkerboard and animal research." (Morgan, age 8)

"To me, Montessori is learning to be kind and helpful. I am very grateful that Dr. Montessori made Montessori. My favorite material is the Test Tubes but the material that helped me the most is the Stamp Game. The Stamp Game helped me with all operations, static and dynamic. My favorite subject is math." (Marin, age 9)

"Montessori has made my life better by teaching me how to be a better person within." (Alex, age 8)

"I love Montessori because you're around people of all different ages. My life here is changing because the teachers are helping me learn by all different ways; they are fun, amazing, great ways! I also love Montessori because we do not have a lot of homework. Montessori is the best school I have ever been to because we don't have to sit the whole time, we are allowed to move and walk around in the class. I wish that there were no weekends because of Montessori. We learn how to be a peacemaker and to love everyone and not to cause or make fights. I love Montessori. Peace, Love and Joy! (Sage, age 9)

"I have been in Montessori my whole life. Montessori means love, family, friendship, and community. I like working independently." (Mia, age 9)

"Montessori is my favorite type of school. I have been in this Montessori school for my whole school life. I learned Algebra and all the operations in this school. I am going to fourth grade next year and it's going to be awesome. Montessori means to me that you learn and get better at everything, and I did." (Sam, age 9)

"I like Montessori because it changes my life, it makes me feel good. It makes me be a better person. I learn math, language, SRA, SSR, zoology, botany, and geometry. I love my teachers. I met lots of friends. In my old school, I didn't learn much and Montessori changed my life. I learned a lot, it changed everything. It is the best thing I could ever have. I love Montessori." (Christian, age 9)

"I love Montessori because it teaches me how to be a better person. Now I am doing better at math. I love to do SRA. It is very fun. I love this school. It makes me feel free. I made a lot of friends. I love doing grammar box and map skills." (Marcelo, age 8)

"I feel really happy when I come to school here and it makes me feel good. I learned about nature and nouns, verbs, adjectives, and more. I learned a lot more than I did before. I learned a lot about peace, love, nature. This school is fun and enjoyable. I feel happy here and excited." (Fenix, age 8)

"I have been to other schools, but Montessori is by far the best." (Farris, age 9)

"Montessori makes me feel free and happy because I get to choose my lessons." (Brielle, age 8)

"Montessori to me means freedom. Montessori spreads love everywhere. I love Dr. Montessori. She filled this area with love." (Tamar, age 7)

"Montessori means to me to learn and have fun with lessons and doing your job. We have freedom to walk around. My favorite lesson is cultural because it is fun and I learn a lot." (Shiwon, age 9)

"It means something special to me because it is free and happy." (Cristina, age 7)

"You have more freedom. You do not have to sit at desks." (Malu, age 7)

UPPER ELEMENTARY STUDENTS (9–12 YEARS OF AGE)

"I am new to Montessori. I have been at a public school for all of my life, and I was nervous when I first came here. At public school, you get assigned a spot and do everything the exact same way that everyone else does it. Montessori school opened my eyes. I was exposed to freedom. Here, you can choose what lesson to do, and when you finish your work, you can do fun things, like use the microscopes. Even though I have only been here for a year, I feel like I found my second home." (Raeya, age 10)

"I like the school because I can pick my lessons and sit whenever I want. Montessori means to me that older kids and younger kids get to stay and learn together. I want to say Thank You to Maria Montessori for creating this idea. The materials help me master things I need help with. The teachers are very nice and they help you learn all the things you need to know for the future. Every week we get new jobs and we learn new things that we will have to do when we are older like: feeding the animals, taking out the trash, and organizing shelves. All the specials are fun but the ones that I like most are Art and Music. When you are in Upper, you have lots of projects to do. They are all fun, even the big ones, like the Science Fair or History Fair." (Victoria, age 11)

"There are many things that I like about Montessori. What I love most are the teachers. I love them because whenever a student needs help, you tell a teacher and they help you. The teachers make me feel safe, loved, and like they care for the students. I also love that you can work anywhere you want, like on the floor, or on the tables instead of desks. I also like the lessons that we have. Whenever we have a lesson, we put the lesson on the rug. I like the rug because I get to use my hands; it helps me learn." (Chloe, age 10)

"Sea Camp taught many Montessori lessons that you need to succeed in life. It taught me that not everything in life comes out as you would want, for example, we were separated into different groups. Even though I didn't get everyone I wanted in my group, we ended up having a great time. We became closer and trusted each other more. I am an independent person and it requires a lot of patience when you have a partner and when you have a lot of patience, you have a great time! Being away from my parents means taking caution, being responsible, and when you are, it can be a life-changing, fun experience! Last year was my first year being away from my parents and I was having a hard time dealing with it. But the people in my group were kind, selfless, and supporting. We even got to call our parents at the end of the day. During this trip, I was prepared. It turned out to be a fantastic trip which surprised me because it was educational and fun at the same time! After this trip, I am more ambitious, brave, and active. Jumping in the freezing cold water just means you must push yourself to do things. Swimming with sharks always sounded scary, ridiculous, and extremely foolish beforehand. I know you shouldn't assume the worst in something until you've tried it. Sea Camp allowed me to use my Montessori education by taking risks and exploring the ocean and the world around me." (Alison, age 10)

"To me, Montessori means more freedom and choices of work. I like how we get more field trips and how it is more about time management to fit in the work. It was very weird when I first went to class but I adapted to the freedom and the freedom is nice. Now it is nice because it is easier for me to learn things I want to learn. Now I am able to fold a paper any way I want to, because in my old school I was not allowed to and I got yelled at." (Davi, age 10)

"Montessori has a completely different way of teaching (and my teachers are a bonus). I get to go at my own pace, and even skip up to sixth grade level math. The only bad thing about Montessori is nothing, although I have so much work to do. I first started in 1st grade, and when I arrived there, it was easy making friends; in fact, I made friends the second I went there. I have a lot more to talk about, but I need to go back to the awesomeness of Summit-Questa." (Raphael, age 10)

"Sea Camp was a lot of fun and taught me things that are the key to a happy future, like the responsibility when you are away from your parents. When people in your group are having a hard time, you should take a minute, and slow down. Why rush, what's the hurry? You should make the person feel safe and comfortable. When you do slow down, help someone out, it will make you feel good inside. Normally jumping into a pool of sharks is not a good idea, but in certain instances you should open up and let go of your fears. It turned out to be a great experience…even if the water is freezing cold!!!! Sea Camp also taught me to be more adventurous and brave and safe at the same time! The people who worked there were very friendly and welcoming. They made me feel at home. The lessons they taught were hands-on, just like our Montessori environment. The Casipoias were fascinating. We wrote about them just like we would do in school. The people in Sea Camp care about their environment, and respect every living and nonliving thing. They are very Montessorian. In all, Sea Camp was awesome and I had a great time!" (Sarah, age 10)

"I love Montessori because you have the freedom to choose what you would like to work on. I also like how the lessons really teach you how to do the work. My favorite year was third grade because you would get to go on field trips that no one else got to go on." (Jesse, age 10)

"My time spent at Sea Camp was a once-in-a-lifetime trip and such an amazing hands-on experience. As a Montessorian, this trip opened up my heart to nature and the ocean. I learned so much and I wish we stayed longer. I was taught at school to always do your best and try everything. I enjoyed living with other people and hanging out with my buddy. At Sea Camp, I learned to appreciate everyone and everything around me. All the stuff I saw, including: coral, fish, squid, algae, sponge, and so much more, has taught me to care about the environment, as I have learned as a Montessorian. I wasn't always a Montessorian, I switched in third grade and I have learned twice as much and twice as fast than I did at my old school. I haven't been a Montessorian for very long, but I have adapted quickly and really enjoy it. I can't wait to learn more! There is so much I wouldn't have learned if I didn't come here. As a Montessorian, I learned about: decimals, states and capitals, animal and plant cells, how to research and write a paper, how to read in front of people, how to be independent, and how to be empathetic." (Mollie, age 11)

"I have been in Montessori since I was three years old, and I am going to tell you two reasons why I like it. The first reason is that the students are able to be involved and encourage fundraisers; for example, we have Pajama Day to help raise money for distressed kids. The second reason is I get to enjoy the school pets and barn animals. My favorite school pet is Simba, one of the school cats, but they have other animals. Simba is an old cat but he is quite beautiful, and he is also a very funny cat. One of the funny things Simba does is stand in the car line and act like he runs the school. Those are a few of the reasons I love Summit Questa." (Lauren, age 10)

"Montessori changed my whole life. I learned so much during the last eight years I was in this school." (Ariel, age 11)

MIDDLE SCHOOL STUDENTS (11–14 YEARS OF AGE)

"Montessori means many things. You cannot simply tell someone what Montessori is just by one explanation. It means things like the freedom to be creative, the acceptance to be different, and the art of learning. In Montessori, they let you be bold and different. It allows you to be creative and it enhances all your styles of learning. You can learn more, and have the freedom to do most anything. It's an amazing program that should be used more often." (Olivia, age 11)

"Montessori means diversity. In our Montessori community, we encourage differences and embrace our creativity. We are free thinkers and individuals who are both caring and creative, as well as intelligent and responsible. Montessori is a wonderful opportunity for young people of all ages. I would also like to thank Dr. Montessori for creating this wonderful style of teaching, as well as being a good role model for young women of today." (Sofia, age 12)

"Montessori to me is the ability and privilege for the child to choose their learning path and/or work ethic. You basically put the children in charge. They are teaching themselves almost. The teachers are here basically to guide you. I would like to thank Dr. Montessori for creating such a wonderful learning opportunity for me. Coming to this Montessori school has changed my life for the better." (Adam, age 11)

"Montessori means that I can be me. That I can be the kind of person I want to be. I want to make a difference in this world. I can do that because Montessori has given me the skills I need to do that. That's why Montessori is not only a good education system, but vital in order to create a world in which everyone is created equal and enjoys life." (Aidon, age 13)

"To me, Montessori means being compassionate and considerate to those around you. It means cooperating with others. It means that you should do the right thing, rather than what you want to do. Montessori is how you deal with situations so that you aren't the only one getting what you want. I would tell Dr. Montessori that she created a foundation that affected the generations to come in a positive way. She changed the way some of us think of the world and those who live in it. She helped us open our eyes and see a world where people can respect their environment and people." (Steven, age 11)

"Montessori means to have fun, learn, and be taught with kindness. It also means to learn many things in many ways and subjects." (Emerson, age 11)

"Montessori means that you are free to learn whatever way is best for an individual. In Montessori, the numbers are so small that you know everyone, and most importantly, the teachers get to know the students. Montessori has helped me out in many ways because I am a quiet student and it is sometimes hard for me to show who I really am. Through this program, the teachers know how the students learn and their abilities. I believe through this, a student can learn more and it is better at their own pace. I don't know how I would have survived in a different environment. I believe this program is the best way to learn." (Liliana, age 14)

"It means closeness, a family, freedom to actually learn, caring, compassionate, and is enjoyable." (Emilee, age 14)

"The impact that Dr. Montessori made makes the soul stronger." (Penelope, age 12)

"For me, Montessori means to go at your own pace. If you're having trouble with something, they help you. Thank you for creating an environment where kids can be not only better educated, but be themselves. Thank you for creating more open-minded teachers, more open-minded students, and a more open-minded system. Thank you for giving students the opportunity to be free from desks. Now, we can be free." (Luciana, age 12)

"Montessori is the passion of our lives, the creativity of our minds. Montessori is a safe, wonderful community where we can be ourselves and learn to love others. I am so grateful for this Montessori environment where I can grow into my own potential." (Sofia, age 11)

"To me, Montessori means *think*. It is an experience that teaches you life skills instead of teaching you what to think. It teaches me to analyze situations. It teaches me to use my brain, not just my memory. Montessori is not a program. It is a gift. From this experience, I have been learning to use my brain, instead of just passing a huge test. It will help me survive in the real world." (Luca, age 12)

"It means that I can have peace, I don't have to be bullied. I can have fun while I am learning. I get to do fun group projects with my friends, or I can even make new friends. I get to learn while being entertained. I would say thank you to Dr. Montessori for making these schools. I respect my teachers and I love my school." (Marat, age 13)

ALUMNAE AND ALUMNI

Anna Biegelsen, Attorney in Washington, D.C., Graduate of Harvard Law School, and St. John's College, Annapolis, Maryland, Summit-Questa class of 1999.

"I went to Montessori school from preschool through 8th grade and I attribute much of my success since then to my Montessori education.

"From an early age, Montessori students learn to be independent, methodical thinkers, choosing which lessons to do and completing each before selecting the next. Over time, the lessons teach everything from the ABCs and 123s, to grammar and advanced mathematics. Later on, the students develop a teamwork approach to learning in more complex subjects. We had no lectures, no busy-work. My middle school algebra *class* involved me and a small group of students reading the text together; working through the problems on a white board, and relying on one another to progress through the material. No one was going to give us the answers; we needed to figure it out on our own.

"These days, I work as an attorney in Washington, D.C. The skills I use everyday—analyzing cases, problem solving, persuasive writing and speaking, and team management—are rooted in my background as a Montessori student. Montessori taught me to learn independently, to listen with intent, and to ask the right questions, and perhaps most importantly, to teach others. And of course, I always push in my chair at the end of a meeting."

Leigh Finnegan-Hosey, Chaplain in Residence, Georgetown University, Washington, D.C., Summit-Questa class of 2001.

"My immersion into Montessori education began in preschool and lasted through 8th grade. From the beginning, I was asked to work alongside students who neither looked like me, nor thought like me. Our teachers asked us to appreciate our differences and to be open to new perspectives, especially when these perspectives challenge the status quo.

"In my experience, this profoundly inclusive approach to learning allows children to experience the transformational power of empathy and vulnerability in both interpersonal relationships and the public arena. As an adult, I have seen these values play out in my work around interfaith dialogue. When I show up as my authentic self, it creates a space for others to feel safe being comfortably and authentically who they are. In these kinds of spaces, real understanding is possible.

"In a similar vein, Montessori teaches children how to work cooperatively with their peers. As an adult, my comfort with collaboration and ability to communicate clearly has proven to be a real asset. Employers want to hire people who they know can mediate conflict, contribute to the collective vision, and recognize when to ask for help. These abilities not only make well-rounded employees, but also well-rounded leaders, parents, and social movements.

"While all of these aspects of Montessori education are invaluable, perhaps the most precious gift I received was the gift of unfettered creativity. Whether it came by way of asking questions, crafting a piece of art, or working together to solve a problem, our minds were challenged to think outside of the box; to create that which had yet to be created. I was taught to see the world beyond black and white categories, to embrace nuance, and to do all of this in the pursuit of peace. Seeing the world and its many problems as dynamic, rather that static, has helped me believe that things can and will get better, and that I have a role to play in the creation of that new world."

Lee Jewell was in the first Summit-Questa graduating class in 1998. He attended the University of Central Florida before joining the U.S. Air Force in 2006, finishing his degree in Intelligence Studies from the Community College of the Air Force in 2014. Lee is currently serving as a Warrant Officer in the United States Army. He is stationed at Fort Gordon, Georgia, where he works as the Officer in Charge of the Counter-Unmanned Aerial Vehicle Team, and as the Executive Officer for D Company 297th Military Intelligence Battalion.

"While attending Questa Middle School, I used to say, 'Everyone has the same amount of intelligence, it just shows in different ways.' That statement was why the Montessori curriculum was so beneficial to me. I was able to learn and grow at my own pace, soaking in every last bit of knowledge and focusing on subjects that I felt passionately about. The emphasis on independence, freedom, and child development allowed me access to an individualized plan—as no two people learn the same—and I was able to perform at a higher standard than I otherwise would have. Early on, I developed a love for education and improving myself; and that continues to this day.

"I remember vividly so much of my time at Summit-Questa that it would be impossible to touch on everything; however, some of my fondest memories were the amazing field trips. As a child, my perception was one of having fun and getting away from parents and school work, but reflecting back as an adult, I have begun to understand more and more how those trips taught me life lessons. On one particular trip to Washington, D.C., I was the student who took the lead on navigating the Metro system. I see this now as my teachers recognizing a talent for understanding unfamiliar places and trusting me to lead the class in the right direction. I use facets of this life lesson in the military today. Understanding people's strengths and correctly leveraging them in the right positions makes for a very effective team. Using these trips as interactive lessons to explore the world around us in order to learn are the cornerstones of Montessori.

"Academically, I was set up for a successful career early on. The emphasis and educational model for core competencies changed how I performed and improved my understanding of many subjects, but especially math. Using physical lessons and tools to explain abstract math concepts gave me a visual roadmap far ahead of my peers. As a military signals intelligence analyst, my job is to deconstruct and analyze radio waves within the electromagnetic spectrum. Often this is done with graphical representations of radio waves and is built upon a complex mathematical formula called the radar range equation.

"Many of these reflections may be subjective as the memories are from that of a young child. One certainty though is that the faculty at Summit-Questa middle school is without a doubt, the most passionate teachers I have had the pleasure to learn from. In every action and lesson I can see that the sole purpose was to make me a better, smarter student. They truly loved and cared for the students and that should be evident by the fact that I maintain such high regard for them and contact with them almost 20 years later."

David Levine, Attorney in South Florida, University of Central Florida, Boston University Law School, Summit-Questa class of 1999.

"It's hard to pinpoint when I first realized that Montessori education, and particularly my time at Summit-Questa Montessori School, was something really special. It may have been my first year in a traditional high school, confined to a desk with two-hour class periods, finding some sense of freedom spending my volunteer hours back at SQ on Fridays. It may have been when I was in college, wondering how my former classmates and teachers were doing, and working back at SQ as a camp counselor and tutor during the summers. Regardless of when the realization occurred, there is no doubt that it was a crucial cornerstone in my development. It instilled a sense of community in me which still persists, almost 30 years after I started there. It may be that sense of community which truly sets Montessori apart from traditional teaching styles. We are family."

Christopher McMullen, Business Manager and Project Coordinator East Coast, Eaton Lighting Division, Aurora, Colorado, Summit-Questa class of 2001.

"My Montessori school experiences from the early age of four until high school have shaped the way I see the world. In the 15 years since, it is clear that Montessori education continues to be an integral part of my life. On a recent vacation to Australia and New Zealand, I was reminded of the many amazing school trips that instilled in me an appreciation for the outdoors and different cultures, thus expanding my horizons. These many trips, ropes courses, and other activities were not only fun, but they helped us develop life-long skills and grow into independent, responsible leaders. I also remember the many group projects that we had to do starting in elementary and continuing through middle school.

"Starting at such a young age helped me to learn effective communication, team building, problem solving, time management, and many other skills that helped me in high school and beyond. At work, as a business manager, I am responsible for a team of employees that requires effective communication, collaboration, and creativity. I credit much of my proficiency with these skills to growing up in a Montessori school. Of course, I constantly work on perfecting these skills; however, I am grateful for the great start that my Montessori school gave me."

Skylar Wilson, MA, is founder of Wild Awakenings, LLC, an organization dedicated to Rites of Passage and transformational education. He is an adjunct professor at the Institute of Ecology and Spirituality in California and leads workshops and intercultural rituals around the country. Skylar was in the first Summit-Questa middle school graduating class of 1998.

"I am deeply grateful for the ways in which the Montessori philosophy and curriculum has supported my journey of coming to know myself and my vocation at large. Montessori was a huge help in guiding my process of self-discovery that eventually led to my work as a wilderness Rites of Passage guide, a cosmologist, and a leader of intercultural rituals for groups as large as 1,400 people.

"I didn't fully realize how much of a help Montessori was until I was talking to my mentor and coworker, Rev. Matthew Fox, in preparation for a talk that I gave to the Jungian Society of Sarasota a couple of years ago. He asked me, 'When did you first become aware of your interest in the human soul and its relationship to the cosmos?' Memories from Montessori came flooding back. Memories of playing, self-guided exercises, reflection time, meditations, creative writing, Native American stories of origin, art, and field trips to places rich in natural and cultural history. It was then that I remembered just how important Montessori was in shaping and supporting my sensitivities and core passions.

"My early experiences of Montessori's holistic curriculum were held within a space of practice and play that encouraged my essence to find me and grow into its own shape. Montessori played a key role in guiding my heart and mind in their attractions. Montessori is where I first practiced listening to my intuitive voice as well as to the voices of others in a participatory, circular format—a skill handed down to us by an array of Native American traditions.

"Montessori is one of the few curriculums that practices cosmology by prioritizing each student's direct connection between herself and the cosmos.

Its experiential curriculum embodies Einstein's reflection that *imagination is more important than knowledge*, as well as the medieval alchemical axiom: 'As above, so below,' that guided many early explorers of science in their search for understanding and integration.

"Montessori sees each child as a mirror of the whole, carrying a unique and important purpose. Maria Montessori believed that each human comes into this world with something to contribute to it. Her goal was to assist students in finding the tools to navigate this complex task.

"Montessori gave me permission at a young age to explore a life-long inquiry into my own unique nature, and the ways that I fit into the earthly and cosmic systems in which I am now consciously connected. In coming to know these origins of myself, I have discovered and rediscovered my own context and purpose while developing sustainable and life-enhancing ways of being human through the practices of ecology, psychology, and cosmology. Montessori watered the seeds that grew into my fascination with life's evolving creativity and the human potential movement."

Kalysta Strauss, high school student and award-winning writer, 2015 Gold Key, Silver Key, and HM-Scholastic writing awards; 2013 Scholastic Honorable Mention writing award; Summit-Questa class of 2013.

"*Montessori*: For me, the word swirls through my mind reminiscing on the best years of my life and the most important lessons I will ever learn. When I was asked to write about Montessori practices and impacts on lives, I knew immediately that I had to do it in order to share the profound impact it has had on my life; but it has taken me over a month to find the words to share that impact efficiently. Montessori, among many fond memories and touching experiences, makes me recall three specific, seemingly random words: rugs, circles, and pigs.

"*Rugs*: The literal ground work for my Montessori education. The rugs not only taught me to keep a central place for activities and to make sure I cleaned up after myself, but also taught me an indispensable lesson. The motion of rolling the rugs took time and had to be done correctly, this moment of peace between lessons has instilled a skill in me for which I am forever grateful. I have learned that sometimes we must take a moment to fully contemplate our actions. It is important not to jump to conclusions (or between lessons) and to make sure we use discretion, patience, and thought when we act or speak (or in order to roll up the rug correctly). I have a unique ability to know when and how to pause, reflect, and act responsibly when making decisions or interacting with other people. This skill—an important one that helps me not only to manage my anger but to change my entire attitude toward a situation in order to handle it more sufficiently—was gifted to me through the simple, engrossing activity of rolling the rug; of making sure the ends line up; of taking a break and reflecting.

"*Circles*: A unique perspective on classroom hierarchy. Circle time was not just a good way to gather students and give group lessons, but it also gave students an interesting vantage point on respect and equality. The balance of teacher and student, the shift to a place of sameness when both adult and child are seated on the floor, displays a vital lesson on how respect and authority are two very different ideas. The authority and guidance of Montessori teachers are the reasons students acquire such deep and wide-ranging education, but the respect the teachers receive is entirely earned—not forced. While obviously our teachers deserve our respect, their choosing to sit with us on the floor and be our equals gave us the opportunity to learn that they deserve our respect in the same way everyone else in that circle—and in life—deserves it; not simply because they hold power over us, but because they are people.

"*Pigs*: This is where I learned a lesson in how to care, cooperate, and change hay. Since my first days of Pre-K at my Montessori school, I was captivated by the goats and pigs on our campus. On beautiful days, my tiny class would line up and duckling our way to the barn behind our teacher. We got to watch the cohabitation of the pigs, goats, chickens, and cats that spent their time in our school barn and sometimes even witness the chaos of the middle school kids' attempt to walk and feed them. Once I was old enough to tend to the animals myself, I quickly learned why the event was so chaotic. Managing to clean the dirty troughs and fill the empty bowls while not being rammed by the wild goats was quite a chore, but more than that, it was an experience that showed me the value of working with and respecting the space of others. Each person who worked in the barn depended upon the other people there to fully complete their task in order for the job to be well done. Remembering that we were guests within the barn, there only as the animals allowed, was important for us to do our jobs to the maximum benefit of the workers and the animals. These practices taught us that when working toward a common goal, it is important to help and rely on those working with you.

"From the practical life lesson of washing a dish to the extensive and paramount understanding of respect gained from working within the school community, Montessori taught me some of the most valuable and beneficial lessons I have ever learned. I loved my years as a Montessori student and look back on that time of growth and education as one of the most beneficial and beautiful parts of my life. I owe some of the most intrinsic parts of my character to the amazing lessons that Montessori teaching guided me through—both those taught in the classroom and those instilled by the world around me."

PARENTS: REFLECTIONS ON MONTESSORI EDUCATION

Sherry McMullen, Montessori parent.

"Like many other parents, I was not sure if Montessori was right for my children. Now, after having four children attend a Montessori school from early childhood through 8th grade, I can confidently answer that question. All four of my children have very different personalities and different capabilities, but all four have strongly benefited from a Montessori education. I am so proud to be their mother and to see what wonderful young adults they have become.

"I have so many memories of their accomplishments: from cutting a piece of bread at age 3 (I would never have let them do that at home at such a young age), to learning their sounds, reading their first books at age 3 and 4, correcting me when I did not describe a ball-shaped item as a sphere, completing the 100 board, circle time, attending their walk-around-the sun (birthday celebration), and how they cared, and most importantly, how they respected their classmates and nature.

"In elementary, they all made tremendous strides in math and reading, along with using their language arts skills to work on numerous projects. Of course, field trips went from day trips to week-long trips in middle school. These trips were not only educational, but helped them to become more independent and strengthened their ability to work and live with others. Throughout the years, they not only increased their knowledge in the educational arena, but they learned the importance of completing their work, being proud of their accomplishments, always being able to communicate with a teacher, working in teams, preparing projects, and learning to speak in front of others.

"Middle school was strong in academics, but also held them responsible for their own work by helping them to perfect their time management and leadership skills. Being located on a 10-acre campus, my children were able to learn to appreciate nature in all its forms (live pond, on-campus barn animals, edible gardens, and beautiful trees).

"I was totally amazed when they were ending their 8th grade year. They could now get up on a stage in front of hundreds of people and could speak as if they were only in front of their family and friends. They all entered high school confidently, able to communicate with their teachers, capable of arranging their extracurricular activities and sports, arrange for a tutor if they wanted extra support, and challenging themselves by successfully taking dual-enrollment and AP classes. With four children, you would think that I would have had to go to their high schools to arrange something for them, but I never had to. The only time I went to their high school was to attend a sporting event, an extracurricular activity they were involved in, awards they received, and of course, to attend their graduations. They took total control of their lives in high school and handled all of the challenges on their own. Unlike some other parents, I never had to worry about my children going off to college, as I knew they were ready to be on their own. Of course, I missed every one of them and still do!

"As to where they are now: the oldest graduated with a dual degree in finance and real estate, is a successful business manager, and is married and living in Colorado; my next child has a business and law degree and is a partner in a law firm; my daughter will graduate with a business degree and is also pursuing a future in nursing; and my youngest is entering college this summer. All four had excellent grades, but what is more important to me is that they all have strong ethics, respect for nature and others, are leaders, are happy, and have a strong love for life."

Monica Berwig, Montessori parent.

"My introduction to Montessori came during my search for a Pre-K3 program for my son. My husband had attended a Montessori school during his early childhood years (Pre-K4 through Kindergarten) and was adamant that it helped shape the person he became. He urged me to research the option for our son. Although I was incredibly skeptical that any preschool education could leave such a lasting impression, I had nothing to lose by investigating it further.

"When we first toured Summit-Questa, my husband was pleasantly surprised by the quaint appearance of the campus—the way the outdoors seemed to meld perfectly with the buildings and how the farm animals that were being tended to by the middle school students brought a touch of the *rural* to our otherwise urban lives. I, however, was not going to be taken in by a few pigs, goats, and blooming trees. This was my son's education we were talking about! I wanted to know about language and math and when he should start reading! So the school set an appointment for us to observe one of the early childhood classrooms in action.

"One week later, I entered a Montessori classroom for the first time. I was immediately struck by the controlled energy in the room. Children were everywhere—working on rugs on the floor, sitting at tables together, at the sink washing their hands. I had never seen a classroom quite like this. It seemed chaotic, yet organized; noisy, but not loud. And then I saw a young girl playing with a very curious set of beads on the floor. What was she doing? The teacher came over to us and explained the Montessori concept of using beads to represent units in math. She showed us how a simple vertical cluster of 3 beads can be used to give the child a concrete example of the number 3; how a chain of three 3-bead clusters can be used to introduce the child to multiples of 3; and how folding that chain into a square introduces a child to the concept that 3 is the square root of 9. I was blown away! Why hadn't I been taught math like that? We were shown many similar Montessori materials in the areas of language and practical life, but by that time, I was sold. We enrolled our son that day and never looked back.

"Now that my son is finishing up his 3rd grade year in lower elementary, I cannot imagine him spending his days in anything but a Montessori environment. He has truly flourished during his six years there. As I expected after our classroom observation, my son was immediately engaged by the Montessori materials. He has excellent math and language skills because of the amazing materials he has to work with and the thoughtful and deliberate way they have been introduced to him by his Montessori trained teachers. Yet some of the most impactful benefits of his Montessori education are things I had not anticipated. Living and learning in a Montessori environment has taught him the importance of working well with others and taught him to value and celebrate the differences that make him and his classmates unique. He has learned to enjoy the company and camaraderie of his friends, but is confident enough to embark on new experiences without them. He is becoming an empathetic, tolerant, and confident young man, and although being in a Montessori school is not the sole reason for his success, he himself would tell you he wishes all kids could go to a school like his.

"My husband passed away when our son was in Kindergarten. Thankfully, it was well after I had been convinced that a Montessori education was the best choice for our son. And although he will never get to experience the amazing person that our son is here on Earth, I know he lives in the smile

that awaits me every afternoon at dismissal. For that smile, and my introduction to the Montessori world, I will be forever grateful to him."

Carol Willis, Montessori parent.

"The Montessori philosophy is so natural it looks easy. Why not let the
children sweep the floor and wash the dishes? They see Mom and Dad doing it. It is an integral part of any given day. It instills discipline and a sense
of purpose. Why not move around at will and then sit on the floor to learn
math using beautiful *toys* to demonstrate the lessons? It stimulates intrigue
and a love of learning. Why not let small mats laid out for work designate
one's private space? It instills respect for one another's resolve. Why not
empower our youth to communicate their ideas to a group by using collaboration as a tool? Overcoming the fear of public speaking can be diffused by
first experimenting in a group. And within those groups emerge leaders and
forward thinkers.

"In very general terms, the traditional forms of education put children
in a box into which information is poured and after which it is spit out for
grading. The Montessori education enables the child to move from interest
to interest when they feel a readiness for that lesson, thus absorbing the
lesson more fully. The Montessori education creates an environment that
is peaceful, where learning is exciting and sharing and cooperation are expected. These are life lessons. They will empower our youth with the skills
and knowledge they will need to sensibly solve problems and to live and
enjoy life fully. We feel very fortunate to have found this truly special form
of education."

Candace Sheitelman, Montessori parent.

"Our older son began his Montessori journey fairly late—in 2nd grade—
but his transformation has been nothing short of remarkable. After two years
of being *bored* and *doing the same thing over and over again*, he was finally
being engaged in a way that worked for him. He was given the ultimate
freedom to explore his curiosities (some of which are a little off the beaten
path) and to learn in an order and at a pace that made him want to absorb
more and more. Although changing schools in grade two was not easy, what
we've seen emerge is comfort in his own skin, confidence in his voice, pride
in and excitement about learning, his interests really beginning to gel, and
meaningful friendships. Our younger son joined him this year at the early
childhood level and is thriving. Watching him experience the Montessori
method and environment early in his education has been astounding. He's
reading and writing; and let's just say I think he loves watching our eyes

bulge and our mouths gape when he discusses things like the state of matter and the work of famous artists we did not study until college art history. Becoming a Montessori family after experiencing the alternative has brought to life all of the possibilities that learning can offer. Montessori expands your mind and your definitions of school and education with consciousness about the child's whole experience—their interactions with one another, with the environment, with their teachers, with the materials, and how they get along with themselves. It builds leadership skills, fosters kindness, rewards inclusion, celebrates diversity, and is giving our boys every opportunity to be the happiest, best versions of themselves. We feel very fortunate to be able to provide them a Montessori education and to be along on their journey."

Jennifer Hudson, Montessori parent.

"As most parents do with their first child, my husband and I fretted and worried, researched, sought advice, and communed with friends about the best possible option for our then four-year-old son. We were curious learners and wanted an environment that would simply allow our son to explore and be the fullest possible version of himself. I remember breathing a sigh of relief when we found Summit-Questa.

"We were former traditional school kids and didn't know anyone who had been taught in a Montessori environment. Multiple intelligence learning? Math that moved from the tactile with materials to the abstract? Goats, chickens, and 10 acres of land? We were hooked.

"I will admit that my son was not always enamored. He's an introvert and at one point, did not seem to appreciate the freedom he was given to explore. He's the kind of kid who wants the Lego plans and can't be bothered to invent a building. From time to time, we questioned whether or not it might be best to move him to a more traditional environment, but at some point, we stopped.

"It became very clear to us that our school is more than just a place of academic learning—it's a community with a keen sense of its place in the context of a larger world. Children recite a Pledge to the Earth after the Pledge of Allegiance. They are encouraged to resolve differences by going to the table with the *peace flower*. Older students tend, feed, and care for the farm animals. The campus cat is known and loved by the entire community. Birthday celebrations include a *walk around the sun* that serves as a teaching moment and involves every classmate. Parents and students with an idea that will enrich learning or benefit the school are encouraged to gather support and bring it to life. When we considered the big picture, we realized that we had actually gotten much more than we expected. And it seems that by the time my son finished fifth grade, he'd finally gotten this as well.

"Fast forward 10 years. Our son is now 14 and heading to high school. He is self-confident, astute, and delightfully witty. More importantly, he is happy. His response to me at pick-up is now a little joke between us. I ask how his day went, and he always replies, 'You know it's always great.' We have total confidence that he is prepared to successfully navigate the next phase of his life—the academic scholarship he won to a notable high school attests to this.

"No learning approach or environment can ever be perfect, but our Montessori experience has resulted in children who are happy and whole. After nearly a decade, I am still breathing a sigh of relief. I'm still hooked."

Mariane DiPierro Pavelic, Montessori parent.

"Having a conversation with Montessorians, it's clear to hear the characteristics that separate them from students taught in traditional schools. There's an air of confidence in their speech delivery, a broader use of vocabulary, and an engaging social tone with an ability to communicate effectively, both with younger people as well as older adults. At least, that has been the personal experience with my two children.

"My nineteen year old son, a college freshman, began his Montessori education at age two. He successfully transitioned into the fifth grade at a private, academically rigorous prep school. My son was many levels ahead of his classmates in geography and science, reading and writing, and excels at creative writing. He remained at that prep school through his high school graduation. Similarly, my sixteen year old daughter began her Montessori education at age two, and successfully transitioned into second grade at the same prep school. She is now a high school sophomore with high honors and seems to excel in both science and math. She is the *mother hen* in her friend group, the most practical of the bunch.

"Their Montessori years taught them many valuable academic lessons, however the practical life lessons benefited them the most. Learning independence, personal problem solving, respecting others as well as their own personal space, observing quietly, being calm, and understanding negotiating as a way of solving grievances; it is in these instances that their personal growth was briskly developed and fostered. My daughter feels that she excels in both common sense and organizational skills. My son is confident in his ability to absorb his surroundings both from a visual perspective, as well as a social one.

"They both have a sharp awareness of their surroundings, an ability to perceive from many senses, and much creativity in developing ideas. They both possess a gift for problem solving, and the importance of respecting others. Their Montessori years taught them well. They learned how to learn. They learned at a young age that exploration and learning was actually play. How clever and brilliant an educational model."

MONTESSORI EDUCATORS

Jeanne Hudlett, Co-director of Summit Montessori Teacher Training Institute, Davie, FL, and former Owner and Principal of Summit Private School, Boca Raton, FL, AMS Certification to teach children from birth through 12 years of age.

"I was blessed to make a career out of something I loved to do. Every day, over the course of 31 years, I drove to one of four Montessori schools that I owned and operated. I spent my day with children, teachers, and parents, who all shared a love of learning in an environment that fostered independence, leadership, responsibility, and community for its students. Montessori is not just a wonderful way to educate children, but a way of life for those who truly embrace the method. Attending a Montessori school for a child and his family is so very meaningful from so many different perspectives. A Montessori classroom is challenging, self-paced, and a place where children can discover the world. Children are truly supported in a carefully prepared environment that facilitates the child's natural desire to learn and develop into a mature, independent person. The parents benefit by being part of their child's education and observing the joy of learning and success that each child experiences. The Montessori school community allows for parents to attend educational sessions where they can learn more about what happens in the classroom. Parents are encouraged to attend school events and cultural activities that take place in the school. A Montessori school is truly an extension of the home.

"So with all this experience, observation, and knowledge about the Montessori method, it only seemed natural when my two grandsons were ready to attend school, we chose a Montessori education. Both boys started at age three in the early childhood classroom of a lovely little Montessori school in Southern California. They enjoyed the hands-on materials and choosing their own *work* from the first day. Since the Montessori curriculum is so vast, they were exposed to daily living skills, sensorial activities, math, language, geography, history, and science over the course of the three years at this level. This environment enabled the boys to acquire the skills they needed for a lifetime of successful learning. In addition to the early knowledge they acquired, they became students who were confident, independent, leaders in their class-rooms, and team players. All of these skills will aid them in their future. The boys are now seven and nine years old and have incredible verbal skills, are wonderful mathematicians, and love to read. They have moved on to a more traditional school this year and were at the top of their class when they entered their new grades. It has been a good transition for them but I know they will miss Montessori and the independence they experienced, and so will I.

"As I reflect on the past 30 years of my Montessori journey, I will forever be grateful to the many amazing students, teachers, and parents who have enriched my life. It has filled me with a sense of hope that the future generations will create a better world where different cultures can live together in peace and harmony."

Dr. Elisabeth Coe, Executive Director of Houston Montessori Center, International Montessori Teacher Trainer, Secondary Principal at School of the Woods, Houston, TX, Past American Montessori Society President, AMS and International Leader and Policy Maker for Montessori Education and Teacher Training, 45 years of experience in Montessori education. AMS Certified.

"I am having an amazing life's journey as a Montessorian. Montessori has given me a framework for this journey, and I am very grateful. The Montessori philosophy is a philosophy of life as well as an educational philosophy, which has helped me find my passions (cosmic tasks) as an advocate, especially for adolescents and peace. School of the Woods, Houston Montessori Center, and the American Montessori Society have encouraged me, supported me, and given me a pathway and the freedom to develop my passions and leadership. I have so many teachers; I have learned so much from my family, the children, the adolescents, the parents, the teachers, the administrators, my colleagues, and the child advocates that I work with each day. It has expanded my horizons in so many ways in how I respect and honor myself, others, and the planet. I have taught in at least 15 countries and cherish the friendships I have developed all over the world. I have experienced that no matter what country or culture, families all over the world are seeking ways to do what is best for their children. And I have great promise for our future by knowing the adolescents that I work with everyday. I am so happy that I discovered Montessori over 45 years ago."

Jane Finnegan, Montessori teacher for 25 years in early childhood classrooms. AMS certified to teach children 3–6 years of age. Jane was nominated for the award of the 25 Best Preschool Teachers in the nation by her students' parents in a national parenting magazine.

"Growing up the oldest of seven children, I recall my parents' desire that I learn the importance of responsibility. They encouraged and fostered in me a desire to become autonomous and that led to a feeling of competence and a desire to seek new challenges. This sense of initiative and the clear understanding of the role that choices and consequences have in all learning are what drew me to the Montessori philosophy of education. The children in a Montessori classroom take responsibility for their own learning and as they become more confident and competent, they realize their important roles in enhancing the learning of all. It was this internalization of trust, autonomy, and initiative that Dr. Montessori saw as the source of hope for a peaceful world. She recognized that these were not merely children at work, but emerging adults with the future of the world in their hands.

"I am always eager to have parent chaperons on field trips with our kindergarten students. I wait and watch as they observe for themselves the children from our class sitting quietly in the theater seats waiting for the performance to begin. The children in the theater from a more traditional school setting are usually the ones who are rowdy, ill-equipped to handle the freedom of movement that being out of the classroom allows them. The Montessori child has experienced in the classroom environment the ability to move about the classroom and freely talk with others with a sense of purpose, self-direction, and respect. Children that come from a learning environment that restricts movement involves getting information from listening to a teacher or a read text, and without the opportunity to explore, question, and experience that information. They have a very difficult time being able to adjust and control their bodies and focus their attention on learning outside the classroom.

"At the end of a very frustrating and difficult week as a new teacher, my director came into the classroom and asked me why I was crying. I told her that I had felt prepared for teaching, but that it was just not going the way my training and manuals had led me to believe it would. She gave me two pieces of advice that have shaped my teaching and my life: 1) Don't expect yourself or the child to be perfect. Perfection is a journey, not a destination. 2) If you love the child, you won't make a mistake that can't be rectified. To love and to be loving is everything."

Patti Sands, AMS certified to teach children 6–9 years of age.

"When I was a child, I attended a parochial elementary school from the late 1960s to the early 1970s. I did well in school and received good grades.

One day, in about the 4th grade, I was sitting in math class and the teacher was doing a long division problem on the board. I clearly remember trying to follow along and make sense of what she was doing. At one step in the problem, I needed her to go back and re-explain what she had done. I'll never forget her response. She said that this was the *new math* and no one, not even our parents, would be able to help us. I remember the panic that set in as she proceeded to move ahead through the problem, and as I realized I was being left behind.

"Many years later, when I became an assistant teacher in a Montessori School in an elementary class, I believe I experienced an epiphany as I worked with a student on a long division problem with the Stamp Game material. The concept of division became so clear and concrete! We loved manipulating the materials, following the patterns, and solving the problem together. It instantly brought my mind back to that time so many years ago when I began struggling with math. I can only imagine the different course my life would have taken if I had been able to make sense of the world in that instant when I felt it all slipping away."

Andrea Trillo, Montessori co-teacher, AMS 6–9 training in progress.

"Montessori education is a way that children learn by doing, assuming responsibility for their actions, their choices, and respecting the environment. The children are encouraged to be independent and to develop self-direction. Montessori education prepares them for life.

"When I ask my students what Montessori means to them, they say it is fun, we have freedom, and the lessons and materials are like games. In fact, they feel like they are playing rather than working.

"Stuart Brown, a pioneer in research on play, establishes that play is fundamental in peoples' lives. Play in childhood makes happy, smart, and productive adults. Play affects human development: cognitively, socially, emotionally, and physically. He interviewed people to study the impact of play on one's life and he observed a strong correlation between playful activities as a child and success in life.

"Play is a critical vehicle for developing self-regulation, language, cognition, and social competence. Children love to play; it is part of their nature. In Montessori education, it is through interaction with the environment that the child learns. Young children develop best when their hands are more directly involved with manipulating materials in their work. The Montessori elementary classroom is a work place in which work is the play and children learn by doing.

"Through the use of the materials, the children reach high levels of abstract knowledge and creative thought. As a teacher, I can see how much my students improve and are able to understand complex concepts by using the materials. For example, when a child uses the triangles by physically moving their pieces, he or she can find out if they are equivalent or can classify them.

"As a Montessori educator, I think it is important to guide children to explore and manipulate materials. They are exposed to a variety of materials that invite them to explore, create, and use their imagination.

"We have a big responsibility in our hands. We are the people who can make a difference in children's lives and most importantly, later on in their adult lives."

Roberta Ackerman, Upper elementary teacher (9–12 years of age).

"My path to Montessori began as an outside observer; continued on as I became a parent of a Montessori child; and finally has brought me to the classroom as a teacher.

"As a college student, I remember being impressed with a bright, articulate neighborhood child who attended a Montessori school. I was struck by the depth and breadth of his knowledge, his interest in the world around him, and most of all, his ability to understand that he was part of a global community.

Many years later, when my son attended Summit-Questa, I began to understand that Montessori was not just a teaching method; it truly was a philosophy, a way of living. I often relied on my Montessori community to support my efforts in teaching my son to be kind, tolerant, and respectful. He learned to value the things that really matter in life, and feels a responsibility to leave the world a better place. He learned these lessons on a daily basis in the classroom and through the example of the teachers around him.

"Now, as a teacher, I have the privilege of watching Montessori change lives. I follow them; encouraging, motivating, and letting them know that I have faith in their abilities. Mistakes are a chance for us to figure it out together. My students are allowed to learn, instead of being relentlessly *taught*. Our days are filled with unexpected teachable moments. Another student might share an interesting bit of knowledge, which often prompts a dozen questions. Research to the rescue!

"Whenever I think about my Montessori students, past or present, I see a love for learning that endures and an awareness of their responsibility to our universe and each other. It fills me with gratitude and gives me hope."

SPECIALIST:

Dr. Mike Rizzo, For more than 25 years, Dr. Rizzo (a.k.a. Coach Mike) has worked with children—and their families—who struggle with social, emotional, behavioral, and/or academic difficulties. Most recently, Dr. Rizzo earned his Diplomate in School Neuropsychology from the American Board of School Neuropsychology. Dr. Rizzo is no stranger to these challenges, as he himself struggled as a child with what was later diagnosed as ADHD, anxiety, and dyslexia. Unaware of the depth and range of his challenges, he and those who loved him were perplexed by his lack of success in many venues of life. His challenges led to academic failures, incredible frustration, and family conflict.

Despite these difficulties, Dr. Rizzo never gave up! On his journey toward completing his education, he took many detours, which later served as a rich experiential base from which to understand the world outside of academia. Eventually, at the age of 30, he finished college and entered graduate training. Against all odds, while working full-time as a school psychologist in the public school system, 37-year-old Mike Rizzo completed his Ph.D.

After 10 years of working as a school psychologist in public education, Dr. Rizzo was recruited to develop the Psychology Department at Miami Children's Hospital, Dan Marino Outpatient Center, in Weston, Florida. While he and his practice, Child Provider Specialists, still have a presence at the Dan Marino Center, as well as at Miami Children's Hospital Nicklaus Outpatient Center in Palm Beach Gardens, Florida, his group has expanded far beyond the walls of these centers. Over 30 clinicians have been trained by Dr. Rizzo to understand the neurobiology of learning and behavior, and to assist families in maximizing the potential of their children three years of age and up. At this time, Child Provider Specialists and Dr. Rizzo's newest venture, the Dyslexia Institute of South Florida, provide a host of integrated psychology and remedial educational services, as well as prescriptive school programming, in a variety of locations spanning the tri-county area of South Florida.

Dr. Rizzo's philosophy is that no child should have to endure the journey toward adulthood that he took. As such, by specializing in the cutting edge science of the brain, he has dedicated his life to ensure that he—and those he has mentored—prevent this for as many children as they can.

"As a consequence of my involvement with hundreds of schools, both public and private, I have visited and observed more learning/teaching environments than most people—perhaps anyone in education.

"Over the years, I always find myself amazed at what I see happening in the Montessori classroom. To the untrained observer, these classroom environments may seem unstructured and even chaotic. In fact, they are just the opposite. Kids are grouped in much larger age ranges. The tasks presented to the children as learning challenges or opportunities are designed to capture all student's readiness levels. Specific developmental sequences are built into the curriculum and kids engage at the level of personal readiness. Eventually, as was Maria Montessori's belief, mastery will come. Mastery does not come with each child at the same day on the calendar. Mastery will come when the individual brain involved is ready. These developmental sequences of learning opportunities are designed around all modalities (visual, kinesthetic/motor, and auditory/language). The untrained observer may not get it, but each *thing* in a Montessori classroom is there for a reason. Each child can engage in learning at the level commensurate with their readiness level (not their exact age or grade) without feeling embarrassed, intimidated, or under pressure to keep up with what the others are doing.

"Following a highly structured curriculum and being compared to one's peers, and either being seen as a success or a failure because a child is the same age and has not mastered a skill yet, is ridiculous. Yet this seems to be the foundation of the typical school in the generic American educational system.

"Creating opportunities for the conditions to be right for each child to have an engaging learning experience at a place/point commensurate with their developmental readiness is what makes the Montessori environment magical.

"A second observation that I've made about the Montessori learning environment has to do with creating an environment in which a student's success and accomplishments create pride and enthusiasm that comes from within. Children are encouraged to experiment, explore, and problem solve in novel ways. Curiosity is not a bad thing; novel ways to take on challenges are respected. Looking at a situation and exploring a variety of ideas to solve a challenge is emphasized, rather than regurgitating information necessary to pass a standardized test. This approach allows the maturing brain to unfold and become a creative, thinking, inquisitive, want-to-learn-more kind of a mind. Learning to love learning because it feels good (reward circuitry activated as a consequence of learning), not because one will receive a reward for doing their school work, is another facet of the Montessori environment that has always intrigued me.

"A third observation I've made over the years is that curriculum delivery is multisensory—highly kinesthetic and movement oriented. The utilization and integration of all senses (visual, motor/kinesthetic, and auditory) in the learning process is typically at the core of most Montessori learning experiences. Modern learning theory confirms that enlisting all cognitive systems in the learning process has proven highly efficacious to brain development, learning efficiency, and retention of information learned. How did Maria Montessori know this over 100 years ago?

"Finally, and to some degree one of the greatest attributes of the true Montessori environment, is the character development and sense of community that flourishes in Montessori environments. The students whom I have worked with feel a sense of pride in the classroom community. It's not only about the child, it's about the group. Each individual's contributions toward group goals support the development of character strengths (endurance, empathy, compassion, forgiveness, tolerance) and are all, again by default, intrinsic to the teaching techniques and the social interactions/dynamics embedded in the Montessori environment.

"To summarize: facilitating developmental conditions to master skills in a sequence consistent with brain readiness; learning to learn for the love of learning; maximizing brain development by utilizing all modalities in the learning process; and developing a sense of community and related character strengths are what makes the Montessori environment a perfect environment to *grow children* into problem solvers, good citizens, and leaders who are driven to do the right thing for the right reasons.

"As I study neuroscience, the more I learn, the more I am convinced that Maria Montessori was, in fact, a century ahead of her time. Understanding the neurobiology of learning, motivation, and character development results in a clear unquestionable *aha* experience that everything Maria Montessori believed is indeed correct."

CONFESSION:

This book is primarily my big picture reflection. Over the past 40 years, in the ebb and flow of my life's journey as a Montessorian, my reflections would have been as dramatically different as the experiences I was having at that moment in time...which is part of the point that our life is a journey. The destination can change many times over the course of one's life, and I believe that it is really the journey that determines the destination. The wonder, awe, and mystery of life are that it is so fluid, depending upon the choices we make along the way. Our view of the world also changes dramatically as we encounter different bumps and turns in the road. Would I have ever guessed as a fearful 20 year old that my life would have taken so many strange and wonderful turns? No, and I wouldn't have wanted to know. It would have robbed me of the learning that needed to take place along the way. I can honestly say that there is still a great deal more that I want to learn so I look forward to the continuation of my journey and the expectation of where the next turn will take me.

This book has free material available for download from the
Web Added Value™ resource center at *www.jrosspub.com*

References

American Management Association (AMA). Critical Skills Survey: Executive Summary: American Management Association, 15 April 2010. Web. 16 May 2011. http//www. P21.org[PDF] AMA 2010 Critical Skills Survey-P21American Montessori Society website: www.amshq.org.

Britton, Lesley. *Montessori Play and Learn: A Parent's Guide to Purposeful Play from Two to Six*. New York: Crown Publishers, 1992.

Burnett, Walt, (ed.). *The Human Spirit*. London: George Allen and Unwin Ltd., 1960.

Burns, M.C. "Interview with Oren Lyons," *Syracuse Herald Journal*, July 9, 1991.

Buscaglia, Leo. *Personhood*. Columbine, NY: Fawcett, 1978.

Conley, David T. "Towards a More Comprehensive Conception of College Readiness." Educational Policy Improvement Center, 8 Feb. 2008. Web. 16 May 2011. http://www.academia.edu/21736140/Toward_a_More_Comprehensive_Conception_of_College_Readiness.

Day, Lori. "Why Boys Are Failing in an Educational System Stacked Against Them." On the Huffington Post. Web. Aug. 2011. http://www.huffingtonpost.com/lori-day/why-boys-are-failing-in-a_b_884262.html.

Elkind, David. *All Grown Up and No Place to Go: Teenagers in Crisis*. Da Capo Press, 1998.

Elkind, David. *Miseducation: Preschoolers at Risk*. New York: Alfred A. Knopf, 1987.

Galyean, Beverly-Colleene. "Honoring the Spirituality of our Children without Teaching Religion in the Schools," *Holistic Education Review*, Summer, 1989.

Gardner, Howard. *Five Minds for the Future*. Boston, MA: Harvard Business School, 2007.

Gurian, Michael, and Kathy Stevens. *The Minds of Boys: Saving Our Sons from Falling Behind in School and Life*. Jossey-Bass. An Imprint at WILEY, 2007.

Healy, Jane M. *Endangered Minds: Why Our Children Don't Think*. New York: Touchstone, 1990.

Heckman, J. J. "The Case for Investing in Disadvantaged Young Children." Big Ideas for Children: Investing in Our Nation's Future. www .heckmanequation.org.

Holistic Education Review, Summer, 1989.

Holtz, Robert Lee. "The Power of Handwriting." The Wall Street Journal. April 5, 2016.

Hughes, Steve. http://www.goodatdoingthings.com.

Institute for Health and Human Potential. "What is Emotional Intelligence?" WEB http://www.ihhp.com/meaning-of-emotional-intelligence.

Itard, Jean. *The Wild Boy of Aveyron*. New York: Appleton-Century-Crofts, 1962.

Karon, Jan. *Somewhere Sage with Somebody Good*. New York: Berkley Books, 2014.

Kilpatrick, William. *The Montessori System Examined*. Boston: Houghton Mifflin, 1970.

Kramer, Rita. *Maria Montessori: A Biography*. New York: G.P. Putman's Sons, 1976.

Levy, Frank and Richard J. Murnane. *The New Division of Labor: How Computers Are Creating the Next Job Market*. New York: Russell Sage Foundation, 2004.

Lillard, Angeline Stoll. *Montessori: The Science Behind the Genius*. Oxford University Press, 2005.

Lillard, Paula Polk. *A Montessori: A Modern Approach*. New York: Schocken Books, 1972.

———. *Montessori Today: A Comprehensive Approach to Education from Birth to Adulthood*. New York: Schocken Books, 1996.

Malloy, Terry. *Montessori and Your Child: A Primer for Parents*. New York: Schocken Books, 1974.

Montessori, Maria. *The Absorbent Mind*. Wheaton, Ill.: Theosophical Press, 1962.

———. *The Discovery of the Child*. Wheaton, Ill.: Theosophical Press, 1962.

———. *To Educate the Human Potential*. Wheaton, Ill.: Theosophical Press, 1963.

———. *Education for a New World*. Oxford, England: Clio Press,1996.

———. *Education and Peace*. Chicago: Henry Regnery Company, 1972.

———. *From Childhood to Adolescence*. Amsterdam, The Netherlands: AMI Montessori-Pierson Publishing Company, 2007.

———. *The Montessori Method*. New York: Schocken Books, 1964.

———. *The Secret of Childhood*. Calcutta: Orient Longmans, Ltd., 1963.

———. *Spontaneous Activity in Education*. New York: Schocken Books, 1965.

————. *What You Should Know About Your Child*. Wheaton, Ill.: Theosophical Press, 1963.

Montessori Websites/Blogs: www.MariaMontessori.com, www.montessori-science.org, www.MontessoriMadness.com, www.macte.org, The Montessori Observer, Aid to Life, NAMTA website.

NAMTA Journal. "The Hungry Mind: From the Casa dei Bambini to Cosmic Education," Vol. 41, No. 1 (Winter 2016).

National Education Association (NEA). "Preparing 21st Century Students for a Global Society: An Educator's Guide to the Four Cs".

National Education Association (NEA) Packard, Rosa Covington. *The Hidden Hinge*. Indiana: Fides Publishers, 1972.

Obama, Barack. "Obama's Remarks on Education." CBS News, 10 Mar. 2009. Web. 16 May 2011. http://www.cbsnews.com.

Palmer, Parker J. *A Place Called Community*. Philadelphia, PA: Pendle Hill, 1977.

Pattell-Gray, Anne. *Through Aboriginal Eyes*. Geneva: WCC Publications, 1991.

Peck, M. Scott. *A Different Drum*. New York: Simon and Schuster, 1987.

Piaget, Jean. *The Psychology of Intelligence*. Totowa, N.J.: Littlefield, Adams, 1963.

Pink, Daniel. *A Whole New Mind*. New York: Riverhead, 2006.

Robinson, Ken. "Ken Robinson Says Schools Kill Creativity." Speech. TED Talks. Monterey, CA. Ted Talks. Web. 16 May 2011. http://www.ted.com./talks/ken_robinson_says_schools_kill_creativity.html.

Rowan, Cris. "The Impact of Technology on the Developing Child." Web blog. 2013. http://www.huffingtonpost.com/cris-rowan/technology-children-negative-impact_b_3343245.html.

Sommers, Christina Hoff. *The War Against Boys: How Misguided Policies Are Harming Our Young Men*. Simon and Schuster, 2000.

Standing, E. M. *Maria Montessori: Her Life and Work*. Fresno, California: Academy Guild Press, 1959.

Sternberg, Robert J. *Wisdom, Intelligence, and Creativity Synthesized*. Cambridge: Cambridge UP, 2007.

Surowiecki, James. *The Wisdom of Crowds*. New York: Anchor, 2005.

Swimme, Brian. *The Universe is a Green Dragon*. Santa Fe, NM: Bear and Co., 1984.

Taylor, Jim. Psychology Today, Web, "How Technology is Changing the Way Children Think and Focus." Posted Dec. 04, 2012. http://www.psychologytoday.com/blog/the-power-prime/201212/how-technology-is-changing-the-way-children-think-and-focus.

Whitescarver, Keith. Web, "Montessori and the Mainstream." http://www.keith-whitescarver.com.

Whitmire, Richard. *Why Boys Fail: Saving Our Sons from an Educational System That's Leaving Them Behind.* AMACOM Books, January 2010.

Wolf, Aline D. *Nurturing the Spirit: In Non-Sectarian Classrooms.* PA: Parent Child Press, 1996.

INDEX

absorbent mind, 25, 95–96
    unconscious phase of, 95
The Absorbent Mind (Montessori),
    47, 103
accreditation, 57–58
achievement test scores, 191
ADHD. *See* Attention deficit
    and hyperactivity disorder
    (ADHD)
adolescents, 141–156
    academic goals, 150
    American Revolution and, 141
    brain, 142–143
    Coe's program, 149–150
    constant complaining stage, 152
    as egocentric, 151
    emotions, 143–145
    formal thinking, 150–151
    intellectual talks, 153
    parents and, 154–155
    physical strength, 151–152
    pseudo-stupidity, 152–153
    psychosocial development,
        153–154
    real-life activities, 151
    relationships with adults, 154–
        155
    teachers and, 154–155
age groupings
    Montessori, 50
    traditional, 50

All Grown Up and No Place to Go
    (Elkind), 172
alphabet
    moveable, 119–121
American Academy of Pediatric
    Neuropsychology, 12
American Management Association,
    192
American Montessori Education, 6
American Montessori Society
    (AMS), 14, 55–56, 57
    Coe's program, 149–150
AMI. *See* Association Montessori
    Internationale (AMI)
"Amrita's Prayer: Embrace the
    Trees," 183–184
AMS. *See* American Montessori So-
    ciety (AMS)
amygdala, 143, 221–222
angry emotions, 219
ASD. *See* Autism spectrum disor-
    ders (ASD)
Asperger's Syndrome, 212
Association Montessori Internatio-
    nale (AMI), 55–56, 57
Atkins, Steven C., 143
attention deficit disorder (ADD),
    211
attention deficit and
    hyperactivity disorder
    (ADHD), 211

attention span, 216–217
auditory learners, 37
authenticity, of Montessori schools,
    53–59
    accreditation, 57–58
    guidelines for, 57–59
autism, 212
Autism Science Foundation (ASF),
    212
autism spectrum disorders (ASD),
    212

bathroom, 74
bedroom of children, 74–75
behavior, 100–101
Bell, Alexander Graham, 6
Bell, Joshua, 15
Bell, Mabel, 6
Bezos, Jeffrey, 15, 26
Bill and Melinda Gates Foundation,
    193
binomial cube, 110
boys, 195–199. See also Gender
    difference
brain, 4, 6, 10, 12, 25, 47
    absorbent mind. See Absorbent
        mind
    adolescents, 142–143
    amygdala, 143, 221–222
    music and, 100
bridging ceremony, 173
Brin, Sergey, 15, 26
brown stair, 111
Bubka, Sergei, 15
bullies, 176
bullying, 52
Buscaglia, Leo, 160

Cadillac of Career Training
    Education, Massachusetts,
    197

Career and Technical Education
    (CTE), 197
Casa dei Bambini. See Children's
    House
Center for Disease Control and Pre-
    vention (CDC), 212
chains, 118
Child, Julia, 15
childhood, traditional vs. Montessori
    philosophy, 27
children. See also Montessori
    schools
    acquisition of oral language, 42
    independence of, 74–76
    inner call, 43
    inner growth, 179–180
    markers for, 172–174
    spiritual embryo of, 96
Children's House, 5, 18, 103
classrooms
    Montessori. See Montessori class-
        rooms
    traditional, 49–50
class size, 47
Clayton Christensen Institute, 190
Clinton, Chelsea, 14
Clooney, George, 15
Coe, Betsy, 149–150
collaboration, 192
color bead bars, 117
color tablets, 111
communication skills, 192
community, 31–32
    ground rules, 159
    peaceful, 175–186
    spirituality, 159–174
community agreement, 45–48
computers, 218
confidence, 35
Conley, David T., 193
consistency, 68–69

corporal punishment, 69
cosmic curriculum, 34
creativity, 193
    and spirituality, 168–171
critical thinking, 193
cube, 109–110
    binomial, 110
    trinomial, 110
cubing chains, 118
cultural revolution, 28
curriculum
    Montessori. See Montessori curriculum
    traditional, 51
cylinder blocks, 110

Dartmouth Medical School, 143
decisions maker, 192
"Deep," 170
degrees, and women, 195
discipline
    Montessori, 52
    traditional, 52
division board, 117
dress code, 173–174
Dyer, Jeffrey, 26

early childhood curriculum
    art, 126
    cultural areas, 123–124
    language, 119–123
    line time or circle time, 126
    mathematics, 113–119
    music, 125
    outdoor time/movement, 126–127
    practical life, 106–108
    science, 124–125
    sensorial materials, 109–113
early childhood curriculum (3–6
    years of age), 103–127
Edison, Thomas, 6

Einstein, Albert, 160
elementary curriculum, 129–139
    geography and history, 139
    language materials, 137
    math materials, 138
    practical life, 137
    science materials, 139
Elkind, David, 172
embryo, 95–96
Emerson, Ralph Waldo, 176
emotional development, 31–32
emotional intelligence (EI), 221–225
emotional quotient (EQ). See Emotional intelligence (EI)
emotions, 32
    adolescents, 143–145
empathy-centered work, 196
encouragement
    language to be used by parents
        for, 72–73
    vs. praise, 70–72
entertainment technology, 216
Erikson, Erik, 27
exceptional learners. See Gifted children

Faithkeeper of the Onondaga Nation of Native Americans, 160
family agreement, 69
field trips, 173
fine arts, 136–137
formal thinking, adolescents, 150–151
Four Cs, 191–192
fraction skittles, 118
Frank, Anne, 15

Galyean, Beverly-Colleene, 159–160
Gardner, Howard, 193

gender difference, 196–199
gender performance, 198
geography
    early childhood curriculum,
        123–124
    elementary curriculum, 139
geometric solids, 112
geometric trays, 112
geometry
    6–9 years, 134
    9–12 years, 135
    early childhood curriculum, 112
Georgia Tech, 197
Germany, Montessori schools in, 21
gifted children, 44
global approach for 21st century,
    189–193
globe of the world, 123
golden beads, 116–117
Goleman, Dan, 221
grades, 36–37, 201–203
Graham, Katherine, 15
Gregersen, Hal, 26
Gurian, Michael, 195

hands-on activities, 199
hands-on curriculum, 197
hands-on learning materials, 30
handwashing techniques, 77
Harry, Prince, 15
Harvard Graduate School of Educa-
    tion, 197
Heckman, James, 191
helicopter parenting, 67
high risk and high reward, 65–70
history
    early childhood curriculum,
        123–124
    elementary curriculum, 139
Hitler, 21

home, Montessori philosophy at,
    74–76
"Hope," 184
Horn, Michael, 190
"How Technology is Changing the
    Way Children Think and
    Focus" (Taylor), 217
Hughes, Steve, 12
human development, 8
hummingbird parent, 67–68
Hunt, Helen, 15

The Impact of Technology on the
    Developing Child (Rowan),
    216
independence of children, 74–76,
    104
individual silence, 178
Industrial Revolution, 29
infants, 99–101
    emotional psyche of, 63
    nurturing, 63
infant/toddler (I/T) environment,
    99–101
inner call, 43
inner life force, 5
Institute for Health and Human
    Potential, 221
intellectual intelligence. See Intelli-
    gence quotient (IQ)
intelligence quotient (IQ), 221
Internet, 217, 219
Itard, Jean, 4

keyboarding skills, 218
Kilpatrick, William, 6
kinesthetic learners, 37
kitchen, 76–77. See also Safety
    issues
knobless cylinders, 110

language development, 42, 96
early childhood curriculum,
119–123
elementary curriculum, 133–134,
137
language use, parents, 72–73
Laren, Netherlands, 14
League of Nations at Geneva, 14
learning attitude
Montessori, 51
traditional education, 51–52
learning disabilities, 210–211
technology and, 216
learning materials, 42–43
learning styles, 37
legacy gift, 178–179
Levy, Frank, 190–191
Lewis, Jerry, 15
life-changing skills, 32–33
"Lights," 169
Lincoln, Abraham, 224
"Living Religious," 170
"Love," 169

MACTE. See Montessori Accreditation Council for Teacher Education (MACTE)
markers, 172–174
Marquez, Gabriel Garcia, 15
materials (Montessori)
for early childhood curriculum,
103–127
for elementary curriculum,
129–139
self-correcting, 104–105
mathematics
early childhood curriculum,
113–119
elementary curriculum, 134–135,
138

Mayer, John, 221
McGill University, Canada, 198–
199
metal insets, 121–122
The Minds of Boys: Saving Our Sons
from Falling Behind in School
and Life (Gurian), 195
misconceptions, about Montessori
method, 44–45
Montessori, Maria, 3–22, 55
death of, 14
goal of, 79
Kilpatrick and, 6
medical career, 4
timeline of life, 16–22
Montessori Accreditation Council for Teacher Education
(MACTE), 57
Montessori classrooms, 58
community agreement, 45–48
infant/toddler (I/T) programs,
99–101
learning materials, 42–43
size of, 47
traditional vs., 49–50
typical, 47
Montessori curriculum, 51
early childhood, 103–127
elementary, 129–139
Montessori educators, 42, 79–92
calling and profession, 86–87
conflict as an opportunity, 80–86
cult-like behavior, 87
parent education and, 87–89
terms used for, 80
traditional educators vs., 50,
86–87
training, 89–92
Montessori Model United Nations,
151

Montessori schools, 14–15
  adolescent program, 148–156
  age groupings, 50
  authenticity of, 53–59
  classroom. *See* Montessori class-
    rooms
  class size, 47
  discipline, 52
  educators and. *See* Montessori
    educators
  false impressions of, 30
  functioning/operation of, 41–48
  goal of, 35
  infant/toddler (I/T) programs,
    99–101
  learning attitude, 51
  learning styles, 37
  misconceptions about, 44–45
  peace education, 175–186
  reasons for, 25–39
  stimulating environments, 37
  time element, 50
  whole child development, 52
motor skills, 43
moveable alphabet, 119–121
multiplication board, 117
Murnane, Richard, 190–191

National Education Association
    (NEA), 191–192
National Health Interview Survey
    of 2014, 212
nature
  interaction with, 34
  peaceful energy of, 182
NEA. *See* National Education Asso-
    ciation (NEA)
neo-cortex, 221, 222
neurological disorders, 212
Nobel Peace Prize, 14

Nurturing the Spirit (Wolf), 159,
    180

Obama, 191
occupational therapy (OT), 43
Onassis, Jacqueline Bouvier Ken-
    nedy, 14
oral language, acquisition of, 42
organizations, 55–56
  accreditation by, 57–58
outdoor classroom, 178
outdoor time/movement
  early childhood curriculum,
    126–127
  elementary curriculum, 137
out-of-the-box thinkers, 30

Page, Larry, 15, 26
parent education, 87–89
parents, 61–77
  adolescents and, 154–155
  behavior, 100–101
  child's independence, 74–76
  consistency, 68–69
  language to be used for children,
    72–73
  risk and rewards, 65–70
  safety issues, 76–77
  social behavior, 76
Pathways to Prosperity, 197
peace education, 175–186
Peace Rose, 182
Peace Table, 182–183
people skills, 190
perceptions, 224
personal power, 176
physical strength, adolescents,
    151–152
Piaget, Jean, 15
Pink, Daniel, 193

pink tower, 110
poetry
    peace, 183–185
    spirituality, 168–171
practical life, 43–44, 75
    early childhood curriculum,
        106–108
    elementary curriculum, 137
praise *vs.* encouragement, 70–72
prepared environment, 6, 41–42
pseudo-stupidity, 152–153
Psychology Today, 217
puzzle maps, 123
puzzles, 124

quiet place, 178

Rajagopalan, Sumitra, 198–199
Rambusch, Nancy McCormick, 14,
    55
reading lessons, 122
real-life skills, 32
    adolescents, 151
    infant/toddler (I/T) programs,
        99–100
record-keeping systems, 203
red and blue rods, 115–116
red rods, 110–111
religion, 159. *See also* Spirituality
restaurant manners, 76
reward and risk, 65–70
rewards, 29
risk and reward, 65–70
Robinson, Kenneth, 193
Rochester Institute of Technology,
    197
Rogers, Fred, 15
Rosanoff, Michael, 212
Rosetta Stone, 218
Rowan, Cris, 216, 219

safety issues, 76–77
Salavoy, Peter, 221
Salonga, Lea, 15
sandpaper letters, 119
Schweitzer, Albert, 160
science
    early childhood curriculum,
        124–125
    elementary curriculum, 135–136,
        139
"A Second Chance," 170–171
Seguin, Edouard, 4
self-awareness, 25
self-confidence, 211
self-correcting materials, 104–105
self-discipline, 32
    natural development of, 105
self-esteem, 35–36, 211
    grades and. *See* Grades
    traditional approach, 51
self-fulfilling prophecy, 202
self-motivation, 51
sensitive period, 6, 96–99
    acquisition of oral language, 42
    overview of, 103–104
    types of, 97
sexual predators, 220
silence game, 125, 126, 177–178
SimCity, 26
size of classroom, 47
skittles, 118
smart phones, 219
social behavior, 76
social networking sites, 219
social skills, 190
social studies
    early childhood curriculum,
        123–124
    elementary curriculum, 136
Sommers, Christina Hoff, 195

sound and reading lessons, 122
sound boxes/cylinders, 113
South Dakota School of Mines and
     Technology, 197
"Speak," 184
special needs, 209–213
spindle boxes, 116
Spirit Naming Ceremony, 171–
     172
spiritual embryo, 96
spirituality, 159–174
     creativity and, 168–171
     markers, 172–174
     special ceremony, 171–172
     theories, 162–168
     Wolf on, 159–160
squaring and cubing chains, 118
standardized tests/testing, 203–208
State Orthophrenic School,
     Rome, 4
Sternberg, Robert, 193
success
     concept of, 28–29
     in new world, 28
Surowiecki, James, 192
surrogate frontal lobe, 155

"Talking to God," 170
Talk So Kids Will Listen & Listen So
     Kids Will Talk (Faber and
     Mazlish), 72
Taylor, Jim, 217
teachers
     adolescents and, 154–155
     Montessori. See Montessori edu-
          cators
     traditional, 50
teacher training center, 14
Technical School for Engineering
     and Math, 3

technology, 215–220
television, 216
time element
     Montessori, 50
     traditional education, 50
toddler, 63, 99–101
toy box, 75
traditional education
     age groupings, 50
     bullying, 52
     curriculum, 51
     discipline, 52
     learning attitude, 51–52
     self-esteem, 51
     self-motivation, 51
     time element, 50
     whole child development, 52
traditional vs. Montessori class-
     rooms, 49–50
trinomial cube, 110
trust, 96
21st century, global approach for,
     189–193

UNESCO. See United Nations Ed-
     ucational, Scientific and Cul-
     tural Organization (UNESCO)
United Nations Educational, Scien-
     tific and Cultural Organization
     (UNESCO), 14
United States
     Industrial Revolution, 29
     Montessori philosophy in,
          29–30
     out-of-the-box thinkers, 30
     traditional educational system, 29
University of Rome, 4

Victor, the Wild Boy of Aveyon, 96
Vision Committee, 180–181

visual learners, 37
visual stimulation, 37

Walters, Barbara, 26
The War Against Boys (Sommers),
    195
Whitby School in Greenwich,
    Connecticut, 14, 55
Whitmire, Richard, 195
whole child development
    Montessori approach, 52
    traditional approach, 52
Why Boys Fail (Whitmire), 195
William, Prince, 15
Wilson, Margaret, 6

Wolf, Aline, 159–160, 180
women
    degrees and, 195
    gender difference, 196–199
work
    child's choice of, 27
    Montessori experience, 27
    new world concept, 28
working memory, 221
World War I, 6
Wright, Will, 26

yoga cards, 179

zamboni parent, 67